The Home Rule and
How the Unqualified of
White Springs
Delivered a Town into
Financial Despair

Karin Fleischhaker-Griffin

ISBN

Hardcover:978-1-966565-32-1

Paperback:978-1-966565-33-8

DEDICATION

I dedicate this book to my daughter, Tamara Lynn Fleischhaker, who has stood by me no matter what the circumstances, giving me advice, laughter and support during my twelve years living in White Springs.

ACKNOWLEDGMENTS

I wish to thank Arlen Scott Gay, CPA, former councilperson, Nicole Williams and the Citizens of White Springs whose complaints to the Joint Legislative Audit Committee of Florida resulted in the Auditor General conducting an audit of the Town of White Springs.

My gratitude to Jessie R. Box. Reporter for the former Jasper News who provided truth and transparency in her reporting of the news relating to White Springs.

My thanks to Stew Lilker of the Columbia County Observer for his friendship and mentoring of some of our articles on the blog.

Thank you, former White Springs Fire Rescue Chief Kevin Pittman and his lieutenant Tom Brazil, for keeping us apprised of the trials and tribulations of the fire department.

My thanks to the Hamilton County Sheriff's Department, for the assistance given by various deputies and especially to deputy P.J. Fouracre and Lieutenant McKire as well as to Amanda Bennett who now serves the J. Harrell Reid Funeral Home.

My thanks To those in White Springs who befriended me Rosemarie (Carin) Copeland, Farron Filya, Jim and Teena Smith and Steve and Donna Jeffers.

I acknowledge and thank Jim Smith for his photography of the bath house on my book cover.

ABOUT WHITE SPRINGS

White Springs is located in North Florida on the Suwannee River. In 2020 its population was 740 and it is the home of the annual Florida Folk Festival. It is a tourist destination known for its historic charm, the Stephen Foster Memorial Museum and Culture Center. Rent a canoe to go down the Suwannee River and take a short trip to the Big Shoals State Forest.

White Springs was Florida's first tourist attraction. People flocked to White Springs by stagecoach, then by rail and finally by automobile to bathe and drink the mineral waters of the spring and its luxury resort environment. The spring water had a "rotten egg" sulfur smell that came from dissolved hydrogen sulfide gas. The Native Americans considered the springs a sacred healing ground. Although the spring resort structure still stands, eventually, the springs dried up.

White Springs is located in Hamilton County which is considered the poorest county in Florida.

Contents

INTRODUCTION: WHITE SPRINGS

The Town of White Springs did not provide Transparency to its citizens. Joe Griffin, the most hated Town activist was criticized for ordering public records. The Town, law enforcement and its officials did everything possible to keep Griffin and his wife away from the political arena, including trying to place the Griffins in prison. The elected officials were ignorant in managing the Town's finances, including the spending of restrictive funds on salaries, legal expenses and even providing funds for those who were unable to work by forgoing timesheets. The officials did not follow the state's regulations requiring adherence to budgets and financials and the Town Charter, nor did the staff retain records and receipts. Florida's Home Rule allows the municipalities to govern on their own without restriction. As such these municipalities could break the rules and the laws without fear of repercussion by the government in the form of criminal or civil prosecution

CHAPTER ONE - THE HOME RULE WHERE THE POWER HUNGRY WISHED TO RULE

The State of Florida has constitutional revision called the **"Home Rule"**. Most states have similar laws, but under different names. The Home Rule allows those of a specific area and its officials of a municipality to rule without State or Federal intervention. The Home Rule in Florida is the right of local governments to make decisions and create laws for their communities without needing state approval. It gives cities and counties the flexibility to address their unique needs and serve their residents' preferences.

Here are some areas which the **Home** Rule in Florida **allows:**

- Local decision-making without needing permission from the state legislature
- Self-government having the authority to create laws that are specific to their needs
- Services: such as water, sewer, garbage collection, storm water systems, roads, sidewalks, fire protection, law enforcement, parks and recreation.

The state retains all taxing authority, so Home Rule does not extend to fiscal Home Rule.

There are certain requirements of a municipality by statute, but the elected officials of municipalities, like White Springs, run with the rhythm of their own drum, deciding which laws they wished to follow or whether they wished to abide by their municipal charter.

The "**Home Rule**" is an excellent concept, especially when different regions have distinct criteria applying to their specific area which differ from other areas. But, let us face it, how well the Home Rule works depends upon its leadership. In Florida, the **'Home Rule"** language was proposed in the 1968 Constitutional revision and was adopted by the people. After several legal challenges, the legislature adopted the "Home Rule" Powers Act in 1973. Since the US Constitution made no provisions relating to city and county powers, this ended challenges relating to Local Government.

Unfortunately, in a Florida county which is financially poor, there are not an abundance of educated or experienced people to lead, or who wish to lead. In most cases, the "Good Ole Boy" rules apply. Those with an education who are newcomers have achieved what goals in their life they desired and do not wish to offer their time to a town, school, or county board. Most are retired because small towns do not produce an abundance of job opportunities for the younger set. But from what I have noticed, in the Town of White Springs, it is that those who have never had the appropriate education, or business experiences, those who have never achieved in their previous jobs despite an education, and those whose employers never saw fit to promote them up the ladder, are those who ran for office and were elected by promising free things or moneymaking schemes.

Yes, there are many successful businesspeople with only high school education or a GED but usually these businesspeople have the experience and know-how to run a business by hiring the best people. Most, however, remain in larger municipalities where their business may thrive, which does not add a wealth of experience or learned leadership skills to small towns.

In White Springs, the officials did not follow most laws. Running for town councils or other offices provided opportunities they would not have had in a larger municipality. There are individuals who did not have the tools to succeed. The resulting failures due to inexperience cost the local citizens thousands of dollars, because of the inability of town managers and officials to manage budgets and financials. Most importantly, there was no transparency, and the citizens did not have a clue of what was happening to their town. The citizens only desired what they were promised by the candidate prior to the election.

Because of the **"Home Rule"** the chosen leaders are free to do as they wish without fear of repercussion by the State or Federal Government. Even the State's attorneys overlook any transgressions which may apply as does the sheriff or other law enforcement. If these towns have their own police force, as White Springs did, the police officers would follow board member advice, rather than protecting lives and property in an unbiased manner. If a board member was questioned as to their decision making. not only would the official make it difficult for the person who dared to question them but, in most cases, would solicit law enforcement to join them in threatening the individual with ordinances and arrests, taking away their Constitutional rights of liberty, quality, and justice. Sometimes they would even take the rights of the citizens to attend public meetings.

the council members and manager in White Springs allegedly have felt they have such power, and knowledge that they may ignore the municipal's charter, and the Town's attorney's legal advice. There are jealousies and verbal and physical attacks as if one is a teenager, back in high school. Each council member works for what they can attain for themselves, rather than being concerned with their fiduciary duties to the citizens. Towns like White Springs cannot afford professionals with accounting or finance backgrounds and will just throw in a staff member with only a high school education or GED to input information and not having the logic to secure the assistance of others or take course studies to improve their knowledge base. White Springs has hired incompetent consultants without the necessary backgrounds to fulfill the positions they were hired for, just to save some money.

In Florida, citizen's complaints are ignored. In order to have the State investigate a claim of violations, a Council Member must draft the complaint and send it to the appropriate State Department. The only rights a citizen has is to secure an attorney and sue the Town and its officials, and most people in small towns cannot afford legal suits and the fear of what the officials may do to them. One should not have to sue a Town to get a response from the State or is it that the senators and representatives are more concerned with ignoring complaints by reason they do not wish votes taken away from them?

You will find in these writings that officials will not include volunteers to assist them who have the experience and education. Control is important to continue the official's personal agenda, and they do not wish for someone to change their decision-making process or provide new ideas or experience. Most develop an ego, and they wish the credit for anything that is favored but if there is a problem, they will not admit it was their decision but blame others. But cannot one be pleased for hiring or bringing in the correct experienced individuals to assist the process?

There is still racism in White Springs, where African-Americans do not trust Caucasians and vice versa. We now have an all African-American Council, but these council members were not voted by their experience and education, nor what they could do to benefit the town. This was a matter of skin color. Benefits such as allowing some to pay their utilities late, are provided to some but not all. It is all about one and only. The citizens are not aware of staff backgrounds or what they are being paid.

One may say that this has to do with individual personalities and their respective temperament. One may say they can vote the individual out of office. And in the case of officials who are elected, they must have a plan for the betterment of the town and all its citizens. However, one must be assured the Town hires the appropriate Town Manager, who has the experience and education to oversee all the duties required. **The council must do background checks as well as requiring a personality test such as Meyers/Briggs or other such profile tests as the private sector does.** No one applying for a high-end position in the private sector would be hired without providing a psychological or personality test. And to find out whether the candidate is serious about a manager's position, what would be wrong with asking how they could benefit the town? **Such testing should also apply to all staff members prior to being hired to assure they are capable of doing the job they have applied for.**

Most, if they had no prior managerial experience, should learn how to interview, but in small towns one must also determine from Human Resource material what one may or may not ask. This is where either the State or an entity like the Florida League of Cities could assist with basic information and questionnaires which would assist, in manual form. Small organizations cannot afford a Human Resource department so a municipality being provided a Human Resource Manual of dos and don'ts would assist the Town Manager and Council Members to follow the laws. It was further obvious that those officials and staff in White Springs had no organizational abilities and did not even know receipts were required or how to handle grant money or other restrictive funds. A local town manager in the area even threatened a staff member with a gun. The state needs to assist small towns by providing material which would be beneficial in running a town. Most importantly, does the candidate understand accounting, finance and insurance? The state could possibly provide an internet tutorial.

There is a failsafe mechanism, which is meant to work for those who are inexperienced in their council duties. It is the Council-manager form of government. It is meant to introduce professional management and remove politics from day-to-day administration. **The council-manager form of government consists of an elected city council which is responsible for policymaking and for hiring a professional town manager who is responsible for the administration of the Town.** The town Manager provides policy advice, directs the daily operations of the town, manages personnel functions (including the power to appoint and remove employees) and is responsible for preparing financial reports and budgets. The council members choose the mayor. The Town council is prohibited from interfering with the manager's administration. but the Manager is directly accountable to the Council and can be removed by a majority vote of the council at any time.

Did I say failsafe? Yes, in theory this would invoke non-political good government, That is if a professional manager is hired. But what happens when a small Town cannot afford a professional manager? And what happens if the Town Council wishes to control the manager? You will be able to make your own assessment after reading what has transpired to the detriment of White Springs.

Voters put Home Rule powers in the Florida Constitution more than 50 years ago. These powers state that any city can adopt laws if the law doesn't conflict with state or federal law. An easy way to understand it is: Local Voices Making Local Choices.

HISTORY OF THE HOME RULE BY THE FLORIDA LEAGUE OF CITIES:

The U.S. Constitution makes no mention of the powers related to local governments – the 10th Amendment reserves those powers to the state. During the 18th century, cities, counties and parishes across the nation derived their powers from their state constitutions, and these local governments relied upon their respective state legislatures for all powers. This was upheld in an 1860's court case, called "Dillon's Rule," which held for most states through the end of the 1800s. An example of the difficulty in a non-Home Rule era would be the issue of traffic control signs: if a city wished to erect signs related to traffic control (horses, wagons, and the newly created automobiles), the city first had to obtain state permission through a special act, or general law of local application.

Cities and counties might seek this permission jointly, or by population category ("all cities over 10,000 in population shall..." but still had to petition their legislators for these bills during each legislative session. It was not uncommon in Florida for more than 2,000 special acts to be filed in a session during this era. In the early 1900s, however, states began to adopt **"Home Rule"** provisions in which cities and counties were allowed to enact ordinances at the **local level** without state "blessing" – or without the enactment of special acts, general laws of local application, or similar measures.

In Florida, Home Rule language was proposed in the 1968 Constitutional revision and was adopted by the people. After several legal challenges, the Legislature adopted the Home Rule Powers Act in 1973, which ended challenges related to city and county powers. The Florida Constitution states in Article VIII, Section 2(b) for municipalities: **"Municipalities shall have governmental, corporate and proprietary powers to enable them to conduct municipal government, perform municipal functions and render municipal services, and may exercise power for municipal purposes except as otherwise provided by law."**

These powers do not extend to fiscal Home Rule: the state reserves all taxing authority unto itself. The most precious powers a city in Florida has been its Home Rule powers.

The ability to establish its form of government through its charter, and to then enact ordinances, codes, plans and resolutions without prior state approval is a tremendous authority. To further be able to enforce them "at home" and to make necessary changes as a city grows is a great reflection of the trust that citizens have in their respective city leaders. Of course, city laws cannot conflict with state or federal laws, Home Rule powers ensure that the cities are effectively and efficiently providing for the wishes of their citizens.

Why I believe the Home Rule requires the legislature to impose rulings which require the officials and managers of municipalities to follow the State and Federal laws or be fined or punished with a violation. It is obvious in my review of what has transpired in White Springs that the Home Rule is too broad or that there is no enforcement by the State to assure laws are followed, unless an official requests an investigation. A citizen's request is ignored. One may advise the various departments of the State of violations of law, but the only action taken is one which advises the Municipality that they should rectify the problem itself with whatever suggestions may be given by the State. The Auditor General findings are an example. What I have not understood is why those laws pertaining to statutes, if broken, are not handled

In small Towns, officials seem to be elected by **nepotism or cronyism** and although the statutes prohibit such relating to staff, there is no statutory definition because the officials were elected by the people.

I propose that the State place together tutorials for small towns to understand financial accounting and that there remains sanctions if such accounting is not adhered to. I propose the State or the Florida League of Cities provide a Manual / Handbook listing all requirements of the Manager and Town Staff to refer to. Since there seems to be a problem for many to read statutes, a simplified manual / handbook would assist the

Towns in handling all duties required by the State to assure that expensive audits need not be performed. After reviewing the Auditor General's report, what was stated therein would be a strong basis for a start. Most of the time, people are fearful of reading anything legal or by statute and I have no answer as to why. But something must be done for Small Towns so that the required procedures and requirements to the State are performed. Manuals and tutorials would be less expensive in the long run.

I also believe that there should be a course work manual pertaining to "How to Hire by Temperament" as well as psychological and personality testing. It would assure the right candidate is hired for the job.

As an afterthought, it is necessary for the legislature to enact within its statutes that independent contractors / consultants may not act as Town Managers for a municipality. Town Managers must be employees because the ramifications relating to a consultant being in charge of all the Town's finances can easily be a problem for all concerned.

How it all started

Griffin's unfavorable recognition may have begun in 2000. Bob Hanelsen, Lake City Reporter authored an article called "Taking on a Town". He wrote where Griffin had a dispute about where he could park his big rig which led to an escalating series of events including arrests, restraining orders and an impending federal rights lawsuit. Griffin, 51, at the time, was at the center of the controversy. Griffin admitted he is *"nobody's best friend"* and succeeded at making himself a thorn in the side of public officials and a disruptive force to a few locals. Griffin along with former town council member Bob D were pointing fingers at the town for not providing public records and showing favoritism to longtime residents.

Griffin and Bob D had erected signs at two locations, displaying their contempt for the town and Griffin has distributed fliers saying White Springs openly harbors pedophiles. They say their tactics are to shed light on the seedy underbelly of White Springs politics. Griffin, known as "Trucker Joe," claims he is only interested in the pursuit of justice. He said he is the victim of a town council that operates above the law. Having been only a resident of White Springs for one year, he was known about in every corner of the town as well as the offices of the State's Attorney Jerry Blair and various circuit judges, who have ruled on his complaints or against Griffin. After months of writing letters in a smear campaign against town manager Townsend, A deputy sheriff arrested Griffin and charged him with disturbing the peace on March 29th at town hall. Griffin, perceived as an annoying newcomer, now was considered a physical threat in his intent on changing the ways of a small town of 832 residents.

Chapter 119 of the Florida Statutes addresses public documents and the responsibility of public officials to release those documents. Griffin made hundreds of requests for everything from minutes of public meetings to personnel files of town employees. He said it has taken the town too long to comply with his requests and there are still documents that he has yet to receive. The town had to hire a part-time employee to help make copies for Griffin.

For a while, town officials with limited knowledge of the statutes had to consult with their attorney, Todd Kennon, about the public records law. Griffin eventually filed several lawsuits against the town alleging public records violations, but he withdrew the suits after he discovered a flaw in his complaint. He still claimed the town had not given him everything he wanted.

Eventually, Griffin went to State Attorney Blair and asked him to intervene. After months of letters, Blair said he tried to appease Griffin by inviting him to his office to look at any file he wished, even saying he could then make copies there. Griffin countered by saying, he did not think the state attorney could deny him the right to pay for the copies in advance and request that a copy of the entire file could be mailed to him.

Blair said it was his intention to resolve the issues, but that Mr. Griffin does not seek public records, he seeks to use the public records law to harass public officials. In a letter from Blair to Griffin dated January 14, 2001, Blair wrote *"I have attempted to respond to your many inquiries in a professional manner.... However, I have spent about all of the taxpayers' time and money I intend to spend in responding to what is becoming increasingly obvious is a vendetta against the town of White Springs and its elected and appointed officials".*

When Bob D and Griffin arrived at Town Hall, Town Clerk Shirley Heath was working with another clerk, Paula Sullivan. She said she was busy and unable to provide Bob D with her file of her Graduate equivalency Diploma (GED). Heath said before she could tell Bob D the file would be available the next day; Griffin exploded and began yelling at her. Bob D joined in. Unknown to both men, town officials had installed a panic button near the front counter for just such an occasion. The Hamilton County Sheriff's office was soon called at Bob D's request because he believed Heath was violating public records laws. Griffin said he was there simply to document what happened and denied acting threateningly in any way towards Heath.

Heath said she had other reasons to be afraid since Bob D worked as a law enforcement officer with the Department of Agriculture, and he was in uniform. She mentioned that Bob D carried a gun when he was in uniform, and the level of the counter would prevent her from seeing whether Bob D was armed with a gun. Bob D claimed he was not in uniform and was wearing a black t-shirt with an insignia on the chest nor did he have a gun on him. It, however, made a great news article.

When Sheriff's Deputy Williams arrived, Heath made him aware of the situation. and he asked Griffin to be quiet, according to the arrest report. Griffin spoke up again and Williams told Griffin to step outside and be quiet or he would be arrested for disturbing the peace. Then Griffin spoke up again and Williams arrested him on a charge of disturbing the peace.

Later, the newspaper, after interviewing Griffin about the inability to secure 119's, attempted to secure paperwork from the Town. Per the statute, the documents should have been provided within a reasonable time in which to find the paperwork and give it to the reporter. When that did not happen after numerous requests, the Newspaper enlisted the support of New York Times attorneys in Tampa to demand the paperwork from the Town. The response given by Town Clerk Shirley Heath and Town Manager Robert Townsend, at the time, was that they had to consult with their attorney before giving out public records. While the records request was granted three days later – the State's government in the Sunshine Laws says the caretaker of the records in this case, Heath, is responsible for knowing which records may be released.

Griffin said he fell in love with White Springs at first sight. It was like he was back in the 1950's. But the love Griffin felt would soon wear off after Mary Lou Cunningham complained to the town council that Griffin's truck broke several branches on her trees, clipped a cable wire and disturbed her when he started the engine in the morning hours. The dispute led to Griffin being told that town ordinances forbid him from driving his truck and trailer on his street. There was also concern that the weight of Griffin's tractor-trailer unit would damage fragile town wastewater systems under the road. Griffin moved his truck but was frustrated that the town took six weeks to show him a copy of the ordinance.

That is when he began his campaign looking into Cunningham's property. He soon discovered that she was living in a condemned house even though Cunningham was a member of the Town's zoning board. The female head of the Zoning Board complained that Griffin's tractor-trailer unit was responsible for damaging the electrical lines on Mill Street, which it could not. The woman was living in one of the two buildings in Griffin's neighborhood which were condemned by a magistrate. Yet the woman lived there, with no electricity or water, stating that Griffin was ruining the value of the properties in the neighborhood. She told the council that Griffin's tractor-trailer unit was depreciating the value of property on Mill Street including her condemned building. She made a complaint to the council about the power lines, but trucks and tractor trailer units still travel on Mill and the power lines were high enough because more than one semi used the roadway and there was no damage to the electrical wires. She also worked at a restaurant Griffin frequented, and Griffin saw her spit in his food. Instead of discussing it with her, the restaurant owner said she would never do such a thing and Griffin left the restaurant.

It so happened that there was no way in which water could be supplied to the woman's building in which she lived so she solicited assistance from a Black neighbor who lived across the street from her. The neighbor placed a water hose across the road so the woman could have water. The only way the water hose would have been damaged is by the weight of the tractor-trailer unit or by any vehicle going across it. But there never was damage to the electrical wires.

At a council meeting Griffin decided to dig into the woman by stating that she as a White woman was making peace between the races (the Town being 50% White and Hispanic and 50% Black). Griffin said he could not understand why her legs were in the air. This caused a commotion at the meeting and then from that day, Griffin was labeled a "stalker" even though he took a wild guess at the relationship.

Griffin finally managed to solicit the help of the right government department, who found the woman another low-income apartment. She stated Griffin did her a favor by his continual reporting of the conditions of the building she was living in. However, from that time on for 18 years, Griffin tried to have the property demolished due to the inherent hazards of the condemned building. No one in the Town would listen even when Griffin forced the Town to take the owner of the property to court. After a year of on and off litigation, It is believed, the Town dropped the case due to the owner being a relative of a Council woman. And there you have the Home Rule. The Council may decide anything it wishes whether it should be against the law or whether someone may sustain injuries or death.

Cunningham said she soon several state inspectors were on her property including one from the State Department of Children and Families, claiming that someone reported she was selling heroin to children. Griffin denied he told the department that Cunningham was selling drugs, and no evidence was found, nor charges filed against her. However, when an inspector from the power company arrived at the property, it was discovered that Cunningham was using a temporary power pole that had been in use for more than five years. Temporary poles are allowed by law, on a piece of property for two years. Cunningham said she found herself homeless. After living briefly in her car, she was able to find an apartment. She believes that her quality of life is much better now compared to trying – albeit poorly – to restore an old house. *"I owe a thank you to Mr. Griffin for improving my life"* she said, *"That will probably make him mad."*

Griffin continued to ask for public records and sometimes showed up to town meetings with a video camera, pointing it at the face of everyone who entered the door. But it was his letters that eventually got him into trouble. In a letter dated September 24, 1999, Griffin wrote to town Clerk Heath and said, *"I am coming after you personally"*. On September 29th, he added *"Why don't you, wonderful Christian people, come talk to me and see if we can work this thing out before any blood is shed"* Then on October 2nd, Griffin wrote *"Stick a fork in you, you're done"*. These types of comments are used by businesspeople. Heath filed a restraining order against Griffin, fearing that his threats implied physical harm. Griffin said that *"blood"* referred to a stock market term used to describe major money changing hands. Griffin admitted it was a bad choice of words and following a hearing with a judge, the restraining order was removed. Griffin was also an ordained minister but did not receive the calling to remain a minister.

As for Griffin, he was an amazing salesperson. As a Meyers/Briggs INTJ he received awards for being the top salesperson for annuities. His closing line was *"Let me help you fill out your checkbook"*. However, when his company asked him to sell other securities, he refused and left the company, even though he had all his Stockbroker series licenses. When he started out, while in college, he sold copy and printing machines. One of his largest sales was for the Black Panthers Organization, who paid him in cash, allowing only him in the future to service and train those in the organization. As a stockbroker, he lived large and I genuinely believe, he still felt he had that kind of money and clout, and everyone should bow down to him.

When I met Griffin, he said that he had been looking for me all his life. I found that although he was walking, he was physically challenged and needed a wheelchair if he walked more than a block. His friend Jim Smith told me that Griffin had not been walking before meeting me.

It appeared he was being treated unfairly and as a result became a formidable opponent to those who dared to say he was wrong. Griffin felt he was smarter and had more of an education than any of these people. And he was going to show them how ignorant they really were. His dream was to be on the Town Council, or to be the Town Manager. He, however, never understood, that taking his disdain and aggressions against the current officials would never allow him to do so. They may have not been book smart, but they were certainly "street smart" and were not afraid to play dirty, as did Griffin.

There was no transparency in the Town and that was Griffin's primary complaint. He felt the officials were not only incompetent, but corrupt. In the time in which Griffin lived in the town, he placed 19 pro se *(acting as his own attorney)* suits against the Town for not providing documentation under Chapter 119 of the Florida Statutes.

Griffin's Pro se Suits

Case No. 99-308-CA Griffin vs. Heath, McKire, Hardwick, McKenzie, Townsend

Case No. 99-324-CA Griffin vs. Heath

Case No. 99-378-CA Griffin vs. Woodard

Case No. 00- 228-CA Griffin vs. Town of White Springs, McKire, Dunn

Case No. 00-329-CA Griffin vs. Town of White Springs

Case No. 01-15-CA Griffin vs. Heath

Case No. 01-16-CA Griffin vs. Hardwick

Case No. 01-332-CA Griffin vs. McKire

Case No. 02-261-CA Griffin vs. John Peeler et al vs. Joseph Mc

Kire et alCase No. 03-56-CA Griffin vs. Town of White Springs

Case No. 03-224-CA Griffin vs. Town of White Springs

Case No. 03-397-CA Griffin vs. Town of White Springs

Case No. 08-283-CA Griffin vs. Town of White SpringsCase No. 09-219-C

A Griffin vs. Heath, Kennon, Rudser

Case No. 09-317-CA Griffin vs. White Springs Town Council. KennonCase No. 10-118-CA Griffin vs. McKire

Case No. 10-174-CA Griffin vs. Koberlein

Griffin's ability to bring pro se suits ended when the Town's attorney brought forth to the Court many banker's boxes filled with paperwork of prior suits. Yet, Griffin advised me that the attorney appraised the court that these banker's boxes applied only to one suit. It was deemed by the judge that Griffin could no longer function as his own attorney. In the future, Griffin was not allowed to file a suit without the engagement of an attorney. The local newspaper published the judge's decision which brought glee to the officials and their followers. The Town felt it won the battle.

Only one of Griffin's suits did not apply to 119's. It pertained to a Fire Chief who came to Griffin, asking for help to recapture the $10,000 his fire department had earned through various money-making events. When the Fire Chief complained that the manager transferred all the fire department money into the town coffers due to an immediate need. His job was then terminated by the town manager. Although Griffin was willing to help the former Chief, the Chief was threatened by officials and the suit was dropped. The various 119 suits made by Griffin ended with a "Motion to Dismiss" in which Griffin acting as his own attorney did not know how to object to the motion.

THE CONDEMNED HARRIS PROPERTY AT 8301

Griffin wished the properties would be demolished after Cunningham left.. He then issued a complaint that the members of the Board of Adjustment of the Town of White Springs, *Nora Lang, Chairman, Board Members Bernard Williams and Watkin Saunders allegedly broke municipal ordinance 98.01, on February 19, 2001.*

Griffin further complained that Town Manager, Robert "Bobby" Townsend, Land Development Regulations admin-istration for the Town of White Springs Florida allegedly conspired with the Board Chairman and members of the committee to break the provisions of the Town's Municipal Ordinances.

Additionally, Griffin alleged that the Town Council of White Springs, composed of Mayor Joseph McKire, Vice Mayor Ralph Hardwick, Council members McKenzie, Dean Dietrich and Tracey Woodard did likewise break said ordinance 98-01, Section 10 for their failure to hear in a timely manner the appeal for an extension of time referred to them by the Board of Adjustment on February 19, 2001.

On or about 09/11/2001 Henry Dunn, the Land Development Regulations Administrator, investigated and reported pm the property at 8301-000 owned by Michael Harris, a resident of White Springs and brother-in-law of Council Member Tracey Woodard. Mr. Dunn found and reported notices of violations of multiple provisions of the Town Land Development Regulations (LDR's). One of the violations expressed to Mr. Harris by Mr. Dunn in his report was for Unsafe buildings. The Unsafe Building Regulations are found in Chapter 10 of the LDR's. On 10/11/2000 Mr. Dunn mailed a copy of his report to Mr. Harris which pointed out the violations of the "Unsafe Buildings".

The report advised Mr. Harris that he was allowed to make an appeal of the decision, including any request for an extension of time to come into compliance. The report gave Mr. Harris 120 days to correct all the violations including the violation of Chapter 10, the unsafe buildings violation.

On 01/2520/01, Mr. Harris, knowing that the 120 days were soon to expire, requested an extension of time to complete the repairs but had not secured a building permit.

On 02/19/2001 the Board of Adjustment of the Town of White Springs held a public meeting to which Mr. Harris had purportedly been advised in a legal manner of what was happening. The purpose of the meeting was to discuss his request for more time to repair the building on property 8301-000. Town Manager Townsend stated that although Mr. Harris had been properly notified of the meeting, he did not choose to attend the meeting, nor did he send his attorney or any representative.

On February 20, 2001, the Town Council met in a public meeting, The Unsafe building provisions clearly stated that the failure of any person to appear at the hearing set forth in accordance with the provisions of the Article (12) shall constitute a waiver of his or her right to an appeal. Griffin stated that since Mr. Harris did not appear at his hearing, his rights were waived to appeal for an extension for repair or demolition of Property 8301-000. Nevertheless Ms. Lang, Chairman of the Board of Adjustment and the two other members of the Board of Adjustment did vote to recommend the Town Council award Mr. Harris an extension to the 120 days contained in the Notice of Violations for Unsafe Buildings.

After 18 years, a businessperson from *Jacksonville* Beach, Arlen Scott Gay, who previously lived in the Town and attended school in Hamilton County, moved into his aunt's house which he renovated. He cared for her prior to her death and was her

Power of Attorney (POA). And because he had plans for purchasing a house across the street for his partner, he also purchased the condemned buildings which he had demolished. This increased the size of the property.

Now one did not have to worry about children going into the building and becoming hurt. The Town never understood the cost of a Liability suit against it and the fact that if an insurer paid out on a claim, the insurance premium cost would increase.

Griffin would try to attend most of the council meetings where he continued being vocal and insulting regarding the Town's handling of finances and not providing transparency. The Town Council initiated ordinances which would apply only to Griffin and other ordinances which would apply to all others. It happened that one of these ordinances applied to Griffin's tractor-trailer unit and other vehicles owned by him. It stated that any such vehicles on the Town's berm would result in a fine. The problem is that a new police officer did not know the rules and fined vehicles at the Telford Hotel, which caused the police officer to be terminated.

The Town continued to retaliate against Griffin's complaints and actions. They drafted **ordinances just for Griffin.**

2006 TRASHY LAWN ORDINANCE:

The Town had to have a special ordinance for trashy lawns because the Town could not enforce the zoning codes also known as MO-98-01. This was because Griffin dismantled the pool and had debris on the front lawn.

ORDINANCE 08-03

ORDINANCE DECLARING THE ACCUMULATION OF WEEDS, UNDERBRUSH, UNDERGROWTH, GARBAGE, WASTE AND TRASH UPON REAL PROPERTY A NUISANCE AND PROVIDING FOR THE ABATEMENT THEREOF: March 11, 2008.

ORDINANCE 07-09

Ordinance prohibiting abandoned or junked motor vehicles or motor vehicle accessories; on property, streets, highways or rights-of-way,

ORDINANCE 03-04

Effective. August 19, 2003 -No person shall stand or park a vehicle upon any roadway for the purpose of (a) Displaying it for sale; (b) washing, greasing or repairing the vehicle except repairs necessitated by emergency; (c) Displaying advertising (d) Selling merchandise from such vehicles except when so authorized or licensed under the Ordinances of the Town; (e) storage, junk, dead storage for more than twenty-four (24) hours), (f) Upon any sidewalk, right of way or swalls (birm) of the Town. Pursuant to hardships due to unique characteristics of a property lot, the owner can request a variance from the Town Council. (g) Shall be unlawful to park or stop any vehicle in such a manner as to obstruct the free use of the streets by other vehicles or in such a manner as to impeded traffic on the streets.

SECTION 4, REGULATION OF SEMI TRUCKS AND TRAILERS:

PURPOSE: To regulate parking anywhere within the Town limits including streets, public property and private property within the Town Limits.

Parking of semi-trucks and semi-trailers on private property is prohibited in the Town unless the property is zoned to allow such parking or otherwise indicated. Parking of semi-trucks and semi-trailers upon streets and other public property (Semi's shall not be parked on public streets or other public property in any zoning district of the town except for purposes of pick-up or delivery. Then they may be parked for up to 30 minutes.) Semi-Trailers not connected to semi-trucks shall not be parked on public streets or other publicly owned property in any zoning district within the Town.

An owner would have to obtain a special exception from the Town prior to allowing parking and those exceptions will follow the Town's Land Development Regulations.

Due to Hurricane Damage in Florida, the average cost of insurance per year is soaring to 11,000. And there are fewer insurance companies willing and able to cover wind damage by named Hurricanes.

When living from paycheck to paycheck, it was difficult for those in a small town to buy either property or liability insurance, much less hurricane and flood insurance. The family and the family's needs came first. Because of the age of some of these homes in White Springs and the materials used to build them at the time, many could not afford specialty insurance, nor could they be offered homeowners' insurance. Flood insurance was not an option because many did not realize homeowners' insurance would not cover floods due to storm surges during hurricanes, rapid accumulation of water during a heavy rainstorm or a river or stream overflowing its banks. Property insurance including Named Hurricanes and Windstorm coverage costs have increased to an average of over $11,000 a year.

CHAPTER TWO – GRIFFIN'S PRIVATE LIFE ASIDE FROM POLITICS

When I moved to White Springs, I certainly had no idea how corrupt the Town was, nor did I realize that Griffin kept "poking the bear" by his continual bullying and defamatory language. When telling me about the Town the conversations were always statements of how corrupt the people running the Town were.

Many in the Town would call Griffin a Narcissist but when I met Griffin, I had no idea that he portrayed narcissistic tendencies. I did not have an idea of what a Narcissist was because I did not find the need to investigate. However. it was noted that Griffin had a desire to control and never could be wrong. Griffin would go through life starting arguments and having an overinflated ego. He had a fake sense of superiority because of his education and felt he was better than anyone else.

After eleven years of marriage and at the advice of police officers, I signed a petition and sworn statement with the circuit court, seeking an ex parte order for Griffin, to have an involuntary mental examination. My husband previously would not take the prescribed tests the Veterans Administration suggested he take. Griffin knew that if he refused to take these tests, any such involuntary act to hold or keep him would result in a charge of kidnapping. He knew he could discharge himself from the hospital when he felt like it and he could refuse all tests. The hospitals and doctors initially felt he was bi-polar, then they said he was mentally ill, but after the examinations, the doctors' found Griffin was well physically and there was nothing anyone in the medical field could do about a **personality disorder**. Yet, he was not the only person in the Town of White Springs who may have been a narcissist, even though it seemed he was more destructive mentally by sucking the energy out of those he dealt with.

Griffin graduated from Lakeview high school, Winter Garden, FL, in 1966. He then graduated from Florida Technological University in Orlando Fl with a BS Degree in Chemistry in 1972. Chemistry was easy for him, so he did not have to work hard to earn his degree. Today, the University is known as the University of Central Florida. Griffin then attended Naval Flight School in Pensacola Florida and graduated in 1972.

While in the Navy, Griffin attended Pepperdine University in Malibu, California in 1976 with an MA in Education in August 1976. This was followed with an off-campus MA program in SE Asia through the American College where he earned his Chartered Life Underwriter and Chartered Financial Consultant master's degrees. Griffin also received a master's in divinity (Theology) degree in 1994. When I met Griffin, he was going to Santa Fe College where he was getting an associate degree in legal studies. He graduated in December of 2012, with $30,000 in school debt and this course did not make him an attorney. but Griffin felt it gave him legal background. In fact, when a local legal office accepted him for his two-week trial, they had him blowing balloons and much work which would not entail legal assistant work.

With Five Master's degrees, Griffin felt he was the most educated person in the Town and certainly the Town should vote for him to be on the Town Council or hire him as the Town Manager.

As a full Lieutenant in the U. S. Navy, he became an aircraft pilot in 1972. Griffin was stationed on a Naval Ship flying aircraft. Griffin then changed over to flying a helicopter in Southeast Asia. Griffin was spot on in blowing bridges and bombing the enemy. His only problem was getting his aircraft hooked on the deck of the ship and that caused many sailors to take bets on the galley. On his behalf, I must say that it takes men like Griffin who have no fear to go after the enemy as he did. He had three tours in Southeast Asia before being a decorated spokesperson for the Navy.

Griffin absolutely refused to ever discuss why he lost his three bronze and two silver star metals. He only stated that they were taken away from him because of his commanding officer. His Commanding Officer (CO) was made the captain of a Naval Ship as an experiment. The CO was educated, and the Navy put him in that position as the first Black Captain without earning the position, Griffin felt. This upset Griffin because Griffin felt he had earned that honor. This may have caused Griffin's bias against African-Americans. But I learned later that as a boy, he listened to two older men who were Racists, and he believed the conjecture they spoke of.

Griffin then apparently decided to do something either against his commanding officer (CO) or to the ship. It is not something he was willing to discuss. Whatever the incident was, his CO was taking Griffin somewhere, in his vehicle. Griffin wished to discuss the incident with his CO, but the officer said he could not discuss anything with Griffin because of Griffin's medals and ribbons, Griffin then, not only took his medals and ribbons off, but asked his CO to stop the car on the edge of the San Francisco Bridge. Then Griffin proceeded to throw them over the San Franciso bridge into the Bay. That is all I was told by Griffin. He did relish later to know that his CO's ship had run-aground, and the CO had lost his rank. I also found out later that he signed off on having his medals, never to discuss them to receive an honorable discharge. He then finished his career as a Captain in the Army Reserve as a helicopter pilot.

When he decided to move into the little Town of White Springs, he immediately had difficulty with the police and the officials of the Town. Although he was friendly to most of the then 800 residents, that soon changed because of the political front; especially once any of his new acquaintances decided to be elected to the Town Council.

Griffin, once ending his military career after 23 years, became a truck driver landing a position operating a semi-tractor trailer unit for an excellent company but parked it in the residential area in front of his home. The Town officials and the neighbors directly across from his house set Griffin up so he would get his third disorderly conduct in 2005.

The neighbors picked a fight with Griffin over his tractor-trailer being parked in front of his house and a police car was sitting at the end of the block ready to arrest him. Griffin confronted his neighbors in anger, he was arrested and charged with disorderly conduct. He paid the fine and was back in town within an hour. However, as soon as Griffin was arrested, Town Manager Townsend immediately called Griffin's employer, Liedtka Trucking Company, to tell them Griffin had been arrested and was in jail. Subsequently, Liedtka fired Griffin who exclusively. had worked for Liedtka Trucking from 1998-2003. I learned this was payback by the Town Manager because Griffin caused enough anger that the Town Manager felt he could not retain his position as Town Manager.

After Griffin no longer had a job, he took miscellaneous trucking jobs because he could not find another long-haul employer with like benefits for almost three years, Griffin jumped at the chance of driving a tractor-tanker. Griffin was hired as an operator of a tractor-tanker by the tanker company on August 3, 2007. On August 21, 2007, Griffin went up the tanker ladder to check the tank compression and he remembered hitting his head on part of the tanker before falling to the cement.

This was after he was Baker Acted and a doctor at the Gainesville VA insisted Griffin was Bi-Polar. Griffin was prescribed three Prozac (Fluoxetine), one Lamotrigine, and an Ambilify which he was to take daily. It was not known if the pills made him dizzy or something else caused Griffin to fall. When he crawled up the ladder to release the pressure in the vents of the tanker, he lost his balance and crashed into the cement, with his head hitting the tanker, breaking his fall. He was rushed to Vanderbilt's trauma hospital in Nashville, where he remained for 11.5 months between hospitalization and rehab.

Griffin shattered his hip, suffered a concussion and other internal organ damage. Griffin was not expected to live. He was in Vanderbilt hospital in Nashville for 11.5 months. He initially was in an induced coma and was not expected to live. He sustained extensive injuries, with the major injury being a shattered pelvis and damage to his bladder. A chain, like that of a bicycle chain, was bolted to his hips to keep his body together since he no longer had a pelvis. The accident happened in 2009, and the doctors told him he would not walk again. But Griffin had determination. Vanderbilt Hospital, Nashville, TN, at the time had two of the three national doctors who could perform this type of surgery.

His sister stated that the lady he had been dating broke up with Griffin at the hospital because she could not come to grips with his disabilities. Once Griffin was released from the hospital, he started to look online for a new companion; one who could do things for him because the only food he could prepare was pizza on his pizza machine. Throughout his military career, he always had servants wherever he was stationed. When he expected his first wife to serve him, she refused, he had an affair, and his wife subsequently divorced Griffin, after five years of marriage. He then continually went to restaurants.

Upon his return to White Springs, Town Attorney Koberlein asked permission of Griffin to enter his home. Attorney Koberlein then went from room to room and Griffin had no idea why the Town attorney was there and did not consider asking Townsend,

Next, within a day or two, Lieutenant Blanton of the Sheriff's office and the Town Attorney showed up and demanded payment for three court judgments. All property was removed from the house, including Griffin's wheelchair even though Griffin was unable to walk. Griffin asked the Town Attorney what he was going to do with the Collection Agency and Griffin was told it was his problem, not the Town's. Sargeant Blanton made certain that Griffin was given his wheelchair back and assisted Griffin into the Sheriff's unit.

Blanton took Griffin to the bank where he withdrew money off credit cards and his bank accounts because he had no time to secure money from his annuity accounts or outside sources to pay for the judgments. Once the judgments were paid, Clerk of Court Greg Godwin did the satisfactions of Judgment on all three cases on September 10, 2010.

Griffin used much of his savings from his Stockbroker days on education, fast cars, travel, and women. Yet in this case, he was in the hospital for almost a year. Griffin's friend Jim Smith assisted him in watching over the property and taking care of his bills. Griffin then was on Medical Disability payments with Social Security, which was a decent income due to him having been a stockbroker previously. He also received military pay and had various annuities; those of which had low balances due to his having paid for his education, except for the recent $30,000.

Griffin spent more than $40,000 in various court proceedings and judgments. Had he hired an attorney, he would have won Chapter 119 cases. He also would have paid less to hire an attorney than to pay court costs and fees. Although he earned an associate degree during the time he met me, as a legal assistant, it did not make him an attorney, especially after the medical trauma he went through which may have lessened that initial 160 IQ.

Then after moving to White Springs, he decided to go into the lawn business with his friend Jim Smith. Griffin purchased a lawn mower with the money received from the ring his former fiancé threw back at him. The problem Griffin had was that he could not even operate a weed eater, so Jim managed the business on his own without a partner. With the way Griffin requires people to serve him, he may despise physical work and that was the reason he feigned not understanding Jim's instructions. How hard is it to cut weeds? At a much later date, Griffin even purchased one for me so I could cut weeds. My birthday gifts included a ladder, a weed cutter, and mops. Otherwise, he purchased pots and pans and appliances for the kitchen including a used mixer with at least ten different attachments. Note, all these items were to serve Griffin in one way or another.

Griffin had tunnel vision when it came to Chapter 119 of the Florida Statutes. There was also the controversy of arguing one of his 119 cases before the Judge, when he did not like the Judge's decision. He called the Judge a "Crook" because the judge did not rule in his favor. Griffin ended up in jail. Since his dog Lump was locked in the house, Lump gnawed a sizeable hole in a wooden door so he could attempt getting out. He also did damage to one of the room's blinds and defecated all over the living room carpet. Griffin did not believe in repairing and maintaining his property unless there was an insurance inspection or appraisal. I do not know how long Griffin was in jail, but it had to be at least a week or two. He told me that he was sentenced to be jailed for 30 days but somehow, he was released from jail early. He had a woman come in and clean, but the living room was left as it was, and I continually had to shampoo the rugs after removing dried excrement from the carpeting.

In 2001-Town Attorney Kennon and Joseph McKire, Mayor stipulated Griffin could no longer attend Council Meetings and that Griffin had no right to question the council nor did the council have to answer him. If he attended a council meeting, the White Springs Police Department would arrest him. Therefore, the only method in which to check the town would be in Chapter 119s of the Florida Statutes.

After we met at a restaurant, Griffin decided to see me where I was living with my daughter in Belleview. He hauled his wheelchair in a small trailer behind his vehicle. When trying to back the trailer, something happened to the tires. One or two tires had come off the rims. I then found out that Griffin had a terrible temper and was using defamatory language kicking his tires which caused the neighbors to peer out windows and doors to see what the ruckus was.

I realized later that Griffin had specific criteria in choosing a mate. He desired a woman who had no children or grandchildren. It should have been my clue that he wanted the attention only, but I did not grasp that initially. My daughter, who was a workaholic like I had been, had not married, and no children were involved. The first time she visited us, because of the friendship the two of us had, Griffin started to brood. He was jealous of her, and I had to assure him that I did not forget him. In time he would be proud of her achievements, which he was. However, that is only if they did not get in a disagreement about the law.

We decided to live together as a trial. When I moved into Griffin's house, the biggest problem was the master bath. There was also a large hole in the ceiling of the utility room which needed repair, so I purchased the materials and fixed the ceiling. The toilet was not attached to the Master bathroom floor and the floor sagged, moving downward when one walked on it. The only sturdy item in that section of the bathroom was the large shower unit. Griffin called his friend Jim and one-half of the master bathroom which was damaged was torn down. Jim then started rebuilding the bathroom and found where prior termites had eaten much of the insides of the wood. The termites were dead or long gone, but the wood taken from the floor was completely light weight, like cardboard. No wonder the floor moved downward. It was amazing that Griffin had not fallen through the floor. The termites ate the insides of the planks. Griffin was upset because he felt I was costing him money.

At one time there was an inground pool but because the cement had cracked, Griffin had it removed. But instead of placing the cement pieces into the ground, he gave the cement to his friend Bob, and he placed old furnishings in the ground so that the ground forever sagged. You noted the aforementioned ordinance regarding the pool removal.

The barn roof remained above what I felt would make a good pump house. Jim built the front of the building with a large window so the air could filter through, and the electrical wiring was protected. With the rest of the barn torn down, no one would bump their heads when going into the pool.

Griffin had a yellow jeep that he purchased as his toy. Everyone in town raved about his jeep. Then came the day when a Black minister came to our door to seek help. The minister stated cars were stuck in the mud around his church and he needed Griffin and his jeep to pull them out. After Griffin assisted those who were in peril, the minister joined us at our house and Griffin asked him if he would marry us in November. The minister agreed and took the necessary courses that allowed him to marry someone. Prior to that he had only officiated at funerals.

Griffin and I were married on November 24, 2012, with the wedding held at our home. My daughter was the maid-of-honor and our neighbor and friend, Bob D., stood up for Griffin. There were fresh flowers in baskets on the hot tub deck which the minister would use as his pulpit. Many guests were invited but some of which could not attend because the wedding was on Thanksgiving weekend. I found out later that Griffin held back invitations for his family so that the invites were not received but three days prior to the wedding.

Tamara, Griffin and I went on a cruise after the wedding. This was to be Griffin's first cruise, which we booked through Carnival. We had a suite with a balcony and before leaving for the trip, I had made up all the details about the schematic of the ship, where we were to go, where we may wish to eat and the activities we wished to enjoy. Everything was great until we boarded the ship. Griffin decided he knew better than anyone where to find our room and where to go. He had the nerve to yell and swear at Tamara and I in public. He told us he was not going to follow us, so we let him go on his own. Little did I know Griffin pushed marriage because he then believed he owned me and could control me.

Although we enjoyed the sites, Griffin decided to drink a lot. It was our first clue when he tried driving his wheelchair up a pillar in the ship next to the elevators. The dining area had a step, and he put the restaurant people through hell, placing a ramp up the step so he could get to the dining table. The people assigned to our table did not seem impressed with Griffin. He operated his wheelchair recklessly, but Tamara and I just ignored what he was doing and enjoyed the trip as much as we could, while the wild man enjoyed his first cruise.

We remained friends with the Black Minister and his family who had married us. The minister even invited us to his family reunion where I assisted Rev. Richard with cooking chicken and small crabs. Griffin just sat with the women because most of the Black men somehow, did not trust him or want to get to know him, from his reputation.

We attended Rev. Richard's church and volunteered for the food drives. Churches were able to secure meat, vegetables, and pastries from a facility where stores would donate items which they did not sell or were a day old. The churches would pay a small percentage of a dollar to purchase the food. Then the food was distributed to the poor. The food offerings were only vegetables from farms, bread and cakes, but one time, Rev. Richard's spouse was able to secure an abundance of meat consisting of beef, chicken, and pork at ten cents a pound.

When I was assisting, I noticed a small amount of the meat was being placed in coolers for distribution, but that was only a fraction of what was in the two refrigerators I helped fill at the church. The refrigeration was turned up to its coolest point and it was obvious that the meat from these two refrigerators would not be distributed to the poor. It seemed strange that only one or two meat items were provided per family. When I donated my time to Interfaith of Ocala, far more food was given to any family. I found out that Rev. Richard and his wife owned an adult living home, where they may use the additional food to feed their residents. This was, in addition to the residents paying for their room and board, which to me, was illegal.

Before I found out about the adult living home, Griffin had started a blog called the White Springs Journal. I of course was a writer on the blog and did research. Griffin also had me author specific stories where he would instruct what he desired and approve or disapprove of the story. He had me do all the work unless someone angered him and then he decided to do his own defamatory writings in capital letters.

It was then that I asked Rev. Richard if I could do a biography of him. He agreed and provided me with the information about how he and his wife started with nothing and worked their way up to having a nice house and began their business, which was the adult living home. He happened to mention the name of the facility which provided the food for the poor. At the time, I thought nothing of providing all the information he gave me. I did not realize that it would be a problem to name the facility.

In 2012 after marrying Griffin, we applied for a loan, only to find that the Collection Agency did not know that the Town received payments in full. The Town Attorney said it would be up to Griffin to manage the collection agency. Sterling King felt the Satisfactions of Judgment had to be falsified because they had not heard from the town nor were they paid. So, to get the favorable loan, the money was paid again, and Manager Farley had to pay $4,800 which was 50% of the fee collected, to the Collection Agency by Credit Card so we could get our money back from the collection agency. The Town Attorney then wanted to sue the Collection Agency for not collecting but then Town Manager Farley thought it prudent to drop the matter

Years after the statute of limitations expired the collection of these judgments never seemed to end. When Townsend's cousin Bullard became Mayor, he told the Town Attorney Hatton again to collect the money for the judgments, believing they were not paid initially, with Townsend's advice. Attorney Hatton did not do her due diligence and after clearing everything with the Delaware Collection Agency, I wrote her a letter explaining how she failed in her duties as an attorney. It may have been with fear of my going to the Florida Bar to report her misgivings, but she elected to give notice to the Town that she was resigning, the very next day. I also mentioned in the letter that when she was an Assistant State's Attorney, she had a bias against Griffin, when she and Mayor Miller railroaded him for five felonies. She also had not done her due diligence to determine whether the judgments were previously paid.

CHAPTER THREE – GRIFFIN'S NEMESES

Sitting on the porch, you would see the police cars escorting Mayor Miller to the area of the Black community. Even though she was voted in by a majority including those who were Black, it took years for her to not fear going into the neighborhood. I thought, what a waste of taxpayers' money. Yet Mayor Miller and her husband provided beer and chicken to the neighborhood so there could be friendship among the races, as well as Black people to manage lawn duties for the mayor and her husband. Mayor Miller became Griffin's nemesis. Unfortunately, after her final term as mayor, she passed away from cancer but not before the worst damage to the Town happened. Even though not all of it was her fault. Like Griffin, she wished to control everything and everyone.

It was interesting to me to find Mayor Miller had three distinctly different resumes. One resume was online through a society she and her husband belonged to whereby it stated she had expertise in strategic planning, technology, education, and training. She mentioned her activities as Mayor in White Springs and her previous positions included St. Edwards University, Exxon USA and EPRCo, Texas Department of Commerce, Texas Engineering Experiment Station, National Center for Manufacturing Sciences and the Society of Manufacturing engineers. She was a consultant and a founding director of both the Texas Board of the Technology Transfer Society. Mayor Miller received the BBA, MBA, and PhD degrees from the University of Texas at Austin.

One resume was to the Town, and one was to apply for a government position of County Extension Director and Extension Agent in Columbia County.

None of the titles of her jobs seemed to be in sync with the first resume and in the resume to the County, she focused on family children and adult family members from June 2000 to 2009. Her greatest achievement was being the mayor of our Town, and her position as mayor was a bit embellished.

Mayor Miller's husband was said to be a diplomat working for various presidents; one of which was President Reagan. Yet, there was no information substantiating that he was a diplomat, but rather another person with the same name was shown on the internet. What one found online was that he was a Consultant for DSI Consulting and a director for Green Planet, Originally, he was a director for Omni Alliance Group until 2008, and for EMTA Holdings until 2009. He remained a consultant. Her husband received a bachelor's degree from Western New England University. He also graduated from the University of Massachusetts without a degree, It is likely he did not complete the dissertation.

Miller was CHU's Government & Urban Affairs Consultant and the Vice chair of FLOW:

"Helen Baca Miller served as CHU's Government & Urban Affairs Consultant, networking communities and regional organizations whose planning needs match the expertise available through the Center for Hydro-generated Urbanism. She was elected the first woman mayor of the historic Town of White Springs, Florida in 2010. As mayor, Dr. Miller advanced water priorities by serving as vice chair of Florida Leaders Organized for Water (FLOW) and as member and chair of the Utilities, Natural Resources and Public Works legislative policy committee of the Florida League of Cities. Prior experience includes work with private companies and public agencies.

The mayor contributed money from the town to FLOW, an organization which was established to provide funds to reverse the downdraw of the Florida Aquifer. The only problem was that the money was for nought because the organization no longer existed. Of course, the council approved all money going to FLOW with a majority vote.

Mayor Miller received the 2012 SRLC Municipal Award for 32 months of service.

Mayor Miller received the 2012 SRLC Municipal Award for 32 months of service. It was for starting a summer enrichment and adult and community education program The 2012 Municipal Official of the Year had worked in cooperation with the University of Florida to complete an architectural visioning for the community and presented the plan at the Florida Rural Economic Summit and to Governor Rick Scott.

The award was nominated for Miller's tireless effort on projects and resolutions that address and attempt to reverse the continued drawdown of the Floridan Aquifer. She has also worked to establish food and fuel banks in her community, hosted a series of community forums to identify the concerns of the citizenry, appointed committees, or individuals to act on citizens' concerns, and initiated the position of Health Counsel for White Springs."

Town Conveyed the Barnett Tract

In January of 2014, the town of White Springs was selected to participate in the Competitive Florida Partnership Pilot Program through the Florida Department of Economic Opportunity. The Town had until June 30, 2014, to complete the deliverables specified in the contract with DEO including holding public meetings for citizens and business leaders, preparing history and previous attempts at economic development as well as preparing a strategic plan for major priorities. Included in this scope of work was mapping of community assets and identification of areas needing improvement, all of which was completed on time.

One major issue that was identified was the lack of lodging – hotels, cabins, RV hook-ups and campsites – in the town that could accommodate visitors and guests during major events at Stephen Foster Folk Culture Center State Park, such as the annual Folk Festival, and various events sponsored throughout the year by the Suwannee Bicycle Association, which draws hundreds of cyclists and nature enthusiasts to the town and surrounding areas.

At the August 12, 2014, meeting, the Governing Board of the Suwannee River Water Management District unanimously approved conveying the Barnett Tract to the Town for the Eco-lodge development. The Barnett tract consists of approximately 180 acres of land adjacent to the town's old sewer plant. The Town did not have money and would need developers.

The Barnett Tract Trail is a four-mile loop that serves as the starting point for the Big Shoals traditional route. This trail features diverse terrain, including swamps, pine flats, and mixed hardwood forests[1]. From the Barnett Trail, you can follow signs to the Big Shoals, where the Suwannee River flows over bedrock ledges, creating a spectacular section of white water.

The property has subsequently been surveyed and a deed of conveyance is being drawn up by town attorney Fred Koberlein. "Once that is complete, it goes back to the SRWMD governing board for their signature," said Mayor Helen Miller, who has been spear-heading eco-tourism development in White Springs. The only restriction is that the town cannot sell the land, Miller explained. The town will be seeking private sector partners to form a public-private partnership to develop and operate the eco-friendly lodge. "The objective is to create jobs in the community by facilitating private sector investment that will result in additional revenue and taxes flowing to the town, which is how the town benefits from that kind of development," said Miller. The town received $40,000 in funding from DEO. Yet since funds for these projects are not kept separately, somehow

$40,000 was rumored lost and it had to be replaced with Sewer and Water Funds.

In addition to biking and hiking, the area is known for its wildlife, including gopher tortoises, and offers opportunities for fishing and picnicking, The Town was conveyed this property but had no money to build an Eco Lodge.

Ahmoglee Okalee Park Business Incubator

Mayor Helen Miller, on behalf of the Town of White Springs, was involved in a joint project with the Development Authority for the building of the Ahmoglee Okalee Park in downtown White Springs. Although the project took three years to complete, the park was opened May 20, 2013, with a grand opening. This park was considered a success and part of a business incubator. However, the park itself could not be a business incubator because it was never built to formulate any new businesses. **"White Springs is small with limited resources, but we do have a vision and that is to restore and revitalize our community by focusing on our cultural heritage and eco-tourism," said Miller. "Those are the two main assets we have in this community, and we must build on that. This park does that."**

There are two entrances into the park, front and back. Brick paved sidewalks, lined on both sides with red mulch and landscape plants and flowers, will guide you to each of the three covered pavilions, which include lighting and ceiling fans. Each pavilion has its own name as tribute to the native American Indian tribes who originally settled in White Springs; the Timucuan, the Apalachee and the Calusa. There are some black wrought iron benches along with restrooms. The park itself rarely is used, and it is next to the telephone building which takes away from what beauty there is in the park.

On March 24, 2015, then Mayor Helen Miller briefed Gov. Rick Scott and the Cabinet on economic development in White

Springs. Miller's remarks focused on year one's achievements of the CFO and the town's current infrastructure projects that include Phase 1 of the Department of Environmental Protection (DEP) sanitary sewer project. The project's objective is to curtail inflow and infiltration, thereby reducing sewer expenses for town residents.

Construction of the new Fire Station

Miller also spoke about the Community Development Block Grant (CDBG) small cities grant for construction of a new fire station in White Springs. Both infrastructure projects were being made possible by matching funds provided by the Hamilton County Development Authority. This project was a success. A new fire department was built but it was found to not have the necessary air filtration system, and the cement was cracked in several places on the floor.

Long Term Lease projects

Miller secured two long-term leases for the Town of White Springs. One was the Nature and Heritage Tourism Center, for which we could not even afford the $500 a month utility. Mayor Miller elected to create an art gallery where the Town had volunteers selling the artwork by various artists. The program was not run like a business because the Town did not hire a permanent manager or staff to oversee the gallery. As a result, one artist volunteer did not pay the percentage of the sold artwork to the Town. The program was a failure. The Nature and Heritage Tourism Center now is leased for only specific events.

Although art exhibitions are mainly run by volunteers, a paid employee must oversee the operations and make the necessary checks and balances. No one seemed to know how to oversee the building expenses nor did they work out a sample budget to determine if they should take the Nature and Heritage Tourism Center under lease

The second long term lease was for the historic Delegal Service Station, and two acres of undeveloped land immediately across from the south entrance to Stephen Foster Folk Culture Center State Park. Yet, no one has sub-leased the Delegal Building for a business and we had initial promises that a radio station would be moving in. Why would anyone secure a lease if you were not assured that you would be able to sub-let it? The building initially housed the library which was moved to a new building.

Historic Signs and lighting

The Florida Department of Transportation (FDOT), Miller added, is at the 60 percent planning stage for installation of historic signage and lighting to enhance the town's aesthetics. This project was successful. The Town was able to piggyback on another municipality's grant in Rhett Bullard's term as mayor. I do not have the full information any longer, but we were required to pay the Municipality who was awarded the grant approximately $11,000 first, prior to receiving the money back through the Grant for which Bullard had difficulty understanding.

Sewer revitalization:

In April of 2014 at the monthly council meeting, then Mayor Helen Miller announced proudly that because of the increase in Sewer and Water rates, the Town now has the $250,000 matching funds for the $3,000,000 loan information Former Town Manager Farley secured. The State was to reimburse the town for 92.5% and White Spring's portion would be 7.5% of the amount borrowed. Later we learned the Town did not have $250,000 reserved for the loan. Instead HCDA was contacted for the funds. When we tried to verify what we had heard in the meeting by the meeting minutes, the statement made by Miller had not been included, nor was it included in the Newspaper article.

Miller spends and hires against the Charter:

Mayor Miller spent over $24,000 (without council's approval) to obtain the University of Florida to perform a study of the Carver School, This information was provided by Rev. Marshall. None of this money benefited the Town of White Springs, nor did the Council approve the plan. On August 29, 2014, the design/planning work for the Carver School began at 9:00 AM.

Children's H.O.P.E Check is used for other purposes

Mayor Miller stated in writing that the Town Clerk should pay for credit card expenses her husband incurred on her behalf, as well as money to the Town Attorney for the Charter School work from a $2,500 check received from PCS (now known as Nutrien). This check was to be given to the Children's H.O.P.E. program, for which the check was issued. When the evidence of the misappropriation of the H.O.P.E.' check was on the blog, the mayor told the Town Council she would pay back the money from her monthly salary; but there was no way to confirm she did. Previously, the town council forbade Mayor Miller from using Town funds for the Charter School because the town could not afford it. Yet she paid the Town Attorney for work he did for the Charter School from the check. The new town manager, Manager Farley, did not know that the Town operated the H.O.P.E. program but in all fairness, the town did not have a 501 (c) (3) either.

After forcing the long-time Town clerk, Shirley, to retire, the mayor hired a person who could not perform as well as Monica who was hired under the H.O.P.E. program. The Chief of Police, the Town Manager, and the Council approved the mayor's choice even though they did not do a background check on the new employee Anita Rivers. Mayor Miller paid Rivers

$2.00 more than Monica, an hour, and did not require Rivers to do the work Monica had easily performed.

The Pavilion Park, the Amphitheatre and Sidewalk to Nowhere:

Mayor Miller and Vice Mayor McKenzie, with the help of the former Town Manager, with a HCDA (Hamilton County Development Authority) grant to build the Pavilion Park, and the Sidewalk to nowhere, which was constructed by Stephen's Masonry in the amount of $70,672, The Amphitheatre, and the park were rarely used by the citizenry and certainly did not produce money.

DEO Competitive Florida Partnership pilot program:

The Department of Economic Opportunity (DEO) set the first partners meeting of the Competitive Florida Partnership pilot program, with White Springs on February 1, 2014, from 10:00 AM. to 3:30 PM. A planning Workshop was held January 25, 2014, led by Ivan Udell who had worked with the Joint Chiefs at the Federal Level intersecting it with the local level. A significant percentage of White Springs youth were not able to participate in military and/or private sector opportunities due to their criminal involvement with law enforcement as juveniles and young adults. This pilot program could have assisted those youths.

The Competitive Florida Partnership helps a community utilize its unique assets and challenges its leaders to set realistic goals to advance their economic development visions. The partnership establishes a network of vibrant communities and passionate leaders who gain ideas on how to reach their goals through the success and lessons learned from their peers. The DEO also provides grants.

I-75 and County Road 136 project:

Town Manager Farley suggested the I-75/CR136 project to Miller. Mayor Miller felt White Springs could add water and sewer pipelines and develop the I-75/ CR 136 interchange in partnership with Suwannee and Columbia Counties. She felt, if developed, it would mean jobs for the juveniles and young adults in White Springs/Hamilton County. An initial meeting was held for the Year two priorities with representatives of Suwannee, Columbia, and Hamilton County, including the State's Farmer's Market on January 25, 2015.

Unfortunately, since the development was in Suwannee County, that county took over the plans, In February 2018, Governor Rick Scott announced that Suwannee County would receive $3.125 million for work at the Interstate 75 and County Road 136 interchange. Gov. Scott announced *The funds will be used to provide water supply and fire protection to the I-75 and CR 136 interchange.* The county also received $3.3 million funding for a wastewater treatment plant at the interchange.

The Town Charter ignored/ Laws ignored:

The Town Charter does not allow a mayor to operate the town, spend money as he/she determines alone without council approval nor does a mayor have the right to hire and fire employees. Miller oversaw all planning and instructed staff to not only bring in chairs and tables for the meetings, what food to serve, and what catering would be done. The Town Managers had no say in the matter, even though the Town manager has a responsibility to provide suggestions to the town council and handle staff issues, providing financial information monthly to the council. The rule was established at the time the State of Florida deemed White Springs Bankrupt. The Town required the Town Charter to have a "Weak Mayor/Town Manager" form of Government. Only the Town Manager could bring forth pertinent criteria for the entire or majority of the council to approve or disapprove. The council members appoint the mayor who has no more power than other council members. She or He is the head of the Town to conduct meetings.

The council, under Mayor Miller, did not conduct meetings in accordance with Roberts' Rules of Order which was required by the charter. The council set a five-minute time limit in which citizens have the right to speak. Once the citizen is finished talking, there are no further discussions and the citizens' responses are dismissed and not responded to for solutions.

There never were discussions among the council members at meetings. Rather, the discussions were determined out of the "Sunshine," by telephone, email or secret meetings between Council Members.

Mayor Miller reigned over the Town Managers (against the Charter), not only breaking the Sunshine Laws, but the Municipal Ordinances. She also retained a reporter to produce articles only on what was favorable to the mayor.

Town Manager Townsend stopped providing the Town with monthly budgets. Since the Mayor and Council Members did not have financial backgrounds. No one knew where the money went per month, what bills were outstanding, what funds were received, or what was paid, and to whom besides payroll, were the funds given. If some bills were brought forward as paid, the Council was approving them after they had been paid and not before.

The Food Bank:

Mayor Miller started the Food Bank, and the Town did not have a 501 (c) 3. She also took away the food bank when Reverand Richard brought up the money the mayor had spent for personal reasons, without council approval. She promised Catholic charities would come into town and that did not manifest even though Catholic charities came to surrounding towns. She then blamed Griffin's blog for listing where the food for those in need came from and she contacted the supplier to advise the supplier's name was shown on an internet blog. The food supplier information was never to be public, or the recipient (Town) would receive no more food. The reason the name was on the blog was due to an interview of Reverand Richard by me, months prior. Mayor Miller, by doing so, took food away from those who needed it and caused additional problems in securing food bank food at a reasonable price (i.e. 10-20 cents a pound)

When she shut the food bank down, Griffin and I set up a new program for Rev. Richard called the "New Hope Food Bank." Griffin purchased a large trailer with Marshall (with specifications by the seller that the trailer be specifically for charity at the low price he charged.) I assisted Rev. Richard with the 501(c)3 applications to the State, but it was never filed by him. Rev Richard, then a minister and a council member, also did not pay the share of money promised to Griffin for the trailer. It was known he used the trailer for which he added refrigeration, for his income earning business, the Adult Living Center in Jennings.

Fortunately, the churches of White Springs started a food bank but even the police could not keep the food secure nor could a lock on the freezer keep the food from being stolen. Some alleged the food, which was stolen, moved to the Adult Living center, but it never could be proven. It may be noted that the licensed food banks provide food for about three months until the recipients receive food stamps (SNAP). In White Springs, food is provided throughout the year to those in need, whether they sold their SNAP cards to buy drugs or alcohol, or did not qualify for SNAP.

Grant Money expended mainly on Salaries/ Some Grant Money lost:

Mayor Miller began the H.O.P.E. program for the Children. In 2013, the Town received a Grant in the amount of $240,000 from the Department of Education. Funds were also received from the Calder Family Trust to be used for education.

Miller hired the Lofton's to oversee the program and those who they hired were paid handsomely. Then the money ran out and there was no money to pay staff. Miller's fair-weather friends left the program. She had no choice but to seek volunteers. The problem was those she contacted knew of the grant. As a result, no one was willing to volunteer their services for the program. Further, those who Miller asked to volunteer were not her chosen friends, and they knew the latter received substantial pay. The mayor could have hired them as well at the beginning.

In March of 2015, Miller had to secure permission to secure $30 from the Special Events committee for an overage spent on the H.O.P.E. program for cookies, sweet and unsweetened tea, water, plates, drink cups and napkins. Most of us would have just donated the $30.

Some grant money was lost, and the accounting for such money could not be found. The officials spent a portion of Grant funds for other than for their intended purposes. All grant funds should be separated as restricted funds to be used in accordance with the Grant's terms.

Miller managed the Police Department and its Chief:

The mayor also ran the police department of the Town in lieu of the Town Manager. More than one officer was also required by the mayor to attend special and monthly council meetings. One police officer was required by the mayor, to sit by Griffin at meetings, because the council previously advised

Griffin that he would be arrested if he attended. This of course was against Griffin's alienable rights.

If the police could have been less biased and fearful of losing their jobs, no one would have complained that the department had a budget of $200,000 in remuneration and benefits but that only one percent of the $200,000 or $2,000 was recapitulated. Griffin suggested eliminating the police department and hiring the Sheriff's department. The Council ignored his suggestions, more than once, because the council would have no control over the Sheriff's Department. Only the Town Manager and Miller had control over the White Springs police Department.

When Mayor Miller initially ran for Town Council, Miller's husband threatened to kill Griffin, if Miller was not elected as mayor. Since it was in a public place, Griffin contacted the White Springs police who did nothing. Miller and her husband retaliated by slandering and defaming Griffin by various letters to all the sewer and water recipients; the postage of which was paid by the citizens.

A $100 Million Bond issue:

After she was elected mayor, Miller attempted to secure a $100. Million bond issue supported by a life insurance company. The purpose was to issue a life insurance policy in the name of each citizen with the Town being the beneficiary recipient. What this meant is that as soon as one died, the life insurance amount on the citizen would make payment to the Town which in turn would make payment to the bonding company. If someone did not die in a year the Town was required money to pay the bond company, would they have killed someone". I am not certain what their plan was, but that was a ridiculous scheme, especially since the Town had no insurable interest in the individual's life insurance. Griffin managed to stop this ridiculous plan since he had sufficient education in life insurance.

The Camel Club was formulated

In 2008, Ed Miller wrote and signed four letters, copies of each of which the Town sent to every sewer water recipient in the Town of White Springs and Mayor Miller assisted him. These letters disparaged Griffin as well as threatened those who stood up for Griffin. This was promulgated because of Griffin's requests for 119's and his numerous suits. Ed Miller offered a $10,000 reward to whomever would have Griffin arrested and convicted. It was said Griffin had requested 20,000 public Records and at that time we checked, there were less than 500 for all those years he lived in White Springs.

Because of Ed Miller's letters, the Camel Club was formed, to continue Miller's work. While in court, Vice Mayor McKenzie told the judge there were nine anonymous writers. These writers said disparaging things about Griffin in his fight for what was legal. Because Griffin received a diagnosis of being bi-polar and was prescribed medications by the VA to even him normally in 2007. The anonymous people ridiculed him as a disabled person laughing at him and saying he was a druggie because of his pills and bi-polar condition.

The purpose of the Camel Club was to defame Griffin for his determination to secure transparency with his 119's. All emails sent were anonymous so I would not learn for three years or so that the Camel Club consisted of the so-called hierarchy of the Town along with officials. The club based its writings on Mayor Miller's husband's four disgusting and crude letters about Griffin ordering public records. There was denial by the Millers, but after Rhett Bullard became Mayor, I found that the letters disparaging Rhett Bullard (*The Rhatt Watch*), which I placed on the blog, consisted of the same fonts as those letters which Ed Miller sent about Griffin.

It would be proven factual that the Millers were the source of our difficulties, when we were asked to place degrading letters about Mayor and Attorney Bullard which the mayor's husband allegedly typed on a typewriter for me to input to the computer, She named the daily series the "Rhatt Watch," and of course, I did the art logos and recapitulated each of his typewritten drafts on the blog. Yet I had difficulty placing the Miller's personifications of Mayor Bullard. It was okay to write about a difference in politics but to bring his personal proclivities into full view and make allegations which may not have been true, was beyond the pale. Yet Griffin was happy to have Mayor Miller's approval again and felt she could assist him in his future run for office.

The Camel Club relished sending Griffin emails daily. They loved to see how angry Griffin would get and how derogatory his response would be. At first, they left me alone, until I supported Griffin. Then I became the subject of their slander, defamation, and harassment. But the Camel Club had a RICO (1970 Racketeer Influenced and Corrupt Organizations Act), side to it as well.

When a new pizza shop opened in Town, the new owner did not know how to make pizza crust and the cost of purchasing pre-made crusts would be expensive. Although he used the pre-made crusts for his opening, he solicited my help for a day in making crusts and training his waitress on the process. At the same time, the owner decided that, for my assistance, he would provide me with a photo of the Camel Club members. He said that the officials of the Camel Club who came to his shop stated they would assist him in making his pizza shop a thriving business. All the shop owner had to do was to include the members one night a month for free pizzas and beverages. This meant closing the shop one night for an exclusive event for the Camel Club members.

A sample of what the camel club would write: (no grammar corrections made)

"Are you so stupid that you don't remember what you write Griffy? Did the lovely Karin forget to medicate you proper? I quote, "One more and I'll report you". Sound familiar Ole Wondering Eyed One? Your stupidity knows no bounds. Like that's a News Flash!!!! Anyway, Lois and I have to start getting ready for a night on the town. Gotta leave early because there is snow in the forecast and my cape tends to ice up. Oh, and by the way, Lois is reviewing your Archives for any possible breeches in the Cyber Laws. How humorous it would be to use your own Blog to take you down. In addition to knowing the Cyber Laws inside and out, Lois has numerous friends in very high places that are willing and able to do Pro Bono work. Food for Thought. As for your list of Camel Club members, if you'll notice, they have their own e-mail address you moron. Even I with all my Superpowers don't know the true identity of the Camels. Till next year. Happy New Year to The Grifter and his Lovely. Looking forward to a New Year of humor from you both."

The Camel Club wrote emails and writings continually. It was our hopes that the State's Attorney Sigmeister would do something about it. But he did not. It was the **Home Rule,** and it may be that he knew some of the Camels were officials who commented on our blog posts and who sent emails continually. At one time Griffin and I provided a large binder of what the Camel Club Members had sent us, but the State and Law Enforcement decided to protect the Camel Club possibly because of Griffin's reputation. Sigmeister also was perceived as a good friend of Mayor Miller. Anyway, the **Home Rule protected Municipalities and officials of those Municipalities.**

Equipment not necessary:

The budget, in one of the years, allocated $6,000 for maintenance equipment. The Mayor, Town Council, and Town Manager, however, elected to pay more than $9,000 for a lawn mower. At the time, the Town was hiring the State to mow the Town's berms and properties, so some questioned the cost. In fact, the lawn mower was so large, it could not mow between light poles. No council member considered following a budget and the town managers did not argue that point.

Sewer and Water

Manager Farley placed the newly installed software at Town Hall, at the cost of $7,000. The software helped the Town to find that the State Park was not in compliance with our utility rates. The State Park had been paying low rates for years, ever since their camping site opened. The software found where other residences were not being billed for sewer and water nor were the meters read. One would think that meter readers would read all meters and report such information to the Town. Further, the town should have kept a record of any favors given to some citizens but never did. But why should those favors have been granted in the first place to the detriment of other citizens and the Town?

Favoritism was amuck during Miller's reign as Mayor. It is not known whose fault it was, but the town kept depleting money.

The State Park system would not have to pay back the difference of those previous years. Perhaps the Town could not charge the State. since a statute of limitations may have expired.

The mayor talked the council into increasing the sewer rates by 25% where older people and families with limited income could not afford their billings. If the utilities were not paid, the water to residents would be shut off.

Miller had control of the narratives to eliminate those she did not like:

As is usual in the blame game, Mayor Miller and the Council blamed the former Town Managers for their budget problems. It was known that the town manager, Townsend, complied with Florida State Mandates by using the same budget year after year with very few changes. Yes, this did cause difficulties, and the Town was in financial despair periodically for unexpected problems. Yet, from statements made, the council believed Townsend was its best manager. The Town hired and or retained him, ignoring all other complaints.

The Town even hired Subic, prior to Miller elected as mayor, who was a traitor to the U.S. which the Reagan Administration did not wish to pursue, for it was an embarrassment. Subic was fired because he tried to have his mistress covered under his health insurance along with his wife. Yet, evidentially, Mayor Miller followed suit by hiring those with unclean backgrounds where she allegedly could control them, and they would do her bidding.

Mayor Miller hired a prior incarcerated felon to be a Town Manager but as a consultant. He was allowed to oversee all finances and decisions without the necessary experience or education. This led to Mayor Miller's demise in the end.

Special Events Committee

The Special Events Committee run by Tom Moore paid for two volunteers to attend the fire school as well as fire gear to the Fire Department. The Special Events Committee had $13,500 in their coffers when the Town decided to take over the funds. The mayor allocated only $5,000 for events in the future for which the Council approved that amount. Eight thousand was used for staff salaries.

It was alleged Mayor Miller ruined the programs wherein volunteers did not wish to apply for various events. Griffin and I were the only applicants who volunteered for the Special Events committee whose applications were rejected by the council members.

Swap Meet

The town manager when Bullard was mayor decided that the Hardware Store swap meets would have to collect $30 from each vendor for the Town. This was because the berms were Town property but used at the Hardware' swap meet. There was no advance notice and the vendors at these meets barely make $30 on the goods they sell. As a result, no vendors would come in and the Swap meets stopped until the owner of the hardware store purchased another building. Miller, who was on the council, did not stop the town manager and from her conversations with me, she tried in every manner to make the current mayor, Rhett Bullard, look bad.

Hamilton County not reimbursed for work on Jewett Street

Hamilton County fixed the road on Jewett Street for which they received no payment for two years until Griffin contacted the County to find out whether the Town paid the County for its work on Jewett Street. After the completion of the work by Hamilton County, the County sent an invoice to the Town Clerk/Finance Director Pam Tomlinson to pay. Pam cited that what the County sent, was not a usual looking invoice because it had charges per job accomplished. The Town had received funds already from FEMA and another source paid the county in part directly. The Town's FEMA funds comingled in the General Fund by the Town and was spent as needed. What was stated by Tomlinson was *"MONEY WAS SITTING FOR A WHILE AND WE SPENT IT AT SOME POINT."*

The County made an investigation after Griffin pointed out that the Town may not have paid the County for their work. Griffin was correct. After Bill Lawrence left, Griffin and I attended the special meeting of August 3, 2015, regarding the $92,662 which we owed Hamilton County for the Jewett Street project. We were correct in that FEMA paid White Springs that amount for the claim and the money received from FEMA was not earmarked for Hamilton County but was placed in the general fund and spent. "The pattern never changes" is a correct statement by Griffin.

A story given by our Interim Town Manager Heath to the Jasper News was a total fairy tale. Heath stated on July 14, 2015, that FEMA documents from Tropical Storm Deby in 2012, were not closed-out; She said Bob Farley took possession of the files and he informed everyone that it had been closed-out. Staff told Bill Lawrence it was not closed-out. **Heath stated the problem was the government shut down and the records were lost. Then she said they grabbed the documents they had and sent them in**

The Government never shut down. And I bet no other prudent town finance personnel. has made the mistake of spending the money without earmarking it to go to the County for work performed.

In fact, per former mayor Miller, Farley stated he had no blame on the matter as Heath had advised our news reporter. (Heath may have been still upset with Farley because he blamed her for not reminding the Council about the yearly increments that should have been made to the sewer and water, but Farley was Miller's man.) The Town received a spread sheet of what the cost was per project accomplished. We also received a copy. In fact, the spread sheet stated, **"invoice"** Another copy of the Spread sheet initially was given to the finance manager, as well as to Bill Lawrence, A complaint was made that Bill Lawrence did not call Farley. Bill Lawrence did not call Farley because, as he stated, it was not his first rodeo. He, however, left information with the finance manager, Mayor Bullard, and Heath before leaving because **Tomlinson was still waiting for an invoice, which she had in her possession via the spread sheet for two years**

Former Mayor Miller also referred to the fact that in the Powell and Jones Audit, the $92,662 came in and then the audit showed that the $92,662 went out, so it looked like it had been paid or why did the auditor not catch that when processing the operating budget? The blame game continued. She further stated that for years, White Springs has had an internal control deficiency. Apparently, the Town has been warned for years about our internal controls.

McKenzie stated people may think we just kept the money; hoping we would not have to pay it out. Then Pam Tomlinson responded that we did keep the money and added she felt that Hamilton County had forgiven the Town from providing a payment because they are so nice to us. Without an invoice that just indicated a total amount, the Town did not pay Hamilton County and ignored the spread sheet. It did not help that Hamilton County forgot to follow up for the payment until Griffin contacted the County.

Griffin was correct, there was no need for the meeting unless we did not save the $92,662 because all we would have to do is issue a check. That was not the case. A decision was made by the Council that $57,997 would be moved from the Enterprise Fund into the General Fund so that the $92 662 could be paid out of the General Fund. That means there would be a balance in the general fund of $61,261 after the payment and $84,762 in the Enterprise Account.

There was confusion for Heath, at the county level, when they contacted Mr. Goodin, who she stated said the County received payment. The County received funds directly from

NRCS for Florida Fill and Grade which was awarded fixing 1st Street, Kendrick and Cauthen

Heath contended that Louie Goodin allegedly stated the FEMA paid the county, but we do not know if this is another fairy tale by Heath or Tomlinson. How did Heath raise the question to Mr. Goodin is a mystery. NRCS paid the County for the streets **other** than Jewett. And Heath kept mentioning FEMA and **we kept correcting her that NRCS paid the County. FEMA did not.**

Hamilton County's engineer Greg Bailey had experience in roadways and assisted White Springs in submitting the original claim to FEMA. That is because the bids varied as follows: Curt's Construction, Inc. $219,599.90 Cauthen – Fl, Fill Gamp; Grading, Inc. $62,878.70 and Curt's Construction, Inc. $99,732.80.

The Town was able to deduct $20,000 from the $ 92,662 owed to the County for the Jewett Street project. This was because the Town spent $20,000 from the Enterprise Account (Sewer and Water) for sandbags.

A Small Bandstand for the East Part of Town

Mayor Miller decided that since the West part of Town included an amphitheater, that the East part of Town should have a bandstand. A small bandstand on skids was built by the University Students. This bandstand was smaller than an event tent and certainly would not logically be used by anyone. It still sits in a field of the Carver School area, unused, deteriorating year after year.

Eco Center as an Artists' Gallery

The mayor secured the State's Eco Center where she had planned to make it a tourist destination. She put together the idea of an Artists' Gallery but did not hire anyone to oversee the financial side or to be a manager. One of the artists did not share the money she earned from selling her art. No other controls were in place either.

Florida Quilt Trail

Mayor Miller along with Merri McKenzie (The vice mayor's spouse} brought White Springs into the Florida Quilt Trail with a dedication and ribbon cutting event held at the Nature and Heritage Center on February 25, 2015. Stephanie and Paul Metts, the creators of the Florida Trail in Trenton, addressed White Springs to the cultural and artistic movement which is growing in Florida. Although Mayor Miller worked with Mrs. McKenzie, this program remained.

Was she serious about starting a Charter School?

Mayor Miller decided she wished to start a charter school, but would not hire Town Manager applicant Tim Day, who had previously started two charter schools successfully. Instead, a friend of Vice Mayor McKenzie, Farley was hired after being fired from Live Oak because of his lack of communication skills. She tried to ruin Day's reputation because he was known as a very educated individual with tremendous skills and background. Like a schoolchild, the mayor even said Day wore a rug and whether he did or not had no bearing on his skills. And the only infractions she could find on Day consisted of a family dispute and an employee who took suit against Day. The Courts exonerated Day in both cases.

The former superintendent of schools, Martha Butler, provided Griffin and I with an outline of how to start a Charter School. This happened after the Town's first failure in completing the application. Martha Butler provided sound information because the mayor, the town attorney and an attorney who was on the council did not follow instructions, or the mayor did not provide them. The information went on the blog in a simplified manner; yet nothing transpired relating to the Charter School. The matter dropped because the Town said there was no money to finance the school. Also, Mayor Miller, with the help of her husband and attorneys, could not follow the directions to complete a charter school application successfully, even with Superintendent of Schools Martha Butler's explanations and instructions.

South Hamilton Elementary School

The mayor campaigned that she worked diligently to keep the South Hamilton Elementary (SHE) school open; but that was never the case. No one maintained the school even when there was structural damage, which would cost $3. Million dollars to repair. Instead, the Town officials and citizens blamed Tom Moffses who was elected the new superintendent of schools, for the White Springs Children having to attend school in Jasper. He was the best superintendent of schools Hamilton County had, but the people were extremely angered so that he was elected for only one term, after the new school was built. When there was water emanating which could have caused damage to the new school, Tom Moffses found the source and had it fixed, saving thousands of dollars.

Awards and work other than for the Town

Mayor Helen Miller was presented with the 2014 **Home Rule Hero Award** from Florida League of Cities Legislative Advocate Ryan Matthews at a meeting of the White Springs Town Council. This award was created to recognize city officials who went beyond to advocate the FLC legislative agenda during the past legislative session.

Miller and representatives of 28 other North Florida counties and 70 cities and towns are asking the Florida Legislature to mandate a more comprehensive mining of the data regarding Florida aquifers. On April 21, 2014, the U.S. Environmental Protection Agency (EPA) and the U.S. Army

Corps of Engineers jointly proposed regulations to revise the definitions of "Waters of the United States" or WOTUS under the Clean Water Act. The EPA indicated that the purpose of the proposed rule is to clarify what waters are and what they are not as covered by the Clean Water Act (CWA). It does not change what the States currently consider WOTUS.

CHAPTER FOUR – GRIFFIN'S
ENDEAVORS RESULT IN FAILURES

GRIFFIN SUED FORMER MAYOR
MCKIRE and NOT the TOWN

Shortly after I moved to White Springs, in August of 2011, Griffin told me that he had sued the prior Mayor McKire. Griffin blamed Mayor McKire for not providing him with his 119 documents or instructing the Town staff to not do so. Griffin filed a suit under what he felt was a civil statue, but it was a criminal statue. The staff used town Letterhead on which public records were denied under McKire's name and signature. With Griffin handling everything pro se, he was not qualified to fight the Town Attorney who brought in three bankers boxes stating to the Judge that he had to put in all this work. Never would this case alone require three banker boxes of documentation.

Although I was not given the specifics, Griffin issued a check for $13,000 directly to the mayor on October 4, 2011. He paid the $1,083.21 balance on January 7, 2012, to McKire, individually, at which time he filed with the Town and the Clerk of Court a request for the interest due. The town Attorney would not provide the Satisfaction of Judgment, nor the interest which was due. A new attorney charged a non-returnable retainer of $2,000 for the investigation even though the interest amount was only $401.96, and the attorney did little work to earn the money. Griffin paid the interest directly to the Town in McKire's name. In the end, Mayor McKire endorsed the check to the Town as was the prior $14,083.21. Griffin finally received the "Satisfaction of Judgement awarding Attorney Fees and Expenses on February 19, 2013, which was prepared by Pam Tomlinson.

When the Judge allowed for a separate hearing, Griffin and I met with another attorney in Perry FL who advised Griffin he

63

was suing under a criminal statute rather than under civil law. As a result, that attorney wrote a letter cancelling any further action in the McKire case so that Griffin would not be in further trouble.

Karma takes hold in part while Griffin aggravates the Town further

Karma has its own way of handling things. Former 3rd Judicial Circuit State Attorney Jeff Sigmeister, in lieu of a maximum of 20 years in Federal Prison, was remanded to spend 40 months locked up for corrupt deals that undermined his office's integrity in return for money. The elected prosecutor for the seven-county 3rd Judicial Circuit until 2019 pleaded guilty in February to conspiracy, wire fraud and tax charges that carried a statutory potential for up to 48 years in prison.

It may be noted that although Jeff Sigmeister listened to Miller's accusations of Griffin, the FBI would have nothing to do with the medals case. The Assistant States Attorney Karen Hatton who worked with the Town to incarcerate and charge Griffin, was forced to leave her position and a new ASA dropped the requirements of the Felony Pre-Trial intervention (PTI) program after reviewing the file. He verbally admitted that the officials and police of the Town railroaded Griffin. It upset Karen Hatton that the FBI would do nothing to intervene and kept calling the FBI, *"the secret service."*

The PTI program is a diversion program operated by the Florida Department of Correction for the purpose of affording first-time felony offenders the opportunity to avoid the stigma of a criminal conviction by diverting their case from the trial court process. It was not without the Town's corruption that the PTI arrangement was stopped at least twice because the Town felt Griffin did not have his first amendment rights. Griffin's attorney suggested Griffin plead guilty and accept PTI because going to trial would cost too much and there would be no guarantees if Griffin could not prove he had military medals, since he signed off and threw the medals in the San Francisco Bay.

Griffin kept trying to be elected to the council

Griffin's desire was to become a council member so that he could end the corruption. His first run to be elected did not work out very well due to the camel club's interventions as well as those of the WSPD.; Griffin ordered all the appropriate signage from Vistaprint, and we passed out brochures wherever we went.

Griffin's platform included lowering the Sewer and Water rates which had just increased, but the Camels said he was ridiculous because their bills were not high. In a town where many were on welfare, food assistance, temporary cash assistance and Medicaid or had low paying jobs, There were many complaints by citizens. And of those who had not paid were not friends of the town or its officials, their water would be turned off.

When the election concluded, Griffin received the least number of votes of all those running for Council. That provided the Camels fodder to rub-in the number of votes Griffin received, through their copious emails. This angered Griffin immensely. His neighbor and friend Bob D told Griffin that the first time he ran, he was not elected either. Bob D found a new building for the Town to continue business and even worked with the local library, but no one had cared, in the first election. He did, however, become a council member in the next election.

A war of emails began between the camels and Griffin and if I dared to support Griffin, I was excoriated, not only for that support but personal attacks were made about how I looked. Every one of the camels called Griffin a narcissist.

The Town had ordinances against animals and birds, but there was an abundance of goats, pigs, cattle, and chickens within the Town. Griffin elected to purchase some pigmy goats, had a fence installed around the property and allowed the grass to grow, including weeds. The pigmy goats would manage to get under the fence and a larger goat was eating all the tree bark. This caused us to purchase ground termite protection because the tree became loaded with termites. The closest neighbor became angry when the Pigmy goats were eating her flowers, so we had to make peace and retribution. I then had to feed goats, which were not my cup of tea. One day, the back sun porch door was open. The larger goat came up the stairs into the room, stood on a ledge and put his horns through the screen window. Now, none of this bothered Griffin, nor did Griffin feel we should maintain the property. Griffin chose not to fix the screen, but I placed a patch on the hole.

Next, Griffin purchased a taller goat, which could easily go over the fencing and that Goat would greet the neighbor lady each morning and see that she was safely in her vehicle or house.

Griffin then elected to go to one of the farms to buy a registered goat. Allegedly, one of the firefighters, or more, was involved with the Camels. The goat was poisoned with something which made his last moments suffer in agony with his body hardening as he died. I called the local police who would do nothing to kill Neptune and take away his pain. Later in the night as I stood by him, his cries and pain subsided. He died. How could people be so cruel?

The Town charged Griffin and the Reverend with buying votes

Soon it was time to elect two council members of the five. Griffin desired to again run for council in 2013, and we secured the necessary signatures so he could. Prior to the election, Griffin and I were still assisting Rev. Richard with the food bank but for some reason, it could not be held at the church. So, we offered our yard to hold the food bank. and I put out flyers. I also provided the Town with a flyer so we could be assured that everyone would receive a notice. I baked cookies and provided coffee for those in line. There was no meat involved but much produce, pastries, and bread. A large group of people attended, and all the food items were given away.

Then the Town Clerk on behalf of one of the officials provided our food pantry brochure to the Florida Election Board stipulating we were buying votes with the food provided at the pantry. As such, it placed a damper on Griffin's campaign because the Camel Club members indicated Griffin was illegal in buying votes and that he would be fined by the election board of the State.

The Town also reported Rev. Richard to the election board even though he was a council member. Yet many of the food recipients had criminal records and could not vote. When Griffin and I provided food for voters, which was commonplace among those running for council, across from the Hardware store, very few people came by. The election was lost again. After the election was over, we would find that neither we, nor Rev. Richard, did anything wrong. Both he and Griffin were exonerated from any crime of buying votes. The Camels won again!

Both complaints sent to the Election Board on Griffin and Reverand Richard were dismissed, but because of the biography done on Reverand Richard, Mayor Miller spoke to the food facility stating Reverand Richard had advertised his source on our blog. As a result of her accusations, the facility told Reverand Richard he could no longer get food from their facility. The Reverand. blamed Griffin for the entire scenario of losing the food bank despite my stating it was because of the Biography he had given me. I did not know that the facility was a secret, nor did Reverand. Richard warn me.

Moore's email of dissatisfaction of Griffin's campaign material:

Subject: *Re: Campaign Material*

"Griffin; Thank you for sending the citizens of White Springs your campaign strategy.

As usual, you make erroneous statements as if they were fact. The tennis court did not cost the Town of White Springs any money. The tennis court was built through donations of the United States Tennis Association, the Florida Youth Tennis Foundation, the Potash Corporation, and in-kind services from local businesses, such as Anderson Columbia. The backboard was built through donations from Home Depot and again the USTA. As for it not being used, I have taught over 100 children over the past three years on that court and am out there nearly every Saturday morning from 9am until 11to teach any child who comes to the court. When they have reached a certain level, I take them to the Lake City Country Club to play on the Junior Tennis team on Thursday nights. Come by and see them sometime. Brownies and pink lemonade at 10 am.

As for the water billing being extended from the 15th to the 1st of the month....IT WAS DUE ON THE FIRST OF THE MONTH. The Town allows a grace period of two weeks. IT IS DUE ON THE FIRST OF THE MONTH. Extending the payment due would not be fiscally sound.

The pavilion park and pathway are the foundation for the future of the retail business in White Springs. It was designed to have parking on Hamilton, the pathway to 41 where hopefully there will be businesses open...or reopened as the Suwannee Cafe. The money for this endeavor was a grant that could be used for this project only and not for all the other ideas and wishes that you proposed during its construction.

You need a greater understanding of the fiscal responsibilities and administration of funds than you show in your campaign strategy.

Tom."

Sent: *Friday, April 12,* **Subject:** *Campaign Material*

GRIFFIN'S RESPONSE TO MOORE

"Thank you for explaining your position. I know you feel my position is in error as you have stated. Yet, I speak for many of the people in White Springs. It is wonderful that you are taking the time to teach children tennis but several children in White Springs are not interested in tennis. Three children a month is nothing to be proud of. Of the future country club set, golf would be of more interest, but the cost is far reaching. Yet, children play basketball behind the asbestos ridden Carver School with no lights. We currently do not have a baseball or softball league that would bring together a wonderful team spirit. For some, they may have a bright future in business; for others, they may excel in sports. Our children need a chance to follow their passion and not just say, you have a tennis court; play tennis.

I understand White Springs has secured money in grants. My reasoning for stating these grants as being a waste is that if you intend to build businesses or bring businesses into White Springs, that pavilion will not do it. A genuine business incubator is based upon a building being built or used for startup business entrepreneurs. For instance, in Ocala, where my stepdaughter works with the EDC and the Chamber, they were donated a city building, whereby with common administrative as- sistants and receptionists for the various entrepreneurial businesses, they pay a low rent and have lawyers, CPA's and Retired Professionals who donate their time to assist them in their endeavors. And this was done strictly by the Chamber of Commerce before the EDC merged with the Chamber in Partnership. What building was renovated? What building was built? If you had such a park within the middle of a facility and started a program, these businesses would flourish. We could have assisted a number of residents with start-up businesses. Yet we have nothing but fenced-in picnic tables that are difficult to use by the fencing and positions.

We do have a Band Shell Amphitheater which has not even been used for a band nor can it house a number of people surrounding it. Tell me how it is that it will bring in businesses? What has the Town done to help its residents For our Town we needed to assist others to utilize their passions by businesspeople assisting those who wish to go into business and to give advice and their time.

Tom just because I was a truck driver when I came here does not mean that I have not been in the country club set as a Broker and Top Insurance Salesman (Yes, I have the award) in the nation. I was the fifth string quarterback for the Raiders and warmed up the wide receivers prior to ball games. I have been a coach for a high school football team who were the champions in the valley (Bakersfield and Stockton.) Tom, I used to be, prior to my accident, a pretty fair golfer and tennis player, having won the Subic Bay Naval Base doubles championship in 1974. So, Tom, please do not for a second think that I do not understand children or how to motivate people for the future. The children here deserve a chance to pursue sports for which they have a passion. Without fulfilling their individual passions, they will never excel or know what it feels like to excel in compe-

tition to be the best that they can be today and in the future.

As far as the water bill, for the fourteen years I have lived here I have never been given a grace period. I just pay by the 15th of every month, so it is hard to believe your explanation. Even credit card companies and the other utility companies give a person thirty days in which to pay. Many companies provide budget payments based upon the prior year and knowing the final payment will be due at the end of the year. Right now, there are leaking water pipes and some individuals, with very high-water bills, have contended the meters have been read improperly or they do not understand that they may have a leak which they may be responsible for. Some utilities through grants allow upgrades for Citizens so that they may be able to replace defective items with latest items and get credits as a result.

Yet, I understand the people surrounding Jewett and Kendrick Streets are still faced with rocks and must go well out of their way. One individual told me that groups from the apartments pleaded with the Council to have the repairs done. Their pleas were listened to but not heard.

There are those who say the Town is run by those who wish White Springs to be another Miami. I do not know, but I do know that certain things are done for special interest groups and other things are left for people or charities to fend for themselves.

The grants sought, especially for the Sidewalk to nowhere and Pavilion Park are prime examples. Our boy Townsend needed a political pick me up. He could have just as easily asked for the seed money for the water project on 25A and Mary Lou Bullard would have agreed. But it still cost us because the Hamilton County Development

Authority Well has now dried up and what have we got to show for it? I say nothing at all is what we got. The second grant was for the amphitheater, the grant read Municipal Park. Where is the park or the vehicle parking for such a park? And yes, you may have gotten grant money from the USTA and other organizations, including the potash mine. But those sources are also dried up to White Springs now. PCS, according to one source close to PCS, will not spend any more money in White Springs without a prior accounting of what the money is to be spent on.

Now on to the biggest waste of government money so far. It is Miller who has stolen over $24000 from the Town treasury, mostly from the Sewer Water Revenue Account for her pet projects including but hardly limited to the FAILED Charter School and the project development funds for the Carver School project (which is years away, if ever.)

And speaking of Miller, where did the Hundred Million Dollar Bond Issue go? Got any explanations for that? What were we to do, bump off people when we needed an infusion of cash to pay the debt service.

If you feel more comfortable voting for a candidate or two candidates who have not given you the first clue about where they stand on the issues of water rates, Town corruption, a medical clinic, a lighted basketball court and the other items in my campaign literature, then please do so. But if you want a person who will truly be on the side of all citizens, country club set or not, then I would appreciate one of your two votes for Town Council."

Attorney's advice

"Let us talk about the mayor for a moment and the fact that she spent seed money that belonged under the Sewer and Water Treatment facility grant. I can give you a listing of causes, but that is not important. It was known that the City Attorney's advice was as follows:

1. *Have the Mayor return the money by paying it back?*

2. *Report the actions of the Mayor to FDLE for their investigation.*

3. *Have the Mayor Step down?*

CHAPTER FIVE – WHAT TRANSPIRED IN TOWNSEND'S TENURE AS TOWN MANAGER

Townsend was the Town Manager who had Griffin fired from his trucking operations, after Griffin was arrested for Disorderly Conduct. Townsend had a record of his own, which Griffin brought to the attention of the Town with his friend and neighbor Bob D. Through his attorneys, however, Townsend's record was always clear, and no one was wiser. But actions which stemmed during Townsend's tenure as Manager never ended.

In 2002, Townsend had taken $10,000 from the Fire Department and terminated the Fire Chief's employment because he needed money in the Town's General Fund. Fire Chief Peeler tried to get a meeting before the council and was denied the opportunity, so he asked Griffin to assist him. Griffin drafted a suit for Peeler to be granted a meeting with the Town Council. Witnesses in the Peeler case backed down for fear of the town using their authority to arrest or intimidate them. The $10,000 consisted of money earned from events donations and contributions. The town spent $7,000 in legal fees so they would not have to give Chief Peeler a public meeting. The $10,000 in volunteer money went to the Town because the town ran out of money.

Going back to Townsend's criminal record, the following infractions happened, although Townsend was never charged by the State or the police, because he allegedly was in line with the correct prominent people and families.

Prior to the Town hiring Townsend as the Town Manager, Griffin and another citizen of White Springs provided the Council Members and the Town with Townsend's background information. Two applications were completed within a week of each other whereby Robert C. Townsend applied for positions with the Department of Corrections and to the Town of White Springs, respectively. In the first, Townsend admitted an alleged child molestation case when he was a deputy sheriff. In the second application to the Town of White Springs there was no mention of the case.

In 1990 Townsend, then a Columbia County Sheriff's deputy, was allegedly prosecuted for a lewd act on a boy. The Judge dismissed the charge against Townsend, but as a result Townsend left law enforcement. Thomas J. Kennon III, Esquire had defended Robert Townsend in an alleged child molestation case when Townsend was a deputy sheriff. With Judge Kennon as one of the Senior Circuit Court Judges, Townsend's case was dropped despite his allegedly being found guilty of child molestation in Clay County. The Lake City Reporter reported this 1990 case including the fact that Townsend was required by the courts to enter rehabilitation for a period of two years.

In 1994, Townsend was convicted of a domestic violence battery, a first-degree misdemeanor, in a fight involving his male roommate.

Because Townsend owed the Senior Circuit Court Judge's firm over $8,000 for his defense, he then had to file bankruptcy. When Townsend became the Town manager, the son of the Judge became the Town Attorney. Both Townsend and the Town Attorney allegedly became hostile toward Griffin because Griffin dared to bring up these facts in a derogatory manner. The subsequent Attorney allegedly also kept the hostilities going against Griffin, since he had previously worked for the Judge's firm before becoming the town attorney himself. The new town attorney admitted at a Council meeting that he had no intention of talking to Griffin.

Townsend had a high school education and no college. Even though the Town Charter requires a bachelor's degree, the council was never concerned. When another citizen and Griffin showed former Mayor McKire the paperwork on Townsend, Mayor McKire said **"He may be a pedophile, but he is our pedophile."**

Townsend's aunt was on the Hamilton County Development Authority (HCDA) board and had the most prestige in the organization. She wished to help her nephew out so he would have achievements of his own. HCDA gave the Town of White Springs $250,000 for a business incubator. Business incubators help new businesses and startups overcome the challenges they encounter through a program which promotes business development, learning and cost savings. Ocala has one of the most successful business incubators and I am certain the director would have helped had one asked.

Also, the Town received grant money from Hamilton County Development Authority (HCDA) for an Amphitheater and a brick sidewalk to nowhere. Although the vice mayor would not admit he had something to do with these grants with Townsend's association with the HCDA board, this was money poorly spent. The trees where the Amphitheater was constructed were removed, so that the heat of the sun could and has caused heat stroke to more than one individual. The sidewalk pavers go nowhere but the Vice Mayor was able to purchase the leftover pavers for his residential use at a lower price based on the overall purchase.

Three individuals alleged Mayor Miller had the Oak Trees removed by the Amphitheater and collected the money. The witnesses could not verify if money was paid to the Millers, but they observed the situation. The oak tree was loaded on a transport with the Millers speaking to the driver, as seen by at least three witnesses. The Town did not indicate the money was in its coffers. Where the money for the oak tree went was a mystery, but a logging truck loaded the large tree, with Miller and her husband giving instructions.

In one of Griffin's Earlier Campaigns for Town council he wrote:

For years I have tried to fight the corruption in our White Springs Government. Because I am honest and believe all people should have equal rights within the law, I have been called many names, the nicer of which is "Idiot". I have been threatened as have my friends. But most importantly, those of you who do not agree with the existing government will be beaten to the ground and you will not receive favors. Many of you already realize the ramifications of going against the Town Government and are fearful of taking a stand.

I have made mistakes in my life. I have realized my mistakes, and I have learned from these mistakes. My mistakes, however, do not include allowing the public to know about a corrupt White Springs government that has gone on for over fourteen years. I have dearly paid the price with thousands of dollars while Townsend used the Town's attorney, the council members who remained and two mayors, in an attempt to run me out of town.

Having been in possession of FDLE's investigation of Townsend. Having provided incriminating files on both Subic and on Townsend when they were hired, our White Springs Government failed to do the right thing. In fact, when brought to Mayor McKire's attention, he stated "Robert Townsend may be a pedophile, but he is our pedophile".

Townsend was in a position of power, and those in our local government including Mayor McKire and the current Mayor Miller allowed Townsend to do everything he desired. Townsend would reward those who were in his favor by making certain they received monetary bonuses or that they would remain hired whether they had the experience for the position or not. Should someone cross him, he would do everything in his power to have police intervein or have a person fired from their job for anyone who allegedly show prejudice against him. Many left the council; some officials were fired when they chose to follow and abide by the law. Townsend's vengeance was great, and he allegedly hurt many people. Many know what the Town did to me, and the current mayor is still wielding her power by attacking me and my friends in every conceivable way, carrying on the work of Townsend.

The town officials, including those in the police department were warned by me and others, yet all turned their heads because if they would not agree with Townsend or the corrupt officials of the town who are self-serving, they would have been attacked as I have or as they have attacked or hurt others.

Because I wish for equal rights for all citizens of White Springs, I have elected to run for Town Council. I represent change and wish for the People of White Springs to have a voice and not be threatened by the tyranny of the Town Officials who wish to control the masses and provide special strokes for special folks only. The mayor and her allies are so concerned about my running that they have tried to hurt my campaign in every conceivable way, including hurting my close friends.

If you feel that you wish to have the Town run as it is today, with the misappropriation of funds, hiring only those who will serve the Town by facilitating corruption, and serving only those who are their friends, accepting money and bribes, (while threatening those who feel there should be a just government), then Vote for your existing government officials. They do not wish Change a thing *and after all, Miller was able to spend some $24,000 (possibly more) on special interest groups, which did not benefit the White Springs citizens. Yet no one would touch her, and the government remains as is has been dictated by Townsend.*

A vote for Griffin is a Vote for Change. Change for the better where people will not have to be afraid to speak to the Council because the government officials will terrorize or threaten them. The needs of the Citizens should be met. The Council and our Current and former Mayors are not looking out for you but for themselves. It is time you, as the White Springs Government took your Town back and together, we may work together for equal rights and justice under the law. The Government Works for us. They are Public Servants, and they are to work for us. We do not work for them.

END OF STATEMENT

Possibly because of the **Home Rule**, the state's attorney Griffin sought help from, sat on the Townsend complaint for so long that Townsend escaped criminal justice, based upon the Statute of Limitations running out. One complaint was falsifying records and not disclosing Townsend pled guilty to a first-degree misdemeanor, when filling out a job application for the Town of White Springs. According to FDLE that charge was in all probability a valid charge, however, the statute of limitations had run out on Nov. 2, 1999. Third Judicial Circuit State Attorney Jerry Blair determined there were no grounds to charge Townsend because the statute of limitations ran out on Nov. 2, 1999.

In 2004, allegations of sexual assaults on a prison inmate while on work release assignment at White Springs water treatment facility were filed with FDLE. FDLE indicated this was a valid case; yet it was held by the courts at length and the Statute of Limitations ran out.

According to the FDLE Reports, both Andrew Greene and Officer Barry Rawlerson knew of **Townsend**'s sexual involvement with a prisoner in 2012 and lied about it, according to the FDLE Report. If Officer Rawlerson knew about the molestation and Andrew Greene knew about the molestation, then Chief of Police Ken Brookings and Council Member Walter McKenzie should have known.

Townsend was not only the Town Manager but also the Water Sewer Operator for the Town of White Springs. He was under investigation by the Florida Department of Law Enforcement (FDLE) for sexual misconduct/attempted rape of a Hamilton Correctional Institution inmate at the Town's sewer plant. Other inmates or former inmates also complained and refused to work at the White Springs plant nor do lawn duties outside of the plant.

Mayor Miller introduced the letter of resignation on April 17, 2012. as having been received from Townsend on that date. Vice Mayor McKenzie was with Mayor Miller and witnessed the signature. The resignation was to have been effective immediately and a motion was introduced, yet pending another motion of delay, until the Town Attorney had the opportunity to review Townsend's possible compensation. Since Townsend's contract required a 90-day notice, Townsend may not have qualified for benefits. Nevertheless, because he was well liked by staff, we believe he was given $8,000.

Soon thereafter, Inmates who had been released wrote letters regarding Townsend's sexual misconduct, but their reports were ignored.

When the new Town Manager, Farley, was hired as Town Manager, Greene took over the sewer plant duties. Mr. Greene was given advantages by the Manager and Staff, which others were not given. Both he and Pam Tomlinson retained the secrets of the Town. Greene was a loyal snitch, and he was favored and paid well. Greene had advised Farley that he noticed a ceiling tile was out of place in the sewer plant office and when he re-aligned the tile, he found Townsend's gay sex paraphernalia, which he destroyed. Greene had full knowledge that law enforcement (FDLE) was seeking evidence of the crime but removed the evidence and destroyed it so that Townsend would not be charged with a crime. It was Townsend's word against that of inmates.

What Townsend brought to White Springs was additional money based on fraud.

Joyce Taylor's (Mayor Miller's friend) Jasper News/Suwannee Democrat article was taken in part by the Associated Press and then printed in the Washington Times. I wonder if anyone ever looked at a map. The town had submitted a claim to the state in 2010 for loss of tourism revenue because of the oil spill.

"In July 27 of 2015—It took five years, but the town of White Springs is about to cash in on a settlement from the British Petroleum (BP) Deepwater Horizon explosion and oil spill that occurred April 20, 2010, in the Gulf of Mexico. As you are aware, **White Springs is not near any coastline whatsoever; but White Springs jumped in when there was an opportunity and cited that Tourist Trade Dropped**. Other than for the Folk Festival and Fat Belly's reputation for tasty food**, I really do not see the Tourists Coming in Droves**. The White Springs Town Council held a closed session meeting at the conclusion of their regular monthly meeting on Tuesday, July 14 to discuss whether to accept a settlement amount of $40,233 from BP. The council, minutes later voted to accept the settlement."

Florida Attorney General Pam Bondi stated the oil spill caused significant impacts to Florida's natural resources and economy. **"Of Florida's 790 miles of <u>coastline</u>, 177 miles received some degree of oiling,"** Bondi said in a settlement fact sheet.

CHAPTER SIX P. 1 – WHAT TRANSPIRED IN FARLEY'S TENURE AS TOWN MANAGER

Since McKenzie was part of the failed Broadband scheme with Farley, Farley was a favorite contender to being the Town Manager of White Springs. In fact, Farley met with council members outside of Sunshine Laws, so that no one would object. The town welcomed Bob Farley with a reception at the Stephen Foster Nature and Tourism Center with a large crowd attending, which probably was by invitation only because many in the town were unaware of the reception. Looking at the larger picture, the $30 million President Obama provided for broadband was a total waste. Most counties and municipalities would not consider broadband because the Florida Rural Broadband Alliance could not even provide financials.

> FRBA received a $24 million-dollar BTOP broadband stimulus grant in 2010 but in three years there isn't anything but lawsuits, federal investigations, and accusations. The investigation into FRBA started in September of 2011 and the Columbia County Observer has been steadily reporting on the problem.

Although Stu Lilker of the Columbia County Observer may have more details, the North Florida Broadband Authority (NFBA) and the GSG, a management firm employed by both authorities, were botched up in the entire grant chaos. There was somewhere along the way $30M spent by the NFBA but no paying customers were in the middle mile network that was not completed. One wonders how much of the money was used to build something, especially when there are reports that they did not pay their contractors or engineers.

At least Farley had an associate degree; however, we did not know what his associate degree was in. He also attended the quarterly North Florida Economic Development meetings at Suwannee River Water Management District Offices in Live Oak. With the Suwanee River and the Beauty of White Springs as a bedroom community, Farley felt there was opportunity for Commercial enterprises as well because of the I-75 interchange. He was the first to suggest water and sewer utilities for the I-75 interchange which Mayor Miller took over the idea and Suwannee County took over the project, since it was in their county.

Farley also fit the bill because he was terminated as city administrator of Live Oak FL on October 10, 2012, by a 3-2 roll call vote. The Live Oak Council Members stated that Farley lacked communication, management, and leadership skills.

Apparently, there were errors in how the fire department's sick time was handled in Live Oak. Since it was a quarter of a million-dollar mistake, the council did not accept that the matter could be put off for six months as Farley and the finance department required.

Farley was also told he did not have a plan for Economic Development and the businesses in the community were not growing. The council felt Farley was lacking in the directing, coordinating, reviewing and analyzing all activities and operations.

Prior to Robert Farley becoming our Town manager, the Town felt they did not have to provide records nor allow the copying of public records. In fact, Vice Mayor McKenzie seemed surprised and irritated and asked if a specific time could be set up, like once a month to answer the records. Thanks to Robert Farley in 2013, the town was told they had to comply with 119 requests. Yet, Chapter 119 of the Florida Statutes still was not followed to the letter.

Hired in January of 2013 Farley soon would orchestrate Mayor Miller's grand plan to not only defame Griffin and Karn's names but attempt to place Griffin in prison with Karin as a co-conspirator. And this was because of an application I completed for Griffin in handwritten form. To the application I attached Griffin's diplomas as well as documents he had ordered regarding his military medals. At the timr, I, Karin, had no idea that Griffin had signed off his medals and I have never been told as to why he did. I asked Griffin to review the application and asked him to determine whether we should include the non-military certifications, and he said "Yes." When we had to secure a Criminal Attorney in Perry, the Attorney advised us that I could not solely take the blame because Griffin's brochure indicated he was a "Decorated Veteran."

EVENTS TIMELINE LEADING TO GRIFFIN'S ARREST

The application for Town Manager and Griffin E. Griffin's resume' including documents I had on file which I (Karin) photographed and included therein were submitted to the Town of White Springs on or about February 24, 2014.

Griffin was qualified to run for Town Council on or about the 10th[h] of March 2014.

Flyers to the voters in White Springs were sent by US Postal Service on or about the 12th of March 2014

When Griffin was campaigning through the neighbor-hoods, especially the Black neighborhood, the majority we met said they were voting for him. Some of the people hugged him; some said they had his flyer; and most citizens, including those of businesses, were upset about the high sewer rates and hoped he would get in to assist them. It was felt that Griffin was the frontrunner, with Jefferson a close second and either Richard Marshall or Woody Woodard would be third, therefore eliminating Miller and McKenzie who most voters wished would be voted out of office. We were also told that Miller expressed her fear to some individuals that Griffin would be on the council.

In fact, this was the first year she sent out a campaign letter as did Vice-Mayor McKenzie. It showed fear on their part that they had to work for their seats on the council.

Postcards reminding Citizens to vote on April 22nd went out on April 9$^{th.}$ These cards had Griffin's e-mail and phone number. Some people called and hoped he would win.

April 15^{th,} the White Springs Police Department (WSPD) issued a warrant. Although we interacted with the Hamilton County Sheriff's office personnel around that time, they did not indicate a warrant was outstanding for Griffin. Since such a warrant could have been issued at any time after the application was filed in February, it is apparent that there was concern on the part of Mayor Miller and McKenzie, the Vice Mayor, that Griffin may take one of their seats.

No background checks were made of the other twenty-four candidates for Town Manager and the application itself states, **"I am aware that any omissions or fabrications in the application may disqualify me for employment consideration** and If I am hired may be grounds for **termination at a later date.** I understand that any information I give may be in-vestigated and I consent to the release of information about my abilities, employment his-tory and fitness for employment by previous employers, schools, law enforcement agencies and personal references." **It did not say one would be arrested and charged with fraud, especially since I had included the material myself (not Griffin) which I did not believe was fraudulent but later found out the papers were not authentic.** Griffin had received certificates from a facility that had past information.

Flyers for our lunch on the lawn for White Springs Citizens were posted prior or after the 15th of April inviting everyone to free lunch on April 19th.

On April 17th, a White Springs police car blocked Griffin's vehicle while we were at the Dollar General Store. Our neighbor's daughter as well as me and others witnessed the officer placing two sets of handcuffs on Griffin (because Officer Klug said "he was a big boy"). I (Karin) asked why Griffin was being harassed. Officer Klug said that he was not harassing him, and that the sheriff's department had five warrants for him. When asked, the officer indicated he did not know what the warrants were for, and that Griffin would find out when he reached the Hamilton County Jail.

5 is was Klug's report: "*On 4/17/2014 at 17:25 Hrs., I (Klug) observed the offender (Griffin) at the Dollar General (16881 Spring Street White Springs, FL) and having knowledge of an active warrant on Griffin, I (Klug) got out and made contact with him (Griffin)*

I (Klug) contacted Hamilton County Dispatch (via the radio) and confirmed an active warrant on Joe E Griffin. Griffin was placed in handcuffs, behind his back, double locked and checked for proper fit and searched for weapons. I (Klug) then transported Griffin to Hamilton County Jail. And he was booked without incident."

It was determined Klug was hired for the sole purpose of securing military information on Joe Griffin. Klug received the following message in an email from Navy Awards:

"*This is an email as a follow-up to your original request for validation of awards. The Department of the Navy has no record of member Lieutenant Griffin E Griffin, USN receiving the award of the silver star. The documents the member provided appear not to be authentic. Member was a Lieutenant in the Navy upon honorable discharge. The Navy Personal Command Retired Records Center in St. Louis conducted a query.*"

Klug also stated Griffin lied about his Chemistry bachelor's degree with FTU, which had he not completed the degree he would not have been in the Navy as a Lieutenant. Klug contacted FTU but it was not the original FTU which changed its name to the University of Central Florida. Had UCF been called, it would have confirmed his degree. This information went on military blogs in which some writers believed a Lieutenant could have received such medals, but for lying about his education, he was labeled as stealing Military Valor.

This arrest transpired at 5:30 pm Easter Thursday (5:25 per Klug). It seemed convenient since the courthouse would be closed on Good Friday and money could not be secured through banking until Monday due to the Easter Weekend. With a $10,000 bond, I was told by the Sheriff's dispatcher that I (Karin) would need 10%, meaning $1,000 to get bail for Griffin. Normally spouses have only one joint checking account and the Camel Club fashioned after Ed's letters and anonymous people have felt I had no funds of my own so therefore the maximum one could get from an ATM would be $500.

It is believed that Joe E. Griffin's arrest would change the residents' vote or since people in the community are intimidated by the mayor and the WSPD, they would fear the same thing would happen to them. Woody Woodard, candidate for council, was concerned enough that he contacted Griffin by phone because he also feared an arrest and inquired about the amount of money needed for bail.

My friend found a list of bail bondspeople and my cellular phone (Verizon) could not get through to two but finally I was able to speak to bail bondsperson, Mr. Ivy. Mr. Ivy indicated he required $1,000 in cash….no checks or credit cards. We went to the ATM, and I was able to pull out $500 from my account and only $440 from Griffin's account due to his having spent some money during the day. As a result, I had $940, and Mr. Ivy stated I could meet him the following day to pay him the $60 required.

He managed to release Griffin on Bond, and we went home that Thursday night.

Joyce Marie Taylor reporter for the Suwannee Democrat and Jasper News picked up the arrest photos and arrest information from the WSPD shortly after Griffin was arrested on April 17th. Griffin's arrest was then on the internet immediately as front-page news. Those who commit murder have never been on the front page of Jasper News. Joyce Marie Taylor had a close relationship with Mayor Miller and Vice Mayor McKenzie, and she prints what they request her to print. The WSPD also contacted and provided information about the arrest to ABC WTXL in Tallahassee. This reporter then contacted Griffin for his side of the story, which was telecasted but removed after the 5:30 news.

An email from Chief Rodriquenz of May 2, 2014, to Karen Hatton with a copy to Eddie Black, State Investigator, included a link from WTXL regarding a phone interview with Me. Griffin. The heading was *"Man claiming to be decorated veteran arrested"*.

Friday, another friend of ours helped me with the preparations for the next day's party on the 19th[h]. She also called some people in the community because I was falling apart from Griffin's arrest and preparing last minute food items was all that I could manage.

Saturday the 19th[h], we moved tables, chairs, food, and banners to offer a free lunch paid for by the candidate Joe E. Griffin for the Town Council.

At around 1:30 pm Mayor Miller arrived at the S & S store across the street from where we were serving food. Since she did not return with packages, it is assumed now, in hindsight, that is when she dropped the flyers of Joe Griffin's arrest at the S and S store. Shortly thereafter, a couple showed up. The woman came directly up to me and said she wished to donate for the food. I told her she could not donate about five times because it was a free lunch for the community. She then asked again, and I finally said, "I can't" and pushed her hand and billfold away. It would violate election laws. I then offered her and her husband food, not thinking about it until others told me they were sure she was a plant of some kind to make me do something wrong for Joe Griffin's election. No one knew who this couple was, and it was obvious she was right in my face challenging me. I noticed also when I kept refusing, the husband or male friend was smirking. I believe that the woman did not get her way and was sent by Mayor Miller to do damage. Yet I could not prove that but I had witnesses.

April 20th and 21st, we drove around and still had everyone we spoke to, telling us they were voting for Joe Griffin; how terrible the mayor is and how Griffin should sue the Town because it was evident the arrest was made to stop him from being a councilman. It was confirmed, the arrest information from the news was photocopied (probably at Town Hall using the Town's paper and ink) and placed at the S & S store where African Americans frequent. Another of my friends stated an African American gentleman was passing this information to people on the street as the Town instructed him. She provided Griffin and I with a copy late in the evening.

April 22nd, Election Day, the area where people stand to campaign was being used by the prisoners to cut grass. Therefore no one could stand on the outside to campaign. It was found later that Joe Griffin lost the election by a landslide because of the arrest. Jefferson had 150 votes, Miller 88 votes and McKenzie 86 votes. Joe Griffin had forty-seven votes. The blog showed where the mayor's anonymous friend wrote. "*They did something of this nature in last year's election with the police helping the friends of the mayor so that Griffin lost as well as a complaint against him with the Board of Elections.*"

90

It was not only Farley colluding with Mayor Miller, but also Police Chief Tracy and staff members Tomlinson and Heath. Tracy was the one who hired officer Klug. who was in the Navy reserves with her husband. Klug did not have a great employment record, having been terminated from his position as a police officer, from a prior department. His hiring amounted to only the time it took to arrest Griffin and check out Griffin's DD214. Which of course had no medals listed. After the arrest it was told by a Police Officer who did not agree with what was transpiring that Chief Tracy had a party in the Stephen Foster Park where Klug parked his trailer for all to celebrate Griffin's arrest. And the hate this Town had was not only Griffin's demeanor but the fact that he ordered public records. I cannot even tell you what disgusting things Tracy performed in the park that no lady would do, especially a cop.

We sent a complaint to the elections board citing voter fraud and were told after the review that if Griffin had not pled guilty to receive Pre-Trial Intervention (PTI), they would have found the individuals in violation. But they also advised Griffin and his attorney that securing PTI would be less costly without court intervention and that the choice was better than a full investigation and trial.

Tracy Capella- Rodriquenz was initially the lieutenant for the White Springs Police Department. Prior to that Tracy was a hair stylist.

At the time Chief Subic was fired by reason that he attempted covering his pregnant mistress under the health insurance policy, Vice Mayor McKenzie wished for Tracy to become the new Chief of Police, but Tracy had just been charged for a DUI after an alleged altercation at a bar in Jacksonville with a Jacksonville police officer. After she left the bar, the Jacksonville police stopped Tracy's vehicle, and she was charged with DUI. Thereafter Chief Brookins became the White Springs Chief of Police and Tracy remained his lieutenant.

She has been rumored to have been charged for giving false. Before the election, she wanted Griffin charged as a Sex Offender for urinating outside in the dark behind Town Hall. And no one saw Griffin until he returned inside.

Prior to Chief Joseph Subic, Jr. (A U.S. Traitor whose charges were dropped, by President Regan) being terminated, he and the investigating officer for an assault charge against Tracy contacted the Assistant State Attorney Teresa Drake at the misdemeanor criminal courthouse in Gainesville wherein he guaranteed to discipline Officer Tracy

She also had an assault charge against her of July 10, 2005, whereby she hit the victim in the face with a closed fist causing small lacerations above the left eye. Tracy was angry because she had overheard a conversation between the victim and another person while inside the restroom of a nightclub where Tracy was the topic of conversation. She had to go to Anger Management Classes. Subic was fired and Ken Brookins then vouched for her, and she then remained his lieutenant until the Chief retired and Tracy was able to take his position.

After assisting Miller with information regarding Griffins, early on, Chief Rodriquenz, on her own time, decided to show a friend how she could operate a motorcycle. As such she crashed and broke several bones and could not walk.

ASA Hatton

There was a person I felt was a weak link in the States Attorney's office by the name of Karen Hatton. Like Chief Tracy, Hatton thought that the **Secret Service refused to make charges** against Joe Griffin, rather than the FBI refusing. Technically many in law enforcement did not feel that having information on an application was a felony but for each medal, Griffin was charged with five counts of "Uttering a Forged Instrument", meaning he was charged with five felonies. If Griffin had all five certificates on one piece of paper, would it have meant only one felony instead of five? But the fact that <u>the application stated</u>: _"I am aware that any omissions or fabrications in the application may disqualify me for employment consideration and If I am hired may be grounds for termination at a later date_ did not mean Griffin should be arrested. The financial gain if hired as a manager would have been a pittance and furthermore, no wonder the FBI would not even consider this matter. **This was a railroad job in its finest**.

ASA Hatton also was reamed by the States Attorney, Sigmeister for taking the case. But it was too late. The damage was done.

Because Joe Griffin kept ordering Public Records and was demanding in his requests and due to the blog still run by me, Mayor Miller felt that Griffin had violated his PTI and ASA Hatton removed Griffin's PTI stipulating there would be further criminal charges. It appeared the Town and its attorney felt ordering public records was a criminal charge. Jason Edward Klug worked diligently to assist the town and charged both Griffin and Karin with Harassment.

> _"I was contacted by White Springs Police Chief, Tracy Rodriquenz in reference to the harassment of the Town of White Springs by Griffin and Karin Griffin via their blog. White Springs journal.com. She states that several employees are being personally harassed on the blog which is discrediting the Town of White Springs. Witnesses state that the Griffins' included on the blog what appears to be hand drawn likenesses of city employees involved in activities that are inappropriate or illegal and statements include calling employees' crooks, liars and using untrue quotes. It is stated that Mr. Griffin emails and sends 119 requests almost daily that include petty and negative statements. It is stated by employees that Griffins attempt to discredit and ruin the character of said employees. (See witness statements and printouts from the website_

provided by City Hall. According to Chief Rodriquenz, there may be more statements and printouts to follow as they become available." 6/19/2024.

By law, if an individual accepts PTI, any other criminal charge or mention of medals would cancel the PTI, and it was in Mayor Miller's purview that both Griffin and I be charged with felonies and locked up in prison. In fact, she and her husband had drafted a letter which Miller sent by email, to the Town Attorney for approval. That letter was behind another email written by the Town Attorney, as evidence after Griffin found it. Instead, the Town Attorney brought it before the council and luckily, Mayor Miller was not the current mayor but rather Bullard. with Vice Mayor Brown and Council Member Jefferson voting against it, while the prior vice Mayor McKenzie and prior Mayor Miller voted for it.

The charges were made to ensure that Griffin would be charged for violating his PTI by criminal harassment of ordering public records and writing on the blog. However, none of these charges are criminal by law. The mayor's complaint to ASA Karen Hatton was that he continued requesting public records and she wished for the blog to be closed. It was not until October 2014, when a new Assistant States Attorney replaced ASA Hatton that he found that **Joe Griffin had been railroaded because the officials were determined to imprison both Griffin and me.**

Town Manager Farley also completed a Victim impact Statement for the office of the State Attorney. When describing his injuries, Farley cited "***Emotionally; Additional Work, his blog with negative comments; calling candidates ahead of the Town; Stirred up citizens against town sta⁾ ; Sta⁾ was concerned about their jobs; His overall attitude about government.***"

The staff also made victim reports which pertained to the ordering of public records, the comments on the blog and cartooning done by me.

It may be mentioned that in an attempt by the Town to take Griffin's PTI from him as well as an attempt to incarcerate me, the Town attempted to place criminal charges on both of us. In the Assistant State's Attorney's letter of September 15, 2014, to each Griffin and I, the letter stated:

"This is to inform you that prosecution in the case against the above-named defendant has been declined by this office for the following reason: There is insufficient information to pursue criminal charges of stalking/harassment in this case. The blogpost referenced does not rise to the level of cyberstalking as defined in the Florida Statutes. As the state cannot meet its burden, our ethical duty requires that no charge be filed in this case. It is understandable that the disposition of this case may seem confusing or disappointing to you. If you have any questions, please do not hesitate to contact me. Sincerely, Arminda W. Janousek, Assistant States Attorney."

I, Karin, alone attended the June 2014 meeting where the council discussed securing the seed money for the revolving loan from the Hamilton County Development Authority HCDA. Since the Town had squandered so much money and had charged the Citizens such extreme rates for sewer and water, Griffin asked our attorney if we could go to the HCDA without having a problem with his PTI. Griffin's criminal attorney said he saw no problem with our attending the meeting.

At the HCDA meeting Farley was presenting on behalf of the town the proposal for a $250,000 grant from HCDA, whereby one of the HCDA members stated" he **had no skin in the game**." The HCDA had provided funds previously to the town and it was not for economic development or to secure jobs but a sidewalk to nowhere, a park and an amphitheater which was to have been a business incubator for the community. Griffin gave a speech stating that he wished the HCDA to provide White Springs with the Seed Money of $250,000 but that he asked they lower the sewer and water rates.

Farley was the one who admitted he found the certificates in the application which assisted in charging Griffin with five felonies. But when he arrived at the HCDA meeting, he sat next to me, and we had a conversation about his retirement and a trip we had taken. After Griffin's speech. Farley gave no rebuttal and left with his head and shoulders down indicating a troubled man. We knew he had not wished to retire but it is believed that Mayor Miller's pressure on him and staff was significant, but I have no proof. Farley provided the ASA Hatton with a statement saying Griffin's requests and comments caused him health problems.

$25,000 apparently was received by the Town and used in the amount of $24,945 by the time Ms. Tebo provided the Enterprise Budget for the period October 2018 to August 2019. Although I never recalled the Council mentioning that the money was received by the Town in 2018 or 2019.

There was no malice in the speech Griffin gave, only how money was misspent and that if the $250,000 was given to the Town he asked that the Sewer and Water Rate be lowered as a condition. However, Bullard, the attorney for the HCDA who recused himself because he was a White Springs Mayor blamed Griffin for the loss. **Yet everyone seemed to forget that an HCDA board member stated the Town had *"No Skin in the Game"* and was against the HCDA providing the $250,000 Seed Money. Mayor Bullard contacted me and advised me it was Griffin's fault that the Town was not granted the $250,000 seed money.**

At the Jan. 14, 2015, meeting of the White Springs Town Council, Police Chief Brookins and Town Manager Farley formally announced their resignations. Farley gave the Town six months' notice and stated he was leaving for personal reasons. The police chief stated he was leaving due to business opportunities. With Brookin's resignation, it gave way for Lieutenant Tracy to become the Police Chief.

CHAPTER SIX P. 2 – WHAT TRANSPIRED IN LAWRENCE'S TENURE AS TOWN MANAGER

Bill Lawrence was the best Town Manager White Springs had ever hired. Lawrence earned a degree in criminal justice from the University of Maine and spent several years in law enforcement as well as undertaking the position of interim Town Manager in Maine. Although there were many applicants for the White Springs Town Manager job, the majority required far more in remuneration, with many not having the experience.

Lawrence served as the town manager of White Springs for eight months. The Town offered only $40,000 a year in salary to Lawrence and the town lucked out because Lawrence moved to Florida to be near older family members. **He started his position as Town Manager on July 19, 2014, and his last day at work, he said, will be June 19 with an official end of employment date of July 20.** Lawrence said he was going back to his hometown in Maine where he accepted a job offer. He left at a critical time for the town of White Springs, due to annual budgets workshops to begin in July..

To show what a technical, logical, and honest manager he was, he continually watched money and even though the council offered him more money, he did not accept it because of the poor financial condition White Springs was in.

As background, one of the things Griffin has always done, is to contact applicants asking them whether they follow the laws pertaining to public records and if they believed in transparency. He also told the applicants that he was a concerned citizen and not an official of the town but that they could read his blog, the "White Springs Journal" to get information on the Town. Griffin contacted Lawrence prior to his hiring, who advised the council at the initial interview. Of course, the council had further anger at Griffin for contacting applicants again.

We would find out later that Mayor Miller would not allow Bill Lawrence to speak at meetings. She conducted meetings as she saw fit. Initially Lawrence advised us that he felt, after reading the blog articles, that this was just a "good ole boy" situation, but as time went on, he found the matter was far worse. Lawrence visited us briefly on March 9th. He could not believe that the mayor had over 1200 emails from her home computer, which is against Policy. In Maine, there were three. Furthermore, she used her personal emails so that they would not be public records, since the emails were not sent through her town council email address but through her personal email.

When Lawrence originally read our blog before taking the Job, he thought this was just a "Good Ole Boy" problem; however, after three months he realized it is far more. The Mayor and Walter McKenzie Vice Mayor control the town and do not allow even the remaining three council members in on what they are doing. Bill Lawrence tried to place what he learned as agenda items, but the mayor ran things and even had checks drafted for whatever she wished.

Bill mentioned how Walter McKenzie has gotten an additional $40,000 from the new Liquor Store owners stating they needed certain things done before they could build the liquor store, and he was proud of it. Bill said that these people have money and if the town continues, there will be a lawsuit.

When Lawrence came to the town, he felt he would have health insurance for his family, but the Council did not provide him and his wife insurance. The Town should have been ashamed because all prior managers were provided with insurance benefits.

He had not decided yet whether he would remain and try to clean the town up or go back to Maine where he received offers from other government entities. He said he knows that if he leaves or if he receives threats from the Town terminating his employment, he would be thrown under the bus for every problem they started.

Regarding the civil rights suit we drafted, he mentioned the mayor questioned him and Tracy Rodriquenz about their depositions. They did not tell the mayor, stating they had to retain secrecy. This is why the Town tries to control every hire. And I do not know how Lawrence, as such an experienced manager, could withstand how the mayor treated him, which was obvious in each meeting.

Kathy **Lawrence** said when she and **Bill** arrived in White Springs, the Millers invited them to a day out in the woods honoring cypress trees and the waterways which neither **Lawrence** appreciated. Usually, a new manager and his spouse are taken out to dinner, but with the Millers, one never knows what to expect.

Lawrence said he was upset that the mayor did not have to be concerned about anything because she felt any claim against the Town would be paid for by insurance, and she (Mayor Miller) will keep doing things because it does not affect her financially. Because of White Springs' reputation, this is why we cannot retain good people.

Lawrence and his wife leased their home in Maine to a family before renting a small house in White Springs which they stated they would be embarrassed in inviting their friends over. Lawrence is not only an intellectual leader but a personable one and treated the citizens of White Springs as though they were family. The only people on the Council who were good to him were Attorney Bullard, Jefferson, and Brown. This worked for the formers' favor when Lawrence showed the three how to get control of the council in April of 2015, eliminating Miller as mayor.

When Bullard was voted in as mayor by council members Jefferson and Brown, Mayor Miller's knees started shaking loudly under the council table. It was obvious she was upset. Lawrence was the only honest person who stated in his deposition essentially that Mayor Miller was out to get Griffin. He did state this to us after he resigned.

Although his decision to move to Florida was due to a sick father in Florida. he was offered a position in Howland Maine after his father passed away and their home in Maine was not sold. He then became the Town Manager for Warren Maine. It was obvious that he could not wait to leave White Springs because he and his wife Kathy loaded their furniture within a day and left that night. In 2019 Lawrence moved back to Florida when he was hired as city manager in Bowling Green.at a salary of $75,000.

Bill Lawrence submitted his resignation to the White Springs Council on Monday, May 18, and a special meeting of the town council was held Wednesday, May 20, 2015, to discuss options to fill the vacancy. At the end of a lengthy and, at times, argumentative meeting, the town Council decided that former town clerk Shirley Heath would serve as interim town manager by a vote of 3-2 until the vacancy could be filled.

Heath was the Town Clerk for 19 years, until Mayor Miller managed to force her into retirement. Tomlinson, who worked alongside Heath, then became the Finance Manager Town Clerk with only a GED. Having only a high school education or GED herself, Heath's claim was that she was a Christian with her husband being a minister. However, it was obvious Ms. Heath manufactured statements, not always leaning on the truth. And she did not have the experience to be a manager but was the interim town manager once before and had 19 years of experience with the town as the clerk. The motion was passed by the council with a 3-2 vote to hire Heath as the interim town manager. Mayor Miller and Vice Mayor McKenzie voted against her hire.

The town council was not allowed to consider Townsend as the interim manager, who served as town manager for eleven years. He had been placed on paid administrative leave after being forced to resign when the Florida Department of Law Enforcement (FDLE) was investigating him. Yet the excuse by Mayor Bullard was that Townsend was out of town at the time.

Vice Mayor McKenzie interjected that he thought *"the town council needed to ..x a broken system ..rst before advertising for a new town manager because the current employment package isn't enough to bring someone in who will actually stay a while"*. He suggested they schedule a workshop to discuss the matter. *"I understand we're on a tight budget… but we've got to ..gure out a way to where we can get somebody onboard so that we won't be sitting here in another 8 months,"* McKenzie said.

The next discussion concerned Heath's salary. Finance Director Tomlinson said that after paying Lawrence what was due him, including vacation and unused sick time, there would be about $9,200 left in the budget to pay Heath for 14 weeks until the next fiscal year's budget is set. *"That would give you approximately a salary of $660 a week,"* said Tomlinson to Heath.

McKenzie said since both Farley and Heath are retired and neither one needs health insurance through the town, the council missed an opportunity to talk to them first and see if they would work for less than $660 per week. Jefferson made a motion that Mayor Bullard speak with Heath to work out the salary issue to see if she will work for less, to save the town some money, or if she would want the $660 a week salary. McKenzie seconded the motion, and it passed unanimously.

Attorney Fred Koberlein advised Mayor Bullard that another meeting needed to be scheduled for the council to approve Heath's acceptance of the position and at what salary, as well as a start date. He also suggested that Lawrence start a **request for proposal (RFP)**_for the town manager position and specify a 30-day deadline.

Miller interjected that she would appreciate notifications of future town meetings. She said she did not receive notice of this meeting because the email had been sent to her old email address that had been closed out for about two years. She also said she had not been notified about a previous meeting concerning the nature and heritage center closing because Lawrence misspelled her name in the email address.

Jefferson made another motion that Lawrence immediately got a help wanted ad posted at the Florida League of Cities noting that the town manager's salary would be negotiable, which passed unanimously.

A notice was sent via e-mail on Thursday, May 21, that a special meeting of the White Springs Town Council would be held at town hall on Tuesday, May 26 at 6:30 PM. to ratify/accept Heath as interim town manager.

On May 23, Heath sent an email to the *Jasper News* with the following statement:

"I am looking forward to working with Mayor" Bullard, *"the council, and staff during this transition period. I will be continuing with the current manager, Bill Lawrence, and the council's vision and plans for White Springs. I am excited to again serve the citizens of White Springs."*

At the May 26 meeting, the council voted 4-1 to accept Heath as interim town manager beginning June 16 for a weekly salary of $660 with no benefits until a new manager can apply and be hired. Mayor Miller, who opposed the motion, read a long letter prior to the vote that detailed why she was in support of Farley being selected rather than Heath, according to Lawrence. White Springs Mayor Bullard presided over his first town council meeting on Tuesday, May 12, since taking office on April 30th.

After brief department head reports, the focus turned to old business and the Visit Florida grant, which consumed a good portion of the meeting. *"5 is was the U.S.P.S. Pictorial Postmark program, which also provided the funding for the Florida Quilt Trail and the White Springs Florida Quilt Trail activities,"* said Miller. "The grant is for $5,000 and it does list the activities that need to be funded by the grant., This is a grant where the town pays for the expenses and when it's complete, it gets reimbursed by Visit Florida."

Miller said what was left to do on the grant program was to use $1,000 for marketing, as listed in the Project Budget Detail, which she said was provided on page 3 of the grant application. **She asked if $1,000 could be allocated to the Nature & Heritage Tourism Center account.** Lawrence noted earlier that PotashCorp-White Springs had donated $1,000 to keep the tourism center open for the month of May to accommodate the Florida Folk Festival.

Another item to be completed on the Visit Florida grant, Miller noted, was to produce designs for postcards, T-shirts and shopping bags based on the Yo-yo Quilt pictorial postmark, and that there was enough money in the grant budget to fund it.

"To get the funds released or reimbursed to us, we have to complete the entire project, so I have asked Mr. Lawrence to provide the authorization to complete the project, so that all funds that have been expended can be reimbursed," Miller told the council.

Council member Jefferson asked where the upfront money was coming from to do the project and Miller told him it would come from the economic development account.

"5 ese are the funds that were generated for the town by performing the work for year one of the DEO Competitive

Florida project," Miller explained. *"5 ese are not revenue funds, and these are not Enterprise funds."* Jefferson turned to **Lawrence, who said he had concerns and wanted to speak with Visit Florida Grant Administrator Susan Gale to see** if the $1,000 for operating costs at the tourism center was appropriate use of the funds. *"I kind of disagree with that,"* said **Lawrence. Lawrence said he was concerned about taking money out of the economic development account because it was down to $15,536.** *"5 e UF pavilion cost us $4,837... $1,475 was raised in donations, which meant we took $3,362 from that account to pay o' the bill so these kids could graduate,"* Lawrence said.

Miller stated after the meeting that she had allocated $1,225 of her mayor salary and raised another $1,000 in donations for a total of $2,225 for the pavilion project, and that Lawrence's figures were wrong.

"We also have a UF subcontract for DEO in the second year of deliverables, one for the I-75/CR 136 site plan that is estimated at $10,000, and another one for the White Springs Eco-lodge planning and development at $15,000," Lawrence advised the councilors. *"Now, these deliverables we will get reimbursed, but by the same token, we signed a contract with UF to pay these when the invoices come in and I was going to pay that out of the economic development account."* Lawrence continued, saying, *"Obviously, if we're on the hook for $25,000, we only have $15,000 in the account before we start getting reimbursed. I feel like we have more debt out there than we can pay and I'm just not real comfortable with that, but I have no problems doing what this council is asking me to do."*

Lawrence and Miller both noted that the deliverables for DEO's Competitive Florida Partnership Program had to be completed by June 15, to seek reimbursement for funds in the amount of up to $40,000. Lawrence said he wasn't sure how quickly they would get the reimbursement money

Lawrence said if after speaking with Visit Florida and being advised that it is appropriate to use $1,000 of the grant funds for the tourism center to keep it open for another month, then he would be okay with it.

Former Vice Mayor McKenzie asked Lawrence if there was any concern that the town would not be reimbursed from Visit Florida and Lawrence said, "No, not to date." **McKenzie then asked Miller whose idea it was to use some of the Visit Florida grant funds for the tourism center. "That's what we submitted it for," Miller replied. "And they agreed to it?" McKenzie asked. "Well, yeah, they provided the funds for the project," said Miller.**

"I don't want us to say we're worried we won't get paid back because we will get paid," McKenzie told Lawrence. *"5 ose statements will come back to haunt you the next time you go to apply for a grant. If we already basically agreed what the grant was and what the expenditures were, and where they were to be spent, and we go to question that or try to change it, I'm concerned that people are going to look at that kind of behavior when we apply for future grants'* Mayor Bullard suggested tabling the matter until their next meeting, so that they could get an answer from Visit Florida.

When asked by Miller, Lawrence said he had no issue with the other items in the **grant "I just want to be sure we're playing by the rules,"** he said. "Absolutely," Miller told him. "That is why I presented the memo and attachments to you earlier today "Miller said if the council chose to do nothing, they would not be reimbursed by Visit Florida for any of the funds that have already been expended.

After a heated discussion, where **Lawrence said he disagreed with statements being made, he clarified that he was uncomfortable taking funds from the Visit Florida grant which were earmarked for marketing and using them for**

operational costs of the tourism center. Brown then made a motion to table the matter until Lawrence heard back from Visit Florida. Jefferson seconded the motion, and it passed by a vote of 3-2 with McKenzie and Miller voting against.

On Monday, May 18, Lawrence advised that he received an email response from the grants team at Visit Florida regarding use of the $1,000 for operational costs at the tourism center. It stated: **"William, be advised, that you are correct, in that the memo is referring to costs that are not an allowable expenditure for the grant program. The allowable costs must be specific to executing marketing programs to publicize the tourism advantages of the state of Florida.**

Today William (Bill) Lawrence is the City Manager for Lady Lake Florida starting at a salary of $120,000 for which he is more than deserving. Prior to that he was the City Manager in Bowling Green FL. Bill Lawrence is one of the best and most personable managers I have ever met, and he deserves only the best.

During our Civil Rights Case it was found that the Town sanitized the emails which were sent to our attorney in discovery. Bill Lawrence assisted us.

Bill Lawrence was the current Town Manager, until June 19th. He stopped by our house on May 22nd,2015 and indicated what we already knew that the former Mayor Miller is out of control. Bill wished for us to know what her trigger points are:

(1) She always has to be right (2) She lies continually and if she is questioned about her first lie, she will start digging herself deeper by not remembering her lies and starting up new lies (3) She likes to be in control and feels she does no wrong (4) She is used to ordering everyone around (5) She will blame everyone if she is caught in a transgression, including Bill and all former managers and current employees (5) For having a doctorate, she does not have a lot of experience or intelligence,

in fact she is like a child (and that is a quote) who just has to get her way.

Bill said that she, Helen Miller, is very articulate when speaking with the attorney for the Town but now even Fred Koberlein is having some problems and Bill plans to speak with the current Mayor Rhett Bullard to see whether Fred and he may do some form of censorship because she is still ordering everyone around and McKenzie (councilman) feels that Helen Miller is the "cat's meow". Although the Newspaper reporter was taken aside by Miller, to give her Miller's views, the Newspaper reported the unbiased truth about the errors. Bill was just trying to keep the town out of trouble and the mayor has always felt if there is an account with money, she can use it as she sees fit.

Since McKenzie now feels there is a problem regarding the Town's inability to keep managers, Bill plans on speaking to the council on how to keep a manager.

Bill Lawrence stopped by also on May 29, 2015. He said that he also told Tracy Rodriquenz that that the Town was attempting to throw her under the bus. "It was Helen Miller who placed the pressure on us: The emails Lawrence will be providing will be those Helen Miller sent to Tracy. Tracy did not with to follow up with Hatton. The mayor asked her if she could go to Hatton and discuss the Griffins. And Tracy told her she could.

Bill also said that Ray Curtis (Griffin's criminal attorney) went up to the mayor, then (Helen Miller) and asked what could be done to get the Griffins off. Helen told the attorney that the Griffins would have to get rid of the blog and not send 119's. Lawrence also stated he is certain now that the mayor does not wish to provide emails from her personal computer because she and Fred Koberlein were attempting to put Griffin away.

Email from our Civil Rights Attorney:

I am concerned about these e-mails magically appearing at this late date. We asked for all e-mails in the Town's possession or control which discussed you or Griffin. For purposes of the Federal Court, I believe that "in the Town's control" would include e-mails the mayor sent in her official capacity even if sent from her personal e-mail account. This is the reason we received e-mails from Fred Koberlein even though he is a private attorney with private e-mail.

The fact that these e-mails are appearing now suggests that they were intentionally withheld. That may be sanctionable conduct on the part of the city.

A reader of the blog made a comment regarding the police department on June 17, 2014:

'It has been confirmed that Chief Rodriquenz has more unsolved crimes in 4 months as chief, than former Chief Brookins had in 6 years. Since February of this year, there are currently 14 unsolved burglaries. There are also Numerous thefts and two robberies and several serious batteries. That is unacceptable by any means. We have a non-working chief who has publicly stated that she pays for the gas in the chief's vehicle, and she will not patrol on her dime. You have her number two officer, Harden, who has been a cop for maybe nine months, and then you have officer Meeks who also has very little lad time. When you have a reserve force who hardly comes out and works, then you have her choice to hire former Officer Klug who stayed maybe two months. The town invested over $1,000 in him by purchasing a bullet proof vest, uniforms and paying for his camp site at the park and then at Kelly's. He was kicked out of the park for having several loud alcohol-fueled parties, some of which Chief Tracy was at. One of the times, she spent the night in Klug's camper. As a 30-year resident of White Springs, I would like for us to consider abolishing the Police Department and get the Sheriff's office to manage the Sheriff is constitutionally required to provide Law Enforcement services at no cost to the county. The public records request I did with the Sheriff's Office show that they are already in charge of 73% of the calls for service already. If that is the case, why do we have a budget of over $200,000 for the Police Department. That money could help lower our sewer and water bills."

CHAPTER SEVEN – WHAT TRANSPIRED IN TEBO'S TENURE AS TOWN MANAGER

There were few applicants for the Town Manager position, after Bill Lawrence returned to Maine. Stacy Tebo was invited to an interview before the Town Council. Her interview consisted of an hours' worth of: *"I started doing this and was promoted to that, etc."* She did, however, indicate that she left DeBary because she had a discrimination complaint against the Manager and City.

Being an incredibly attractive lady with a Master of Public Administration degree from the University of Central Florida she did not do the research on the town and made no suggestions of how to make the current state of the town better. It was apparent, she needed a job while she sued DeBary and its manager for discrimination. She also admitted she had never heard of White Springs prior to the town calling her for an interview.

After her interview and in a separate meeting, Councilman Jefferson said, **"I want that girl."** Mayor Bullard contacted Ms. Tebo by phone to set a starting date. What surprised me is that Mayor Bullard advised Ms. Tebo that she would have to take a drug test and to stay off drugs for two weeks. It may have been Bullard's sense of humor, but was it? Stacy Tebo served as the town manager from September 9, 2015. To November 2019.

Much later in her employment, it was verbally admitted by Ms. Tebo that she was taking Percocet after Chief Tracy Rodriquenz found a pill on each of the bathroom floors.. Initially the Chief blamed one of her officers who denied the allegations. Tebo said that she had a prescription for years. Why would a doctor prescribe Percocet for years, since Percocet was addictive and an opioid? Yet Police Chief Tracy Rodriquenz confirmed the Percocet was prescribed to Tebo by a physician, in a deposition. When deposed in DeBary, Tebo made no mention of Percocet when asked what medications she was taking by the attorney.

Although Tebo did not have a friendly disposition, in her first year, she made one of the finest budgets White Springs had ever seen, using all the appropriate government codes. But that would change when the auditor and the council wanted the budget to be simplified with fewer codes.

Tebo's disgust appeared to be with former Mayor Miller who she felt wished to control everything, even though she no longer was the mayor or spokesperson of the town. And of course, she was disgusted with Joe Griffin's complaints. Tebo construed Griffin joined forces with Miller, which he did in the end prior to Miller's death from cancer.

Tebo witnessed Miller telephoned Rivers every morning at 9:00 a.m. and had a long friendly conversation with her. Tebo said in an earlier disposition that she refused to listen to anything Miller suggested.

Tebo worked as White Springs Manager from September 2015 to November of 2019. She had worked in local government since 1996. Tebo was employed by the City of Sanford Community Development Department for seven years. After she was laid off from Sanford, she worked for Volusia County for six months. From April 2005 to May of 2015, Tebo was employed by the City of Debary as their City Clerk.

After a year, Bullard no longer chose to be mayor, Spencer Lofton had a short stint as Mayor before moving to Lake City. Once Lofton left, the Council turned the office back to Mayor Miller. At the time Tebo's renewal was due, Councilman McKenzie stated he had concerns about renewing Tebo's contract for two years. McKenzie was loyal to Miller, but most agreed with his comments relating to holding workshops to discuss the position, which never happened. Mckenzie stated, *"It is a concern of mine how we have a manager that manages with too heavy of a hand sometimes." He stated he would like to see a more cooperative atmosphere.*

It may be mentioned that Tebo took more time off by leaving for her home in Volusia County every Friday, than any other manager. She lived in a room in Lake City during the weekdays and spent the time she had in the office allegedly working on her lawsuit. Although she filed a discrimination case against Debary, and the City Manager, **she won her case due to "retaliation" not being easily disproved by the courts. Discrimination was not a factor in her case since such complaints were based upon the treatment of other people and pay raises, not hers.** As such the Judge awarded Tebo $287,500, of which her attorney would receive approximately $118,634, The City would pay the $5,000 deductible and the City's Liability insurer would pay the balance.

Once the court case was won, Ms. Tebo would have the opportunity to seek other employment opportunities since her salary with White Springs was $55,000 initially; then raised to $58,000 and White Springs had financial problems. This was not due to Stacy Tebo's lack of experience as a manager but because the council was spending money without adhering to budgets.

The players during the first year of Tebo's reign were **Mayor Bullard, esquire Vice mayor Brown and Councilman Jefferson.** Together with Mayor Bullard, we have what was referred to as the **"Power of Three".** Others had seen the three make decisions prior to meetings in violation of the Florida Sunshine Laws and the three vote as one. Mayor Bullard would start the motion or discussion and the two would readily make or second the motion, each taking turns at council meetings. The motions and seconds to the motion were swift, so that the other two councilors would not have an opportunity for discussion. Yet, this is not verifiable due to the Finance Director, Tomlinson, overseeing the recorder at meetings. She allegedly shut down the recorder with respect to anything which would appear damaging to the **"Power of Three"** or the Town Manager. Even though I had information in my notes and in the blog, the recordings did not include that information. **Did she cleanse the recordings, or did information disappear on its own?**

Various citizens also alleged they saw Tomlinson take home the unlocked early voters' box prior to bringing it to the voting place. Likewise, the meeting minutes were void of information. I, of course, took my own meeting minutes and placed information on the blog.

Mayor Bullard did not place any of his requests in writing but rather like Miller, had the Town Manager Tebo do his bidding for which he provided protection for her with the **"Power of Three"** That protection may have constituted a violation of their fiduciary responsibilities to the Town's citizens, yet there were no formal complaints just criticisms.

When asked whether there is a cap on **legal expenses**, Mayor Bullard told the citizenry at a meeting there is no cap and should money be required over the $20,000 in the current budget for legal expenses, it would be taken from other areas of the budget. This was wrong but the African American population as well as those impoverished were afraid to bring forth information against the three for fear of retaliation such as increased water and sewer bills, police arrests, and harassment. Each citizen was given five minutes to voice their comments or complaints, but all complaints or requests were ignored; sometimes tabling them to be brought to staff.

Rivers, while employed as the Administrative Assistant for White Springs, submitted a complaint by electronic mail of discrimination. She sent it by email to the Town Attorney Frederick L. Koberlein, Jr., esquire, Mayor Bullard, and Town Manager Tebo.

We did research into her background from the application and found only one previous employer out of six would rehire Rivers. Joe E. Griffin received the blame for drawing cartoons of the officials and staff when it was I who did the drawings. After noting a charge of kiting a check, I produced a cartoon of Mayor Miller providing Rivers with money on the blog. That did not go well.

The River's Case

On March 22nd, 2017, Tebo sent three work-related emails to Rivers. She sent them before realizing Rivers was unable to receive emails. Rivers made a request to the Town's IT Department, who was not responsible for assisting her. After the representative, Jason called Tebo about Rivers' help request, Tebo asked Rivers if she sent the help request and Rivers confirmed. Tebo then asked Tomlinson to *"reset her password"*. When Tomlinson reset Rivers' password, she notified Tebo, who notified Rivers. Rivers loudly stated *"Really?" "Are you kidding me?" "She couldn't tell me herself"* referring to Tomlinson.

Tebo claimed that while Rivers was making these comments and complaining about Greene not communicating with her, Tebo admittedly yelled *"Stop it." "I just want you to do your work. Can you just do that?"* Rivers stated *"What?" "Am I not allowed to complain?"*

Some of the complaints included Rivers asking Tebo what she could become a poll worker for the elections. Tebo in February 2017 referred Rivers to Laura Hutto, the supervisor of elections, and Rivers completed the 30-minute training class. Because of Joe Griffin's intent to contest the upcoming elections, Tebo decided none of the staff would work as poll workers. But Rivers felt it was unfair to her. Then because Greene did not respond to Rivers' call immediately but connected with Officer Brownfield, Rivers complained about Greene not communicating with her for years and pre-dating Tebo's employment.

Several have testified to having difficulty connecting to Greene due to his busy schedule and lack of cell phone coverage in the fire station and water plants. Greene also denied ever ignoring or mistreating Rivers. He also has never witnessed Rivers being mistreated by any town employee or council member. He denied ever knowingly or intentionally failing to respond to Rivers' emails, phone calls and/or text messages. In March 2017, Greene claimed that Rivers *"would not speak or acknowledge him"* and that all she would do is communicate with him is "shake her head yes or no" This was the only time Rivers had ever acted this way towards Greene.

During Miller's tenure as mayor, she hired Rivers as the Administrative Assistant. The two had an excellent relationship due to Rivers being able to perform any tasks which the mayor gave to her. Tebo was unhappy about the relationship and as a background leading up to Rivers' complaint, **Tebo theorized that Rivers created it as a diversion to cover up her incompetency.** In March 2017, the town was undergoing two separate audits, a financial audit and FDLE audit. These two audits revealed several areas of non-compliance.

Tebo stated with respect to Rivers, the financial audit revealed that the Town has been overbilling its sewer customers for 17 months and underbilling-billing its commercial garbage customers for a lesser period. Tebo contended that Rivers' claim is false relative to not being provided training in changing the garbage rates on the computer. Accordingly, Tebo claimed that she was going to discipline Rivers for not making the sewer and garbage rate changes, but Rivers filed the instant complaint deflecting her deficiencies before Tebo could do so.

What may be mentioned also is that the CPA blamed Rivers, by name, for all the errors in a **public council meeting.**

One does not single out one individual who technically the manager is responsible for. In fairness, Tebo did state she bared a portion of the responsibility.

When Tebo became Town Manager, Rivers asked her if she could go to the clerk training class. According to Rivers, Tebo initially stated that she would **"look into it"**, but then later told Rivers that she did not *"see the need for it"*. Rivers stopped asking Tebo after that.

Tebo recalled Rivers and Tomlinson having a similar argument in April 2016 over garbage rates. Yet Tebo also claimed that she could have disciplined Tomlinson for not checking behind Rivers to ensure that the rates had changed. She also stated as the Town Manager she bears the responsibility for these rates not being changed.

Tomlinson admitted that on July 27, 2016, she told Rivers *"5 at is your damn job"* out of frustration. She explained that the statement was made only after Rivers had said that crediting customer utility payment was **"not my job."** Yet. Others have heard Tomlinson yell **"do your damn job"** to Rivers.

Tomlinson was addicted to her cigarette breaks so to remain in the office, she smoked e-cigarettes. The vapor gave Rivers' headaches, so Rivers complained to Tebo. Then at some point it happened again, and Rivers had to leave the office because she was becoming ill. Tebo explained to Tomlinson that smoking e-cigarettes in the office could no longer happen. Tomlinson then took several cigarette-breaks outdoors, during the day when she was not on the phone with her to-be ex-husband.

In addition to the audits, Rivers had taken off two days in March and as a result, no late fees were inputted on certain customer accounts. No one had credited the accounts for those customers who paid their utility payments in cash for those days. Tebo, Tomlinson and Greene then began checking customer accounts for discrepancies. Tebo believed this was upsetting

Rivers and recalls Rivers making comments about **"people checking behind me."** Then on March 23, when Tebo requested that Rivers charge the late fees on the accounts, Rivers attempted to blame Tomlinson and stated loudly, **"You didn't put the late fees on?"**

In River's complaint she alleged concern for her failure to receive training on how to make garbage rate changes. She alleged that after she was hired, Greene only trained her on how to enter bills, take payments and put new customers into the system. She claimed she was never shown how to add or change garbage rates.

Although Rivers was not the Town Clerk, she wished to be a deputy clerk, which would allow her to apply for the Town Clerk position when the Clerk retired. When Bill Lawrence was the Town Manager, Rivers applied to attend a training class, which he allowed. When Tomlinson discovered that Rivers was going to clerk training, she *"threw a ..t"* and *"went to screaming and yelling at Lawrence,"* asking why Rivers was attending and telling him that she should be the one going to training since she was performing some of the Clerk's duties. Lawrence still allowed Rivers to attend. After Tomlinson did not appear interested in attending the next two classes, Rivers again asked Lawrence if she could attend the October class. When Tomlinson discovered that Lawrence had once again approved Rivers to attend the class *"she . ew o' the handle" and made him change his mind"*

Tebo mentioned that she had a good relationship with Rivers initially but there was tension in the office that resulted in a division between Rodriquenz and Rivers on one side and Tomlinson and Green on the other side. After Tebo started she noticed that Rodriquenz and Rivers had stopped going to lunch together. She believes that former mayor and council member Helen Miller had something to do with it.

Rivers is African-American so there always would be fear of repercussions from the ALCU. Mayor Bullard, in his protection of Ms. Tebo, told her to have Fred Koberlein secure Robert Edward Larkin, III, Esquire, to manage the Rivers Case. Attorney Larkin had recently assisted Attorney. Koberlein in a Lake City Employment Case where the judgment was in favor of the city.

When Ms. Tebo contacted Town Attorney Frederick L. Koberlein, Jr., to secure Robert Edward Larkin in Rivers' case, both attorneys were assured by Tebo and Mayor Bullard that the White Springs Town Council **approved** their hiring in a formal meeting to make an investigation in this case. Yet the entire council, other than the three, did not have any knowledge of what was happening. It was not voted on in a public meeting.

Rivers intended for the Town Attorney to assist her in her complaint of discrimination and as a whistle blower into the actions of Town hall. Rivers stated she had no intention of securing an attorney or a lawsuit at the time but only to settle her claim of discrimination against Town Manager Tebo, in-house.

After much cost and no mediation, it was deemed there was no discrimination against Rivers and that Tebo was not discriminatory. There were comments made that Rivers could not have written her professional complaint by herself, inferring that perhaps Mayor Miller had assisted her.

Prior to Rivers' March 27, 2017, complaint, the **"power of three"** led by Mayor Bullard dismissed all complaints made by citizens, even if the violated laws were included in the complaint forms. This included a petition signed by citizens who are African-Americans, relating to a May Day Celebration. Mayor Bullard just ignored the petition even though councilor McKenzie said the Town should respond.

Tebo in her infinite wisdom decided not to allow the May Day celebration to be at the Carver School area without fencing, police, and canines. This made those attending feel as though they were prisoners. However, it did stop out-of-town activists from causing problems.

Town Attorney Koberlein also addressed that "Robert's Rules of Order" per the Town Charter must be abided by the Council. Mayor Bullard's response was *"We are a small town and cannot be expected to follow those rules."* When questioned, Bullard stated *"You want us to admit we did not follow the law?"*

The Rivers' case was not made public nor to councilors Miller and McKenzie until the money for Attorney Larkin was addressed in the council meeting. Our Town Attorney Frederick Koberlein secured a court reporter and chose the building where statements were taken under oath. His total charge including legal services was $13,965.22 with Attorney Larkin charging $12,000 for his legal services, for a total of '$25,965.22, which the entire council did not vote on, nor was it decided upon at a public meeting.

Mayor Bullard made no attempt to mediate the situation between Tebo and Rivers, but he felt that he could hire an outside attorney through our own Town Attorney without securing full council approval. When he was asked why approval was not sought, **Mayor Bullard just stated he did not do it, our Town Attorney did**. In other words, Mayor Bullard placed all the blame and liability on our Town Attorney even though Mayor Bullard instructed Tebo to hire Larkin. Due to a lack of money in the Town coffers, the legal expenses had to be deferred to our 2018 budget.

In the meantime, Frederick L. Koberlein and Robert Edward Larkin, III, by omission, **felt there had been council approval for their legal services**. In fact, Attorney Larkin thanked the White Springs Council for hiring him in the summary provided to White Springs. The Town's clerk refused to send us the paperwork in Rivers' case, but Attorney Larkin did by electronic mail.

Yet Rivers would have done better if she had gone to the EEOC or private attorney with a retaliation charge. The financial director, Tomlinson, with her GED would not assist Rivers and would tell her **"Do your job"** and **the Manager Tebo was heard by others screaming at Rivers, who ended up shaking and in tears**. Tomlinson should have been disciplined by the Town Manager and told she needed to be more civil to her work associates and to customers.

The Town spent $25,950 plus on the Rivers Case.

Tebo's Contract was not renewed accidentally

The Town Attorney, at a monthly council meeting, stated that Tebo's contract was not renewed from September of 2016. Counselors Miller and McKenzie brought up the findings that Ms. Tebo was using Percocet, an opioid drug. As such, there was concern about renewing her contract without an investigation regarding her drug use and whether a physician prescribed it or whether it was bought off the street. Mayor Miller questioned her taking medication, after I provided Miller with all my research papers. This was due to the apparent mood swings Tebo seemed to have, rendering her to remain in a closed-door office for most days, and sending emails as the only form of communication with the Town Staff

Mayor Bullard interrupted Miller consistently, and appeared to be screaming at her, telling Miller that she could not discuss Tebo's medical condition. **He stated it was private; however, Town Attorney Koberlein concurred with Miller that the statements made regarding her use of Percocet was a matter of public record.**

Mayor Bullard then decided to quash this discussion and asked Attorney Koberlein whether he could prepare an extension to Stacy Tebo's contract. **Attorney Koberlein said he could not do that and until the matter was decided with a new contract, Tebo was an "at will" employee and he explained the term of "at-will employee" at the public** meeting.

Not listening to Attorney Koberlein, Mayor Bullard then said, we will extend the contract for ninety (90) days and the remaining power of three made the motion and seconded it for a verbal three-month extension. **Attorney Koberlein again restated that since an extension could not be made to the existing contract verbally or in writing, there could be no 90-day extension**…. for which the **"Power of Three"** ignored him.

Mayor Bullard stated a discussion of Tebo's contract would take place at a special meeting, soon. He continually called the ninety days, an extension even though others corrected him that Tebo was now an "at will" employee.

An at-will employee can be fired at any time, for any reason (except for a few illegal reasons), If the employer decides to let you go, that's the end of your job--and you have very limited legal rights to fight your termination.

Discussion of Tebo's contract pulled from agenda (Jasper News article) By Alexis Spoehr Oct 20, 2017

"WHITE SPRINGS — Town Manager Tebo's contract was not discussed at the White Springs Town Council's Oct. 10 meeting. Although it was on the agenda, Vice Mayor Brown made a motion to delete the discussion of the Town Manager's Contract under old business, which was seconded by Council Member Jefferson. The item was asked to be placed on the agenda by Council Member Dr. Miller.

During discussion of removing the item, Council Member McKenzie asked: "Isn't this an opportunity to talk about it, so we can see if we want to renew it when the time comes?" Brown said since they gave her three months they had to wait until the three months are over to discuss the issues with the contract. Miller and McKenzie both disagreed." (The three-month extension referred to was unlawful.)

"Plus, if we go back to how that motion was made to stop the discussion, I believe that was made improperly," Miller said. "I had the floor, and I was making relevant comments, the town manager interrupted me over and over again, which she did not have the right to do. The mayor did not exercise his duty to curtail the interruption.

"Finally, I think you made an improper motion, which the mayor allowed for a vote." "Miller brought up that the motion would need a two-thirds majority vote, but only received 60 percent majority vote based on Robert's Rules of Order. McKenzie reiterated that the council reconsider voting against the motion because the contract needs to be discussed before the three months are over. The motion passed in a 3-2 vote deleting the discussion of the contract from the agenda. "

END OF ARTICLE

Miller the rogue council member case

Thereafter, Mayor Bullard and the Town Manager, who admitted she disliked Miller under oath, decided to rid themselves of Miller by forfeiting her seat. **It was mentioned by citizens who went into Town Hall that Mayor Bullard, Tebo and Finance Director/City Clerk Tomlinson went through various records for a period of two weeks to see what they could find against Miller.**

In a subsequent meeting, Mayor Bullard had Tebo read various accusations made against Miller. These Accusations initially involved old items for which Miller had council approval when she was Mayor. **Mayor Bullard would not allow Miller a chance to respond, unlike what Jasper News printed. Miller had not received a copy of the complaints which Tebo verbally read.**

The Jasper News - Town manager calls Miller a 'rogue council member'

By Jessie R. Box May 19, 2017, Updated May 22, 2017

WHITE SPRINGS — White Springs town manager Tebo called council member Miller a "rogue council member" at the May 9 meeting. During the manager's comments, Tebo read a prepared statement regarding Miller. Tebo said Miller inappropriately used town funds when orchestrating a "Beautiful Dreamer's Awards Banquet" last February. According to Tebo, Miller purchased food, drinks, supplies, decoration, plaques and more without consulting her. Tebo added she did not know about the purchases until she received the credit card bills and invoices the following month.

Tebo said Miller has violated Section 3.02 (b) of the town charter by directing the town staff. According to the charter, the directing of staff is a power vested in the town manager. Examples Tebo provided included Millerr directing public work staff to set up tables and chairs in the Tourism Center to get ready for a dinner and banquet and instructing Police Chief Tracy to be available by phone for a meeting with the Department of Juvenile Justice regarding the Invest in Children Program the town was applying for.

Tebo said Miller also directed her to pay the HOPE Program employees after they had not been paid by the Hamilton County School Board. The HOPE Program is a summer youth program run by Miller and the school board was acting as the fiscal agent at the time. Tebo said she recently learned Miller was working with the Stephen Foster Folk Culture Center State Park to hold the summer HOPE program there this year. "There has been no communication regarding the HOPE Program between her and myself, nor the council," Tebo said.

"Council member Miller is a rogue council member operating on her own, making decisions on behalf of the town, and speaking on behalf of the town. I am bringing this to the full council's attention in this forum and ask you to address the problem.

It was not addressed at the May 9 meeting as the issue and was tabled until the June meeting. "I want to know why this wasn't presented as an agenda item so that we could do a little bit of background research into it," Council member McKenzie said. "It sounds almost prosecutorial, and we had no advance notice of it." Miller declined to comment.

END OF ARTICLE

Miller hired Mark Herron of Tallahassee FL who was an attorney for various congressional people, to represent her at her upcoming hearing. She needed to save her seat on the council. Because of this, **Mayor Bullard appraised the council that the Town had to pay for an attorney to defend Stacy Tebo. Not only did Counselor McKenzie object but Town Attorney Koberlein objected, citing that such a thing has never been done and cannot be done.** (i.e., paying for a staff attorney to sue a councilor). It is outside of the Town's insurance due to it being a willful and a malicious act and one employee cannot sue another of the town council and expected to be granted defense under municipal insurance A municipality is covered by its insurance when a third party sues the municipality.

Mayor Bullard, however, was determined and started Tebo's defense budget at $7,500. He also said that Tebo could choose her own attorney from those she would be contacting. The remaining power of three, Brown and Jefferson, made and seconded the motion respectively despite our Town Attorney's objections.

At the next meeting, Tebo advised that she had chosen an acquaintance of hers, Attorney Darren Elkind, to assist her. Mr. Elkind had "worked" with her in Sanford and although he charged far more than our Town Attorney, Koberlein (who could and would not represent her), Mr. Elkind had litigation experience. The Town attorney provides legal services for the Town and its Councilors in their usual business to the town. **Thereafter, the council agreed to 30 days of advertising for a new town attorney to represent them since the Koberlein Law Offices provided the Town with a 30-day notice of intent to terminate his agreement with the town on October 4th.**

McKenzie encouraged the council to do an exit interview with Koberlein's office. Mayor Bullard refused and said this happened because Koberlein is now the attorney for Live Oak whose meetings are on the same date. **McKenzie, however, called Frederick Koberlein to find that the termination was due to the way in which White Springs manages its business.**

Miller's hearing was held October 25, 2017, in the White Springs Council room.

Darren Jay Elkind represented Tebo and the staff. Attorney Mark Herron represented Miller. Town Attorney Koberlein officiated the hearing.

The councilors were to serve as judge and jury based upon the information received. However, the decision of the **"Power**

of Three" already had been made in the darkness, to charge Miller with malfeasance in all four complaints, even though she broke no laws. Mayor Bullard had been collaborating with staff to make certain Miller would be removed from her seat on the Council.

My recollection and notes of this since I attended the hearing and reported it on the blog, are as follows. Miller's attorney, Mark Herron, initially requested a continuance because the charges were different than those initially cited in the newspaper against Miller. Attorney Herron said he did not have sufficient time in which to secure the appropriate witnesses because the current charges were not received until October 19, 2017. Herron provided this request in writing as well as vocally at the hearing. He advised that he had only two hours to go over the material with Miller. Attorney Elkind, Tebo's attorney, said he was against the continuance because all emails and paperwork were forwarded to Attorney Herron well prior to the recent charges being made. He further stated that Miller did not have the right to ask for a continuance or see the complaints against her.

Mayor Bullard verbally went into rapid antics, saying that a continuance would not be acceptable in any way, while condemning Miller. Council member Jefferson said *that "we have waited for months and there should have been enough time to prepare"*.

Not all the emails Attorney Herron requested had been provided to him by the Town. There was an omitted email where Tebo appointed Miller as the White Springs H.O.P.E. administrator. That email would offset the complaint. Miller took liberty which she did not. Fortunately, Miller retrieved copies establishing Tebo's appointment of her. As the HOPE administrator through the Hamilton County School Board, Miller was accepted to manage the program by the Town Manager and did nothing wrong. The conditions were set up by the benefactor for the benefit of White Spring youths. If the money sent by the donor was necessary to make a payment to the program immediately, any one of the staff could have called the County. The money was available, but this was the first year the benefactor did not wish to allow White Springs to manage the funds. Or, one of the Staff could have contacted Miller to contact the county. Instead, Ms. Tomlinson refused to issue a check and blamed Miller for the money not being in the White Springs Account. Yet by Contract, the Town had the obligation of paying the employee whether there was money. As such Hamilton County did release the funds and the employee of the program received payment within two days.

Nevertheless, Mayor Bullard blamed Miller for the lack of funds. Yet the Town Manager was to provide the council monthly financial reports by Charter but has not done so in her tenure. And furthermore, the hearing established that none in the Town, including Bullard, who signs the town's contracts, has ever read the details and stipulations of said contracts. Of course, when Tomlinson was initially told that Hamilton County was to administer payroll, before anyone read the contract, she laughed and said she was happy that she did not have to do the payroll because it was less work for her.

When Police Chief Tracy was questioned whether she would assist any council member who asked for her assistance, she said of course, she would assist anyone. However, either she had a memory lapse or did not intend to be truthful initially, because she stated only Miller had requested anything from her. That led to McKenzie stipulating he had requested something from her relating to the Bike Club and then Brown admitted something about hot dogs. **McKenzie stated, that if a council person may not ask for assistance from the Staff or from the Town Manager, then everyone should be ousted from the Council.**.

When Attorney Herron elected to bring forth information which had similarity to this case from Tebo's lawsuit in DeBary, Mayor Bullard, who is also a lawyer responded contrary to the law, objecting to this line of questioning. As if Bullard considers himself the most knowledgeable litigator and had the right to comment on Mark Herron's defense, Mayor Bullard said that was **unnecessary but a** *"good legal ploy"* to bring Tebo's former employer to the forefront. Yet Attorney Herron continued to show similarities of what happened in DeBary is now happening in White Springs to a council member and former Mayor Miller Of course, Mark Herron ignored the comment which was made by Bullard.

Mark Herron, Miller's attorney included definitions as shown below relating to Fla 119, Supreme Court of Florida STATE ex rel. v. COLEMAN May 26, 1934, relating to Public *Employment* Conduct or Misconduct in General "Malfeasance" *as* did Town Attorney Koberlein. Nevertheless, **Mayor Bullard and the remaining power of three voted that Miller violated the Charter and charged her with four counts of Malfeasance, without allegedly understanding the meaning of Malfeasance was or ignoring its definition under the law.**

Stacy Tebo even contacted the court reporter **prior to the hearing** and told her a court reporter **was NOT necessary to take statements** at the hearing. When the court reporter confirmed that with Attorney Koberlein, he stepped in and set the record straight advising a court reporter was necessary to take statements.

The cost for Attorney Elkind's services to and from the hearing and defending Tebo and staff at the hearing was $8738.50. Again, by law, the town of White Springs and its citizens had no right to pay for Tebo's attorney. Miller was paying for her own attorney.

129

Throughout the years, Dr. Miller has received money from the following benefactor so that she could assist White Springs Children. Although she may have spent the money foolishly at times, in my opinion, by paying high salaries to friends, she should still receive credit for securing the money from her benefactor and thanked by the parents of the children who benefited.

"H.B. Calder, Ph.D.

26 June 2017

Letters to the Editor

The Jasper News P.O. Box 370 Live Oak, FL 32064

Dear Editor,

I am writing concerning an article entitled "White Springs council votes to declare Miller's seat forfeited" which appears in your 22 June edition and subsequently appeared on your website. Since the actions discussed predominately concern funds which I provided, I believe it appropriate to provide my insights.

I have had the privilege of knowing and working with Dr. Miller for nearly twenty-five years. While in Ann Arbor, Michigan she maintained full-time employment; volunteered in the City to plan, fund and implement a wide range of infrastructure projects oriented towards improving public safety, and served as president of the Ann Arbor Huron High School Athletic Booster Club, working throughout the entire public school system to restructure and expand girls and boys athletic programs, implement fund raising programs contributing in excess of $500,000 annually to pay for sports activities, infrastructure shortfalls, awards events and more and to implement a school system-wide alcohol and drug *diversion program (which subsequently was deployed State-wide, including the University of Michigan).*

When Dr. Miller retired to Florida, she recognized the needs of White Springs' youth and decided to bring her experience and expertise to the challenge. Working with church groups and community leaders, one of her first activities was to put in place a summer program. Though I personally have no ties to White Springs, I gladly offered to help fund these efforts through my Charitable Giving Fund because I felt that the programs would impact the lives of young people and because I knew that Dr. Miller would be successful. Between 2010 and 2015, I contributed $134,500 directly to the city of White Springs for the purpose of supporting Project HOPE and the summer activities for the youth of White Springs. In 2016, I contributed an additional $15,000 to the Hamilton County School District for the exclusive benefit of White Springs youth/Project Hope. In this regard I provided funds to be spent at the exclusive direction of Dr. Miller for any general expenditure she deemed appropriate to facilitate her summer, or other programs; a provision agreed to by the White Springs Town Council in 2010. I visited White Springs several times and observed first-hand the ongoing activities, I was impressed with the activities and continued my funding on an annual basis.

I have known Dr. Miller to provide nothing less than the highest quality work at the highest level of integrity. The expenditure made with funds provided by my contributions were proper and well within the grant guidelines. I am proud of the results that Dr. Miller's tireless efforts have achieved for the White Spring's community and for its youths.

Sincerely H.B. Calder, Ph.D."

"SLIPPERY SLOPE – SUWANNEE DEMOCRAT EDITORIAL"

Editorial: Council starts down slippery slope

As both Mark Herron and Darren Elkind, the two opposing lawyers in the Oct. 25 public hearing regarding Miller Miller's seat on the White Springs Town Council, agreed: the council took upon itself a solemn responsibility with the hearing.

It was the council that charged Miller with malfeasance, misfeasance or non-feasance while in office at its June meeting when it moved to declare her seat forfeited. It was that same council that then heard the evidence at last week's public hearing and issued the verdict on whether Miller would indeed have to give up her seat. But in doing so, the council started down a slippery slope.

One of the four charges heard at the quasi-judicial hearing against Miller involved her asking if staff could move chairs from one building to another to host a dinner for the Suwannee River League of Cities, which Miller serves as the organization's president. Herron, Miller's lawyer, called the charge "probably one of the most trivial charges in terms of trying to deprive the people of their representative on this board that is imaginable. We agree that it's hard to imagine how making a request about moving tables and chairs can lead to someone losing their elected office. Watergate, this is not. In fact, Elkind even admitted that the charge seemed petty, although he quickly touted the importance of not interfering with employees' jobs and responsibilities. Petty and trivial as it may be, the council — by virtue of a 3-1 vote from Mayor Bullard, Vice-Mayor Tonja Brown and Willie Jefferson with only McKenzie voting against — decided it still constituted a willful violation of the town's charter. They also voted Miller in violation on the other three allegations of questionable employee pay requests and overstepping through unilateral direction to city staff.

And in doing so, the council opened itself up to the potential for more seat forfeiture hearings in the future. McKenzie earlier in the hearing admitted to having made requests of Police Chief Tracy. "I've asked Chief Tracy to do things, I've asked her if she would mind taking care of the bicycles for the Suwannee Bike (Association) that were donated to the kids for the Christmas program," McKenzie said, later adding that he also contacted the supervisor of utilities about a water main break that flooded his yard, which could be interpreted as a no-no: "According to the way we're doing business here tonight, I could be charged with a violation of the charter. And I will openly stand up and say, 'Yes, I did that.

That admission seemed to have jogged Rodriquez's memory, who had just said that Miller was the lone council member who asked for her help. "Everybody asks me to do things," she said. "He's absolutely right in that he's come to me about the bicycles, and I believe Miss Tonja has come to me about hot dogs. "It's whatever the community needs." Except, requesting help to fulfill the community's needs apparently is a willful violation of an express prohibition of the charter. At least, that is what the council declared last week"

END OF ARTICLE

<u>Doner-Advised Funds and B. Faithful:</u>

All contributions to a donor-advised fund are irrevocable and cannot be withdrawn by the donor himself/herself.

Following the donation, assets contributed to a DAF are solely owned by the sponsoring organization. Donors retain advisory privileges over the assets in the DAF account and can recommend an investment strategy as well as where the funds can be sent, for grantmaking purposes. The sponsoring organization has a legal responsibility to ensure that DAF assets are used for charitable purposes only and will work to honor the donor's intent as closely as possible.

Since Miller no longer trusted White Springs to assist with the H.O.P.E. Program, Rivers and Nicole Williams introduced Bea Faithful Coker, their cousin from Lake City, who needed funding for a children's summer program. Miller elected to contact Calder for funding and the restriction to Coker was that White Springs children would be able to enjoy the program with those children of Lake City. Miller was honest about the DAF and advised that she could not guarantee if the DAF would provide $13,000 to B. Faithful and she provided the necessary agreement to Coker, establishing the fund would be the sole decision of the sponsoring organization. The sponsoring organization would have researched Coker's organization since it was a new entity, to ensure they were a charitable organization. This in turn delayed the payment.

As time went on, it could not be determined whether White Springs children were welcomed into the summer program, and the money B. Faithful sought included rents and utilities for the building which some stated had not been paid previously and should have not been part of the donation given. Only $10,000 was provided by the DAF and B. Faithful elected to threaten White Springs with a lawsuit for $3,000. And when Vice Mayor McKenzie offered $3,000 if the suit was dropped, B. Faithful considered the matter bribery and Rhett Bullard would not listen to the fact that it was a DAF, out of the control of Calder or Miller. B. Faithful, nevertheless, kept calling Calder to the point that he allegedly paid the $3,000 through his own checking account to silence her and to add to the matter, The White Springs Council voted to pay $3,000 to B. Faithful. Bullard and the council members blamed Helen Miller for the payment the Town made. Calder refused to send any more funding to White Springs, and Miller, Rivers and Williams had to start a "Go Fund me page for the following year.

Although the information in the Jasper newspaper regarding this matter no longer existed and may have been removed by Coker, there was another article as follows, relating to bribery, but this time it was not a charge against Vice Mayor McKenzie but Mayor Rhett Bullard:

White Springs council members accused of threats, bribery.

By Alexis Spoehr Feb 22, 2018

WHITE SPRINGS — Members of the White Springs Town Council have been accused of threats and bribery, according to at least one town resident. At the council's Feb. 13 meeting, Nicole Williams addressed the council about intimidation from three of the council members and accusations made against her from those members. "Instead, I want to speak about the intimidation about those who wanted to sign the petition but felt that they would be harassed by the members of the council," Williams said about a recall petition circulating through town in regard to Mayor Rhett Bullard, Vice Mayor Tonja Brown and councilman Willie Jefferson.

Williams stated that she did not believe the threat and bribery at first until she had a conversation with Bullard over the phone. She said he tried to bribe and threaten her. She said if the members of the council try to contact those who signed the petition they would file a lawsuit. Bullard stated that he was trying to figure out a way to discuss the complaints with her that were being made. He did say the conversation got heated at points but did not try to bribe her or intimidate her. "I can say for a fact that I had nothing to do with any kind of bribery or intimidation of citizens," Bullard said in phone call with the News.

Both Karin and Joe Griffin spoke about how there is injustice in White Springs and how it should be fixed. Joe Griffin even brought a shovel for three of the members "to help with their digging a hole for themselves that they are already in."

The former ASA gets hired as the Town Attorney

After advertising for over thirty days for a new attorney to replace Frederick Koberlein, Jr. who had resigned October 4th, 2017. No one attorney or firm applied by the deadline. Mayor Bullard then contacted former 18-year Assistant State's Attorney (ASA) Karen Hatton, who was let go or retired as an ASA, and she started a private law practice in Mayo, to apply. The Town received her information one day after the deadline.

Our Town Attorney Koberlein provided rules relating to Roberts Rules of Order as well as explaining that with complaints, the council members are judge and jury in a quasi-judicial hearing. Attorney Koberlein outlined the procedures for handling Citizens Complaints in his memo dated August 4, 2016. Mayor Bullard at the meeting held January 10, 2017, stated that the Town could choose which portions of Robert's rules of Order the town would follow and which it would neglect to follow at the Council's choosing. This was despite a ruling from the State Attorney General which *said, "If the agency has adopted Robert Rules of Order, then that method of conducting meetings and business must be observed"*. The Town Charter requires that *"Robert's Rules of Order shall govern the procedure of meetings"*. In his memo, Attorney Koberlein gave examples of where the Town would incur liability should a substantive right of an individual or entity be affected. Griffin and I provided the Town Council with a Robert's Rules of Order manual and four cheat sheets to follow.

Since Karen Hatton's costs were much higher than former Town Attorney Koberlein's, Bullard **told Stacy Tebo to re-negotiate Karen Hatton's fees**. It is the council's duty to negotiate but Bullard had Tebo do everything he apparently was responsible for. This happened during the council meeting. When an objection was made, Bullard said **"But that's her job."** Joe Griffin said he had better not give it to her (Stacy) and Councilor McKenzie said in accordance with the Charter and Sunshine laws**, it was the Council's duty to interview Ms. Hatton.** Thereafter, a special meeting was set to interview councilor prospects to fill Miller's seat and for the council to interview and negotiate fees with Ms. Karen Hatton, who became our attorney as of December 27, 2017.

Dr. Miller's Attorney in the interim filed on November 21, 2017, **A "Petition for Writ of Certiorari" in the Circuit Court of the Third Judicial Circuit** in and for Hamilton County. Then on January 31, 2018**, Circuit Judge Andrew J. Decker III is**sued an order directing respondent (The Town) to file a response to petition for Writ for Certiorari stipulating a review of the Petition **appeared to demonstrate a preliminary basis for relief.**

Since Darren Elkind previously defended the Staff of White Springs at the hearing. Mr. Elkind only provided the Town of White Springs with one contract covering only said staff. However, the writ involved actual "Town of White Springs". We asked for a specific contract to be drafted, showing Mr. Elkind's fees. We asked for the new contract from both the Town Staff and from Mr. Elkind himself. Yet we knew that there was no prior council approval for Mr. Elkind to defend the Town in this action since there was never a vote at a regular or special meeting.

We were advised Elkind did not need to provide *a separate contract. Obviously, the Town Manager was not concerned since Bullard has covered her infractions.*

On December 21, 2017, Darren J. Elkind, Esquire, stipulated the response if ordered, would not be an "answer" to a complaint but rather would be an appellate answer brief.

The judge directed the Town to file a response to the Petition for Writ of Certiorari dated January 31, 2018. Miller petitioned the Court for a writ of certiorari to review the order of the Town, concluding she had forfeited her office as a member of the Town Council because she *"willfully violated an express provision of the Town Charter"* or that she committed acts constituting *"malfeasance and non-feasance in office"* **The Writ stated the findings and judgment of the Town Council are not supported by competent substantial evidence; and the action of the Town Council to Forfeit Miller's Seat departs from the essential requirement of Law; The town Failed to provide Adequate due process.**

It then went to the appellate court and Griffin, and I attended. Of the three appellate Judges only one Judge was in favor of not supporting the Town's response to the Writ for Miller. The court stated the record of the case contained substantial, competent evidence to support the decision of the Town to remove Miller from her position as Council Member. Her case against the Town was "dismissed with prejudice." Yet even though she no longer had a seat on the council, she was able to run in the next election. The citizens of the Town voted for Miller and elected her to be a member of Town council with a lead of nine votes only.

Although Darren Elkind had a contract for the hearing to defend Stacy Tebo and staff, he was not the attorney of record to represent the "Town of White Springs" under which the Writ for Certiorari had been made.

A complaint was made to the Florida Bar. after telling Mr. Elkind that the White Springs Council must approve his defense of the Town of White Springs by contract. **Elkind said he did not need to contract with the Council, because Mayor Bullard allowed Stacy Tebo to make the decision to hire him, without approval or a contractual basis.** In the meantime, we, the citizens are expected to pay higher fees for Mr. Elkind who lives two hours away from White Springs rather than having our Town Attorney Karen Hatton take over the case since she is the attorney who represents the Town of White Springs…and at a lesser cost.

The response received from the Florida Bar.

Joshua E. Doyle Executive Director
www.FLORIDABAR.org January 19, 2018

Re: Darren Jay Elkind; RFA No. 18-8079

Dear Mr. Griffin:

I have received and reviewed your January 4, 2018, inquiry regarding Mr. Darren Elkind, Esq. The issues raised in your inquiry appear to be issues that can be raised in the civil court system, perhaps as part of the pending matter referenced in your inquiry. The Supreme Court of Florida has ruled that the disciplinary process and proceedings are not to be used as a substitute for civil proceedings and remedies. See The Florida Bar v. Della-Donna, 583 So.2d 307 (Fla. 1989). As such, The Florida Bar is not the correct forum in which to have your allegations adjudicated, and resolution of those issues must be left to the appropriate tribunal. In the event the proper tribunal makes a finding or enters an order which supports your allegations against Mr. Elkind, you may resubmit your complaint along with a copy of such findings or order. At that point in time, the

Bar would not be in a position to further address the issue.

For the foregoing reason(s), our file remains closed. This decision does not preclude you from seeking the advice of counsel or from pursuing any legal or equitable remedies to which you may be entitled. Pursuant to the Bar's records retention schedule, the computer record and file will be disposed of one year from the date of closing (the date of closing is January 18, 2018).

Sincerely, Jack Franklin Wise, IIL Bar Counsel Attorney Consumer Assistance Program ACAP Hotline 866-352-0707

cc: Mr. Darren Jay Elkind (w/ enclosure)

Joe Griffin also requested a motion to join the action of the Miller case as a Friend of the court. He stated that the Town of white Springs has violated Florida State Statute 286.011 in hiring an attorney, to represent the Town in this present defense. This was denied by the court.

The Town spent $14,565.67 on the Council Seat Forfeiture and $25,950 plus on the Rivers Case for a total of $40,515.67 plus Opinion

Bullard had attempted prior and after he was elected to remove Miller PhD from the White Springs Council by reason, she would question items such as why we should buy Greene a new truck so that he can go to and from work to Gainesville to be with his fiancé" We only needed a pre-used vehicle for utility work. Dr. Miller further felt the complaints should be decided upon, in accordance with our Charter. Furthermore, the White Springs office should remain a drug free zone.

The City of DeBary fired Stacy Tebo as the City Clerk. She first filed an EEOC complaint against that city, then sued the City of Debary as well as her former manager Dan Parrott as soon as she accepted a position with White Springs. The suit related to sexist remarks and pay discrimination of women, even though she herself has not been the recipient of these remarks nor inadequate raises.

It was Ms. Tebo's Intent to have her previous job back at DeBary and a settlement; however, it did not appear favorable for her. But because of the time she has required for meeting with attorneys, depositions and the like as well as going to her Orange City permanent home in Volusia County on Weekends, Ms. Tebo had taken a substantial amount of personal time off; such time was not acceptable in accordance with our personnel manual and her contractual Ms. Tebo took Friday's off and did not return much before noon on Mondays When questioned, Bullard stated on her behalf that **she had doctors' appointments every Friday.**

Since we had common problems, the City of DeBary and we shared public records information. And since both Ms. Tebo's attorney and DeBary's attorney were advised of Ms. Tebo's Percocet use, this is what Ms. Tebo relayed under oath in her deposition in DeBary of August 2017:

> *The attorney asked whether Stacy sought any psychiatric, psychological counseling related to the incident in this case, the incidents in this case? To which Stacy replied "No." When she was asked whether she was taking any medication, she said "Yes". And the Attorney said, "Are you taking any medication that might have affected your ability to recall testimony you've given here today, and she said "No".*

Yet instead of saying she is taking Percocet; she said she had been taking Xanax at the time her employment was terminated in DeBary. She stated now she asked the doctor for Bupropion, the generic name for Wellbutrin. She has been going to three to four doctors who may see her on Saturdays. Two are general practitioners and one is a gynecologist.

Fear is the contributing factor to how the White Springs office treats others. Tebo may not be scrutinized, which employees have stated under oath, and she spends most of her time behind a closed office door, authoring emails and working on her personal cases.

Rivers' employment with White Springs ended on May 12,2017. Rivers, even though she had paid a portion of the late fees, had not turned her water off and paid the fees, which ordinance 15-01 requires.

Tebo provided Rivers with a memo dated May 12, 2017, in which she stated she began looking through accounts and checking adjustments. While doing so she noticed Rivers had not charged her account the $30 reconnect fee on three occasions, nor had her water turned off in November, January, and February. In November, the cut-off day was November 7th with a past due amount of $137.70. On November 8th, Rivers paid $65. In January, the cut-off day was January 12th for a past due amount of $78.26 and $80 was paid on January 18th. In February, the cut-off day was February 6th with a past due amount of $76.42 and Rivers paid $70 on February 8th. Tebo stated Theft is a serious violation and terminated Rivers from the town of White Springs. Rivers was required to turn over all Town property in her possession and the clicker remote for the gate and keys to the safe and drop-box for First Federal town Hall as well as for the Community Center.

Not realizing Robert Larken was not her friend or attorney but Stacy's, Rivers sent the following email to Larkin.

"I was just terminated by Stacy Tebo for stealing according to her. She is claiming I made payments to my own water accounts after the cut-off date and did not charge myself the proper reconnect fees. This is

ABSOLUTELY not true. I have reason to believe that she went into the system and changed the payment dates to support her allegations. I will be getting my bank statement for the dates I made my payments with a credit card as proof. That is the reason I believe she had me limited to certain things on the billing system. I will be hiring an attorney. Thanks for all of your help and I would like to receive a copy of your findings from the current investigation when it is complete. Thanks. Anita Rivers May 12, 2017, at 1:51:14 PM CDI"

Not only did Stacy terminate River's employment with the Town, but she also decided to send evidence and **a letter to State Attorney Jeff Sigmeister,** advising him of the theft.

"The town of White Springs requests the prosecution of its former employee, Anita Rivers, for theft. Ms. Rivers was previously employed by the town as its administrative assistant and billing clerk. She was terminated on May 12, 20017, when I discovered that she had not charged her personal account the reconnection fee of $30 on at least three occasions in the current fiscal year. I have attached the termination memorandum with the associated documentation from our billing software.

In late July, I researched her account further back to her hiring in December of 2013. I discovered that she had failed to add a reconnection fee of $30 on May 6, 2015, which was our cutoff date. She paid a portion of her past due balance on May 7, 2015.

Ms. Rivers also failed to charge her account the $15 late fee on four occasions during her employment. This happened in November 2014, January 2015, July 2015, and November 2015. Her complete billing transaction history is attached, and I have highlighted the months in which she failed to add the fees.

Ordinance 15-01 outlines the town's fees that I have referred to in the corres-pondence. It is included in this packet. During her employment, Ms. Rivers essentially stole $180 from the town of White Springs.

The same rules do not apply to the **power of three**. Mayor Bullard purchased a home he had previously rented from the Methodist Church in November of 2016. The Water Utility Deposit of $300 is due for any change in ownership. The only exception to not paying the $300 is if one purchases another home in White Springs and sells their existing home, then the $300 Deposit will move to the new home. Bullard told Town Hall that the water transferred with the sale of the home to him by the Methodist Church. However, our Ordinance stipulates there may not be such a transfer so Bullard technically owes the Town $300 but because he is the mayor and makes his own rules, the Town will not receive the deposit. The Town does not return its deposits, and the ordinance does not state that the deposit will be credited to the payor's future billings, at some point. They Town should not call the money "deposits." If this were a deposit, the Church would have received their $75 or credited it toward the final utility bill. Years back the deposit was only $75.

Rivers claimed that her relationship with Tebo began to change in August or September 2016. Since that time Rivers felt her co-workers Tomlinson and Green were not speaking to her or including her in workplace decisions. On one occasion she discovered a sticky note that Council Member Brown had dropped, where Tebo had written that Brown was not to talk to Rivers about something, which further bolstered her perception. Rivers assumed this was related to the Carver School Grant issue. Tebo had attested that the Carver School Grant had become political in White Springs and according to her, Rivers friends have authored a letter of protest advocating against its demolition.

Rivers stated the relationship she had with Tebo officially changed when she stopped organizing "movie night" for the Town in October 2016. Rivers stopped because of the claims she received from Councilwoman Brown and Mayor Bullard who would do this to purposely aggravate her like not paying for candy and food and complaining during the movie.

Going back to 2016 and the Carver School Demolition

This was the meeting in which verbal protests began regarding the George Washington Carver School where Bernard Williams was one of its educators:

There was no formal documentation either by the Citizen's Advisory Task Force (CATF) nor by the governing body as to what the citizens' needs for the grant were.

COUNCILMAN WILLIE JEFFERSON STATED AT THE SECOND HEARING THAT THE 100 OR SO PEOPLE THAT HE TALKED TO THOUGHT A COMMUNITY CENTER WOULD BE A GOOD IDEA. FROM HIS COMMENT THIS MEANS THE CITIZENS WERE NOT ASKED WHAT THEIR NEEDS ARE BUT THE COUNCIL ITSELF DECIDED UPON A COMMUNITY CENTER AND BROUGHT THE IDEA FORTH TO THE PUBLIC WITHOUT PUBLIC INPUT OF NEEDS IN THE COMMUNITY.

This meeting was NOT published in a local newspaper, BUT THE REQUIREMENT OF NOTICE OF at least five days prior to and no more than 20 days before the date of the second public hearing. WAS ADHERED TO.

Reverter Clause

At the May 13th Meeting, Mr. Ted O'Donnel, our Grant Writer, from Jordan & Associates, advised that with respect to our CBDG Grant for the Community Center and to build a Park, at the Carver School Property the Town would need to have the Hamilton County School Board remove a "Reverter" Clause. Mr. O'Donnel told the Town that it needed to apply for funding by completing the FRDAP application in August or September.

In 2011, the School Board agreed that the Carver School Property would be Deeded to the Town of White Springs if said property would be used for a community center or park. That "Reverter" clause expired five years later in 2016. No one noticed when White Springs had applied for the CBDG Grant in 2017 that the Town intended to demolish the Carver School and build a community Center if the Grant was awarded on Land which reverted to the Hamilton County School Board, since neither an extension was made or a request to remove the clause.

The Hamilton County School Board met in their chambers in the administrative building on May 28th. After Mayor Miller walked into the Chamber Room, Councilman and former Mayor Spencer Lofton became incoherent in his speech and stumbled for words talking about the award of $600,000 to build the community center to which Chairperson Johnny Bullard indicated he had heard of the award. Lofton then asked for a clause to be removed so the Town could have the Property, but he stuttered and paused between words which seemed inarticulate for Lofton as if his mind was elsewhere. He probably was worried that Helen Miller had not been contacted and that she could pull rank since it was not Lofton's job to go before the School Board...only the Mayor or Vice Mayor in the Mayor's absence and of course, the Town Manager since she is the CEO per see.

Ms. Tebo had originally authored an email to the Hamilton County School Board requesting this information and stated she would come before the board but did not show up for the meeting. Instead, Lofton and Councilwoman Tonja Brown came to the meeting to support each other in Tebo's absence.

I figured the Town of White Springs would apply for a FRDAP Grant, as seed money for the CBDG Grant. The $600,000 would be insufficient to build a community center as Tebo and former Mayor Rhett Bullard decided with the demolition of the Carver School. We understood Ms. Tebo asked for $400,000 from Senator Montford and Representative Chuck Branford. And of course, Ms. Tebo allowed Lofton to negotiate with the Montford and Branford staff members for the extra money

FORMER MAYOR MILLER CHALLENGED THE NOTIFICATION TO CITIZENS IN THE NEWSPAPER

Former Mayor and now council woman, Helen Miller, stipulated that proper public notification had not been provided to the public. The grant writer at the behest of the White Springs Council Members, specifically Mayor Bullard, elected to advertise the FIRST PUBLIC HEARING in the Gainesville Sun. Mrs. Miller contacted the Sun and was advised that approximately 10 papers are sold and there are only three subscribers to the Gainesville Sun from our Zip Code.

Mrs. Miller asked why the notification was not in the Jasper paper since more people in the area read the Jasper News. Mayor Bullard gave the excuse that the Jasper News only publishes once a week and that a larger circulation was required. Mrs. Miller contended that more people subscribe and read the Jasper News.

NIKKI WILLIAMS CHALLENGED THE GRANT WRITER AS WELL AS THE COUNCIL.

Ms. Nikki Williams stated that the council obviously wished to keep the information from the public and that the matter was kept secretive. She stated that it does not matter if one makes a complaint or wishes something other than what the council decides because the council does what they wish. Councilman McKenzie stated it was not a secret The grant writer and Mayor Bullard stated they were within the rules. Mayor Bullard stipulated that the citizens have known for a long time that it was the intent for the council to provide a community center.

Simply stated in the minutes, "Ms. Williams asked why the notice of the public hearing was not posted in the places where the Council agendas are usually posted. Ms. Tebo responded that the agendas for the public hearing, the workshop and the second public hearing were posted on the bulletin boards, outside of Town Hall, and outside of the old fire station, which are the same locations that all Council agendas are posted for the public to see."

Nicole Williams' family has been a prominent family in White Springs. Her father Bernard (Pi) Williams sought a grant to fix the Carver School which has great historic value for the Town. Mr. Williams told me at the time, Town Manager Robert Townsend stated that the land should be set aside for housing. Ms. Williams was enthusiastic about why the Carver School should not be demolished.

Mayor Bullard ended the public hearing after other complaints were heard and the council was to vote on the second public hearing acceptance. Former Mayor and Councilwoman Helen Miller stated she would abstain her vote because the rules were not followed. Mayor Bullard stated that if Miller abstained the vote would be considered affirmative per Robert's rules of Order. Miller had removed herself from the council chair. After Maor Bullard stated such, Miller walked out of the council room and building until the vote by the other four council members was made and passed 4/0.

> *To abstain means to refrain from voting and consequently, there can be no such thing as an "abstention vote." Abstentions have absolutely no effect on the outcome of a vote because it has the same effect as a "no" vote.*

Nicole B. Williams and Bernard L. Williams Letter of February 20, 2017, to Mayor Rhet Bullard, Tebo and the Town follows:

"We are writing to protest your abuse of Rule 73C-23-0041. Florida Administrative Code as applied to White Springs' application under the Department of Economic Opportunity FFY 2016 Small cities Community Development Block Grant (CDBG) Program for a neighborhood revitalization project.

As you are well aware, the application process requires that you hold at least two public hearings, and that both public hearings be given proper public notice as defined in subsection 73C-23-0031(35), F.A.C. Rather than provide public notice (of both meetings) to the citizens of White Springs through notice in the Jasper News and through postings on the town bulletin boards at Town Hall an across the street from the U.S. Post Office (in front of the old volunteer fire department) you chose to advertise in the Gainesville Sun and the Lake City Reporter. We believe you chose to deviate from long-standing community norms (and program requirements) in a deliberate effort to reduce/or eliminate opportunities for citizen input, comments and views that are opposed to your project – contrary to the intent of public notice.

In this letter, we will address the required first public hearing. You advertise the first public hearing on December 29, 2016, in the Gainesville Sun. The Circulation Director for the Sun reports "we have three subscribers in that area (zip code 32096) and sell an average of 20 papers Monday-Saturday in the retail outlets and 30 on Sunday" Of these three subscribers, only lives in the Town of White Springs and the other two live in Hamilton County. In addition, rather than post topic-specific notice (CDBG First Public Hearing) of the first public hearing on the Town's two bulletin boards, as has been municipal practice in the past, you choose to position notice as new business on the Town Council Agenda which was posted on the town bulletin boards on Friday, January 6, 2017, before the Council Meeting on Tuesday, January 10, 2017, thereby violating the 5-day notice rule.

Why this conscious effort to reduce community awareness, participation, and discussions of the project? We believe the answer lies on PG-6 of the application. The CDBG application "Application Profile, Table G-1, asks under the heading of "Historic Preservations. Will the project impact a building, public improvement or planned open space that is 50 or more years old? If yes, documentation must be provided in Appendix I, of Part 9? You checked "No" in the answer to this question – contrary to the truth.

In fact, this project will dramatically and forever impact the historic George Washington Carver School, constructed in the mid to late 1940's. A critical milestone of the overall project is to "demolish and remove all these buildings currently referred to as Old Carver School." In *response to your request for in-kind support for this project. Hamilton County has agreed to perform "the demolition and clearing of the property," estimated at a value of $160,700. The Old Carver School is the core of what remains as evidence of Black History in White Springs. During previous Council Meetings, Council Member Jefferson promised to hold public meetings for the express purpose of discussing and developing a consensus on a plan to address the "Old Carver School Property. He failed to do so, and in fact, said at the Council Meeting on February 14, that he had talked to people and all were good with your proposed project for the Carver site. Council Member Jefferson's statement of personal conversations is different from conducting an actual publicly notice community meeting to elicit, discuss, and modify a plan that addresses the range of views in our community. To submit this application during Black History Month adds insult to injury.*

Your lack of honesty in completing the CDBG application brings dishonor to the entire White Springs community. Your arrogance and total disregard for the application process and administrative requirements speaks to your lack of respect for federal, state, county and municipal laws – you hold yourselves above the law. Your lack of interest in the needs of the community is disheartening, and your confrontational approach when dealing with citizens who disagree with you has led to a demoralized citizenry."

Both Nicole and Bernard Williams signed the letter.

Tebo's stamp of receipt was dated 2/20/2017

The County agrees to demolish the Carver School at No Charge

The Town did receive the CBDG grant of $600,000 and the Town citizens refused to accept only a community center but desired a hurricane shelter. It was then that Hamilton County elected to charge nothing for the demolition of the existing Carver School and Mayor Miller kept working on what additional money she could secure. During the tenure of Manager/consultant Jones, she made the following statements

In Mr. Louie Goodin, Hamilton County Coordinator's letter of February 13, 2017, addressed to Stacy Tebo, Town Manager, it was stated The Hamilton County Board of County Commissioners has agreed to demolish and remove all those buildings, currently referred to as "Old Carver School", provided there is no discovery of asbestos or lead paint. The County would utilize its Road Department employees and equipment to perform the demolition and clearing of the property.

PCS (Nutrien) provided the $13,000 to have the asbestos removed. Whether there is Lead Paint, I am unaware nor do I have a record of that.

Mayor Miller indicated that the Retention Ponds could be dug deeper, and the dirt used for the Community Center which would be a $12,000 savings. Jones was going to speak to Mike Williams in the hopes that Nutrien would have some funds to spare so that we could secure the additional $48,000 we need to complete the Community Center so that it would be Hurricane Proof. Since that would not include the Generator, Mayor Miller suggested that Mr. Jones request $50,000 if Nutrien is willing to provide a contribution because the building would help employees of Nutrien and their family members.

Mayor Miller also suggested that Home Depot and Lowes be contacted to see whether they could discount the price of a generator. Also, First Federal and Duke Energy each provide

$2,000 for communities who need the money. Mayor Miller said this was the first Phase of the project.

It was stated, there is nothing on paper with respect to the FLORIDA RECREATION DEVELOPMENT ASSISTANCE PROGRAM (FRDAP) Grant. Yet upon my calling the FRDAP, I was advised the Town was accepted for a previous FRDAP grant but the paperwork had not been completed. Yet there were more problems which were not considered:

It was further advised by FRDAP that the Governor has not signed for any funding for FRDAP in this current year and it is expected no funding will be received.

I then received a phone call from another Staff Member of FRDAP who advised that there is a problem with the Bailey Ogburn Park Grant in that they still had not received the appropriate paperwork. I passed the information on to Miller.

THE FLORIDA COMMUNITY DEVELOPMENT BLOCK GRANT PROGRAM

The Florida Small Cities Community Development Block Grant Program is a competitive grant program that awards funds to eligible cities, counties, towns, and villages. There are approximately 249 eligible communities in Florida. To be eligible for the Small Cities CDBG Program, a city must have a population under 50,000, and a county's population must be under 200,000. The Program awards sub-grants in four categories:

Economic Development Neighborhood Revitalization Housing Rehabilitation, and Commercial Revitalization.

WHY THE TOWN OFFICIALS FINALLY WISH TO BUILD A COMMUNITY CENTER

Because the Town of White Springs has done nothing to assist those in the community; including dropping the after-school program Councilwoman Helen Miller had worked so hard for with then Superintendent Tom Moffses, Councilman Willie Jefferson and Mayor Rhett Bullard have elected to secure a Community Development Block Grant to provide a Municipal Community Center near the old Carver School Area

Council Member McKenzie stated in prior meetings that a citizen's advisory taskforce was not necessary. It is true that the council makes all decisions and obviously is responsible for printing notices in the newspapers for which the Community may not get the proper notices. Yet one needs to review the statute which requires a CATF.

Back to 2019

At the June 2019 Council Meeting, the Town had decided to sell the old jail building which required a number of repairs and maintenance.

Dennis Price had written a letter to our Town Manager Ms. Tebo with an offer to purchase the old jail building which is adjacent to his property. His intent is to use the building for the sale of crafts and made an offer of $25,000. Mayor Miller indicated it would be on the agenda at the next council meeting and stated a 30-day notice should be given to the tenant of that building, Shaunda Wirts.

Later in the meeting, Mayor Miller apprised Dennis Price of the decision to bring his offer to the Council. Shonda Werts arrived with Arthur Natteal, hearing the conversation. Shonda first went up to the podium and stated that her pantry may not have paid any money in the lease but that it was important to at least five hundred people. Arthur Natteal scoffed at Dennis Price's offer and Dennis had explained that the building had not received any revenue and had been sitting vacant for a long time. Price had talked to the Tax appraiser who said the building was appraised for$25,000. Initially it had shown the value as $35,000 but that included the Park, and the appraiser broke the price down to show the building value only at $25,000.

Arthur Natteal continued to scoff at Dennis Price, mentioning the building was prime commercial real estate and could be worth $300,000 or more. Arthur Natteal had no real estate experience, nor has he conducted real estate appraisals. Mayor Miller requested a real estate appraisal be done. Tebo made no recommendations, which a manager should do.

> *A real estate appraisal will be based upon the Market Value of the Property. It is an opinion of what a property would sell for in a competitive market based upon its construction, its features, and benefits of that property (value). Also taken into consideration is the overall real estate market supply and demand and what other comparable properties have sold for at the same condition the old jail is in. This is usually the initial determination before a Market Price is determined.*
>
> *The Market price is what a willing, ready and qualified buyer will pay for the property and what the seller will accept for it. Price is determined by local supply and demand, the property's condition and what comparable properties have sold for without adding in the value component.*
>
> *The difference between market value and market price is that the market value, in the eyes of the seller, might be much more than what a buyer will pay for the property or its true market price. Real estate is like economics. Value can create demand, which influences price. But without the demand function, value alone cannot*

influence price. As supply increases and demand decreases, prices go down and value is not influential. As supply decreases and demand increases, the price will rise, and value will influence price. Market Value and Market Price can be equal in a balanced market.

White Springs is not a hot spot where real estate prices are sky high. Is there a rush for people who wish to move to White Springs? It is a beautiful little village, but it is not the first place a commercial business would wish to buy property. The old jail had was leased to an outfitter and then to a beauty shop and neither considered purchasing the building and it could be that there was insufficient business in our little Town of White Springs to support the costs.

The Tax appraisal value, for which Mr. Price was extremely fair in his offer:

The tax appraised value of a home or property is a figure that county tax offices use to determine what a property owner's annual property tax will be. The county provides basic services to residents (e.g., fire and police service, road maintenance) which are paid for from the money collected from property taxes. Sometimes, local tax levies (such as for schools or county disability boards) are attached to property taxes, but the residents will first have had to approve the levy by simple majority vote in a local election.

In most areas of the country, a property's tax appraised value is a straight percentage of its fair market value, the old jail does not include a homestead exemption, so the appraised value is NOT reduced. Some counties have instituted an annual increase based upon an inflation index which I do not believe is the case in Hamilton County. Furthermore, since counties must pay for property tax reappraisals, they often only have appraisals done every 5 or 10 years, or upon the sale of a property.

A motion was made by Council Member Moore and seconded by Walter McKenzie to get a certified appraiser to establish the value of the property. The motion passed 3/2. Voting against the motion were councilmembers Spencer Lofton and Tonja Brown. A motion was made by Vice Mayor Walter McKenzie and seconded by Mayor Helen Miller to give "Bebish, Inc" (Shonda Wert's Company) sixty days to vacate. The Council withdrew the motion after a lengthy discussion. Councilmember Tom Moore suggested that the item be tabled until the July 9th meeting.

The Town elected to not sell the old jail building which Price would have purchased as is, making the necessary repairs as his cost. Instead, he built a separate building which added value to the main street.

Tebo removes Pittman as Fire Chief

Although there was ample time for Stacy Tebo to stipulate a **Memorandum of Complaint** regarding Chief Kevin Pittman, **Stacy Tebo did so one hour prior to the January 9, 2018, council meeting.** The council members had not received her complaint in their council packets nor had Kevin Pittman received the complaint to review until the meeting started.

Tebo states that she had requested his resignation as Fire Chief, and that he could remain a volunteer if he wished on November 29, 2017. She did this because she wished to avoid any public embarrassment caused by disciplinary action. **She stated, *"knowing that any public records created for that purpose would certainly be publicized on a local blog". "I was also mindful that anything I created would become part of his personnel ..le which could be reviewed by potential future employers and anyone that wished to see it."***

Tebo also states that the Charter provides that only the Town Manager, town attorney and police chief are hired by the Council. Again, *the Charter does not discuss the Fire Department, which technically has equal billing to the police department; therefore, it should be under the auspices of the Town Council not the Town Manager, but currently the Charter has no mention of who is in charge. Secondly all volunteers are approved by the council with a vote and our ..re..ghters are volunteers.* Stacy Tebo did accredit Andrew Greene for giving her the name of Kevin Pittman to be fire chief.

Chief Pittman organized an in-house course to get our volunteers certified. The Town does not pay or reimburse our firefighters to attend Fire College and for room and board so Kevin Pittman, who had a previous certification as an instructor, trained our firefighters so they could pass the 206-hour course.

Tebo's major complaint relating to Kevin Pittman was that he <u>was</u> a CERTIFIED INSTRUCTOR until his certification expired on June 30, 2015, and he did not opt for the one-year extension until 6/30/2016 because he did not take the 40-hour course. *Therefore, instead of thanking him for what he had done personally with the firefighters to assure they would pass, the Fire College did not accept Kevin Pittman's signature.* As a result, one of the students who he assisted was fired by the Division of Forestry because the lack of certification. Yet other Chiefs signed the certifications on Pittman's behalf.

> *IT HAS NEVER BEEN REQUIRED THAT OUR FIRE CHIEF BE A CERTIFIED INSTRUCTOR AND THERE ARE NO SPECIFICS WITHIN OUR CHARTER. NONE OF THE OTHER CHIEFS WERE CERTIFIED INSTRUCTORS. PITTMAN ASSISTED THE FIREFIGHTERS WHO HAD NO MONEY TO PAY FOR THE COURSE AND THAT IS ADMIRABLE.*

Tebo also blamed Kevin Pittman for having major repairs completed on the newly purchased pre-owned fire engine in October before the Council had even approved the agreement. She complained he ordered decals for the engine and removed the Windsor decals. She was upset with him about the purchasing policy and although she apprised Mr. Pittman that he should maintain the pre-used fire engine, she was angry that she did not get the cost in advance. $3,702.51 was required for repairs, mainly because of the Turbo which Stacy did not understand was essential to be repaired. When she initially was asked by Kevin Pittman and Thomas Brazil, she told them to get the maintenance done and did not tell them to secure an estimate first. Furthermore, if Thomas Brazil and Kevin Pittman did not tell Stacy Tebo that Windsor was having a title problem, the vehicle was still in the Town's possession which is nine points of the law.

Stacy Tebo did not have a copy of her complaint for Kevin Pittman but rather Mayor Rhett Bullard gave him a copy. Mr. Pittman was given five minutes to read the complaint and essentially called it crap and resigned. When there was a complaint made that a copy should have been given to Kevin Pittman in advance, Rhett Bullard said he should have known what he did wrong. Then the members of the fire department who were there stood up and Bullard told the firefighters they were out of order, and we were done with Fire Department Business. Thomas Brazil was the first to say My name is Thomas Brazil, *I'm a Fire..ghter engineer for White Springs Fire Department and this is my resignation.*".

We were told that Andrew Greene Assistant Fire Chief would not allow the Fire Department to spend money even though they received $17,000 from the County for fighting fires outside of White Springs. They required breathing apparatuses and Andrew Greene said such were frivolous or something to that effect. He said Stacy would not provide it because we did

159

not have money. Then Stacy blamed Mr. Pittman for not securing a grant for breathing apparatuses when it is the Manager's duty to coordinate and place together grant information.

Andrew Greene used the new SUV fire truck personally. Not only did he receive $120 per month but all maintenance and fuel was paid for by the Town, even when he took frequent trips to Tampa, and he lives in Lake City. This left other volunteers who have to catch up with the fire truck using their own vehicles which they maintain and for which they pay all costs of fuel.

When it comes to Tebo however, we will pay her legal fees with no applicable limit or cap; but we cannot allow the volunteers to use the fire truck for which the grant was meant for, nor can we provide them with breathing apparatuses. Yet Rhett Bullard gives her complete control and will not agree to mediating differences.

White Springs fire chief, six other firefighters resign

By Alexis Spoehr Jan 11, 2018

WHITE SPRINGS, Fla. Seven members of the White Springs Fire Rescue, including Fire Chief Kevin Pittman, resigned at Tuesday night's town meeting. The resignations came after discussion at the December meeting in regard to Town Manager Stacy Tebo asking for Pittman's resignation Nov. 29. Also, during that meeting, members of the fire department asked for support in a vote of no confidence against Assistant Fire Chief Andrew Greene.

The council then decided to move the issues with the fire department to the January agenda. During Tuesday's meeting, Tebo submitted a Memorandum of Complaint

against Pittman, providing each council member a copy. Several citizens asked for a copy of the memo as well as Pittman, who said he had not seen or heard of the memo. "This document was created today and was finished right before the meeting," Tebo replied. + Pittman said: "Since it involves me, I would like to be able to read through it."
According to the memo, Tebo asked for Pittman's resignation in order to avoid public embarrassment and keep disciplinary action out of his personnel file. Tebo added that when she asked for Pit-tman's resignation it was just as chief, that he could decide whether to remain as a volunteer firefighter.

In the memo, Tebo outlined the reasons that led to her decision to seek the resignation, mainly stemming around attempts to get certification for the town's volunteer firefighters. According to the memo, Pittman allegedly had told Tebo he was a certified instructor and with the help of another instructor would hold classes to provide certification for the firefighters.

Last summer, Tebo and Pittman had talked about recognizing everyone who earned their certifications publicly at a meeting, according to the memo. The recognition was rescheduled from June to July because not everyone had received their certificates. The recognition was held at the July 11 meeting. However, Tebo states in the memo that she received a call from Hamilton County Emergency Management Director Henry Land on Aug. 2, stating one of the individuals was not certified and Pittman's signature was not being accepted by the fire college. Land offered Tebo assistance in getting students certified and could sign off on the certificates, according to the memo. Tebo told Pittman and he allegedly stated it would not be necessary.

161

In the memo, Tebo states she then looked further into Pittman's previous employment and certifications where she found an expired instructors' certification. It expired June 30, 2015, and was given a one-year extension to June 30, 2016. While looking into his previous employment at Suwannee County Fire Rescue it shows he was terminated on July 12, 2012, and is stated on his resume that he worked with SCFR through July 2013. "He was dishonest to me about his instructor certification," Tebo wrote, adding "he was also dishonest on his resume. "The integrity of the Town, the Council, and myself was compromised as we unwittingly participated in the deception." Also, in the memo, Tebo documented issues surrounding the purchase of a fire truck from the Windsor Fire Department. The memo states that Pittman had spent money on repairs and decals for the truck prior to the council approving the agreement, also alleging that the repairs were done without her approval.

After being given a chance to read the memo and prior to the memo being read aloud at the meeting, Pittman resigned. "I have been fired before and I have quit a lot of jobs, so effective right now you have my resignation as fire chief for this department," Pittman said. "Tomorrow I will return the truck, personal items and the keys, my keys to the town. "There is no point in going through this, this nothing but… crap. I am just going to say it and I am not going to have my name put out there and walked on." Following Pittman's resignation, six volunteer members of the department resigned as well. "Hold on. We have moved on from the fire department, there is no…" Mayor Rhett Bullard said before the six volunteers cut in stating: "Let's just do this right then right now. If you are going to move on, then we are going to move on. My name is Thomas Brazil, I am a Firefighter engineer for White Springs Fire Department, and this is my resignation." Brazil was joined by Antonio Perez, William Register, Peter Shanks, Andy Stormant and Andrea Thompson in submitting their resignation, leaving nine members at the fire department as of Wednesday afternoon.

END OF ARTICLE

At the December 12th meeting, the firefighters had approached councilors on their way to the meeting to protest the firing of Kevin Pittman. Mr. Pittman did not attend the meeting. Rhett Bullard pretended that he knew nothing about the request to remove Kevin Pittman as fire Chief and made no admission. Walter McKenzie warned the council that if we remove Mr. Pittman without a fair hearing, we will no longer have a fire department. Currently under Kevin Pittman as Fire Chief we have had more volunteers who are certified and who have protected White Springs and the surrounding area as no other town has had.

On behalf of all the Firefighters, one firefighter read the following to the Town Council in the December meeting:

WHITE SPRINGS FIRE RESCUE December 12, 2017, VOTE OF NO CONFIDENCE

We, the members of the White Springs Fire Rescue, have composed this letter to express our dissatisfaction with the current Assistant Chief, Joseph Andrew Greene. Unfortunately, circumstances have left us with no other recourse. We have lost all trust, faith, and confidence in Assistant Greene's ability to lead this department. Asst. Chief Greene's lack of dedication and inability to perform his duties in a timely fashion has damaged the department's performance. These problematic tendencies

163

are very crucial in a field where mistakes and divisive behavior can cost department members and citizens their lives. He has not upheld his position or responsibility to the Department and has not attended any department trainings, functions nor Station shifts since April 29, 2017.

Records show since July 1, 2017, a total of (51) responses have been required in and around White Springs. Chief Pittman has responded to (35) of those calls. Firefighter Brazil has responded to (29) calls, Firefighter's Perez and Register have responded to (27), Greene has only responded to (7). Other members of the department who are not able to reach the station in an adequate response time are often performing shifts and duties at the fire station on their days off from full-time employment. The only shift Greene has participated in was a contractual paid event. During that shift, both he and member Dominique Greene were dismissed from their duties for inappropriate behavior and misconduct within a patient care area.

His lack of leadership, mismanagement and poor policy decisions have damaged the relationships within the department. In June of 2017, Chief Pittman met with the Town Manager, Stacy Tebo, on behalf of the department to discuss Assistant Chief Greene's lack of communication and his deliberate avoidance of training and department procedures. Attempts to address workplace problems with Assistant Greene have gone unheeded by the Town Manager regardless of the number of complaints.

During Hurricane Irma, several members were present at the station for up to (72) hours each to perform their services needed due to the catastrophic impact of the storm. Greene, who is also the town Utilities Director, was not present to fulfill his duties in public works and the fire department, before or during Irma. No contact was maintained with the department during this time and several individual members were approached by contractors, city employees and citizens attempting to contact Greene. This was a major devaluation of Greene's dedication to the department, as Chief Pittman was present for the entirety of the storm including preparations and cleanup efforts alongside other responders, maintaining clear communication with all members.

Greene refuses to address issues presented to him by department members, answering inquiries in a dismissive manner showing disregard to the chain of command and the need of the department. When approached by department personnel regarding essential firefighting equipment needing repair or replacement, he deflects questions and says, "I do not have to explain myself". In other confrontations, he has told members that Town Manager Tebo has not allotted any budget for the department's frivolous spending" and the equipment shall have to suffice, even though we must stress that the difference between life and death for firefighters is the degree of functioning equipment they possess.

With (8) certified Firefighter One members and (2) Firefighter Two members in the department with only (3) functioning air packs, this places all members in dangerous situations. Greene's lack of care for the issue shows his total disregard for department members. He does not show respect to the livelihood or wellbeing of the firefighter's safety.

In October, Assistant Chief Greene and Town Manager Tebo removed personnel access to the station's computers required for reporting runs and other necessary information. Taboo's memo claimed that Greene would be taking full responsibility for the logging of paperwork and the running of reports. Since this was enacted, Green has not performed his duties in a timely manner, often requiring members to tape reports, receipts and requests to his office door. This attitude of poor management has sown distrust with his refusal to communicate properly.

We feel that the relationship with Assistant Chief Green is irreparable. He has brought morale to an all-time low with his lack of leadership and poor management style. Greene has established a pattern and practice of inequitable treatment of department personnel. A bad manager can take a functioning staff and destroy it by causing the best employees to leave the Department and those which remained, to lose all motivation.

In closing, we would like to reiterate one last time that the members of White Springs Fire Rescue have lost all trust and faith in Assistant Chief Andrew Greene's ability to lead this Department. We therefore ask that you support our VOTE OF NO CONFIDENCE and relieve Assistant Chief Greene of his duties and responsibilities pertaining to the Fire Department.

Respectfully yours,

The Members of White Springs Fire Rescue

END OF LETTER

Making a vote of no confidence in Andrew Greene, in a public forum, was their last hope for the towns' officials to do something about the problem. It was brought to Stacy Tebo's attention in a meeting she and Kevin Pittman had. When he asked her who appointed Greene as Assistant Chief an She stated Stith did (*A former chief who quit twice who used Greene as an administrator only but neither fought fires as volunteers*).

166

Pittman also informed her that he was going to remove Greene from the Assistant Chief spot and just do away with it because it was not needed due to the quality of leaders he had under Greene. Stacy Tebo said" *No; You cannot remove Greene again.*" She was told Greene could remain as a firefighter but not as the Assistant Chief again. She said "No!". Much of this information was received from the firefighters themselves.

Andrew Greene handled the Wastewater Treatment plant, and he assisted Townsend former Town Manager and a cousin of Mayor Bullard's prior to taking over the utility when the former was fired. Although he was appointed Assistant Fire Chief by former Fire Chief Steven Stith at the direction of Bullard, and former Town Manager Townsend, he has never been inside a structure fire or been to one in three years. He has shown up to two fires in shorts and flip flops, handing water to the other firefighters. Yet he uses the new SUV for personal use and shows up at the annual Christmas parade, various restaurants in Lake City and various areas of Tampa.

One reason Bullard protects Andrew Greene is because his number one client is Andrew's grandmother Ethen McGhin, so there is a clear conflict of interests and ethics. Bullard won't let any harm come to the boy because it affects him financially.

If you want more proof on Andrew's blacking out condition, we were told one should look into Andrew's use of sick leave at work. One of the firefighters told us. Some of those days may have been because he was sick but some them may have been covering his seizures and blackouts. Specifically, days when Andrew may have come to work but then at some point in time had to go home sick.

The members of the Fire Department on the night of the council meeting did not intend to resign but when Ms. Tebo did not provide the memo to Mr. Pittman in advance of the meeting so he could defend these allegations, the firefighters felt they would be treated the same. The members decided that they had no other choice but to leave the department because if Tebo did it to two different chiefs and Bullard would not stand up for the department, who would be next? *"Just know we as members are sorry that we could not do more for this town but just know we gave it our best and we did, all we could do, with NO SUPPORT FROM THE TOWN OFFICIALS,"*

Pittman was the only chief that worked for this town/department that stepped up to do the job to get everyone trained to hold meetings, family dinners, and events for the kids in this town. He stepped up when no one else would take a broken-down department with little to nothing and bring it into the 21st century. The Town had no dedicated members before he took over. It is known first-hand that previous members of the department did not show up for calls in the middle of the night during the day or even come to wash a truck. When Chief Pittman took over, the fire department gained some of the best members any department could ask for. They showed up to calls, cleaned and manned the station, cleaned the trucks and took care of the equipment. The firefighters tried to give the best of the best to the town, and we were constantly shut down by city hall.

We had the most members of any department in the county now this town is left with nothing but three even though the town manager stipulates there are seven firefighters. *"It doesn't matter how many names you have on a piece of paper it matters on how many show-up. How many show up in the middle of the night to help you? How many show up when you need them at your most critical times is what counts? The list means nothing and holds no water when no one shows up."*

Kevin Pittman was a certified Firefighter II, a medic, a hazmat tech, and a fire inspector. He did not lie to her about everyone being certified as he stated to her that the firefighters have completed the required class of 206 hours and were awaiting the state certification at this time. The firefighters were aware that there was an issue with a signature, and all were aware that it was being worked on and it was taken care off. Just know Chief Pittman did everything for this town. He was the only fire chief I have seen show up in the middle of the night for medical calls, fires, crashes, Landing zone set ups. He showed up. The firefighters said it was not the same for the previous chief or the assistant chief. Chief Pittman showed up when this town needed a chief and a leader. He single handedly turned a broken run down untrained unstaffed department and turned it into a full-on working staff and trained a loyal department

ORDINANCE 12-01 amends Section 5.06 of the Charter of the Town of White Springs as follows:

The Town of White Springs, Florida has the responsibility for providing fire protection services, whether by or through a White Springs Volunteer Fire Department or by and through an appropriate contractual relationship with a third- party fire agency.

The Town Council shall have the sole discretion in determining the manner for providing fire protection services for the safety and wellbeing of the citizens of White Springs, Florida. Nothing herein shall prevent the White Springs Volunteer Fire Department from assisting agencies as the need arises.

Regarding Mayor Bullard giving the second fire truck to Greene for his personal use.

There are no Town Regulations regarding Staff personally using the fire trucks. At one time Tracy Rodriquenz was allowed to drive to and from Jacksonville and she was required to pay a portion of the fuel cost. In the case of Andrew Greene, Helen Miller stopped the Town from purchasing a new Vehicle, a

169

pickup 4/4 so Andrew could travel back and forth to Gainesville. Since Bullard and Pam Tomlinson favored him, they were upset, and a motion was made before the **power of three** could vote against Helen Miller's motion.

Greene was of course upset with us as well and the fact that we reported him driving the bush truck. He would display lights and sirens when coming by our house and would throw firecrackers at our Jeep and house along with one of his cousins. We had to report it to the police.

Griffin's complaints were being sent to the Attorney

Joe Griffin made three complaints. One was against the council and Tonja Brown for being silent on reasons for voting for/against items. The second one was against Spencer Lofton for approaching school board for the lease of South Hamilton Elementary School *(Mayor Miller suggested getting a legal opinion from the attorney)* and the third was against Spencer Lofton for negotiations with Hamilton County Board of Commissioners regarding the fire Service Agreement *(Again this was being sent to the attorney for legal advice)*.

KENNETH HUTCHERSON PUBLIC WORKS EMPLOYEE

Kenneth Hutcherson was our Public Works Employee. He was not a contract employee and was not supervised by any Town Manager. Although it is stated in the personnel manual, the Town Manager may approve additional leave, when Mr. Hutcherson was critically ill with cancer, he was unable to work for over two years. Yet payments were made to Mr. Hutcherson, including additional benefits during a period of two years when he was unable to work from 2016 until his death. Town managers are allowed to make payments of up to $2,500 before securing permission from the council, so advantage was taken to make such payments without council approval.

When securing a packet of Kenneth Hutcherson's time sheets; none of which had been signed by him for two years, it was shown that then Town Manager Townsend, provided a "leave payment" to Hutcherson which was done under contract with the then City Attorney Kennon:

Contract regarding "Employee Sick Leave" dated January 14, 2008

Pay Rate: $18.45

Number of Hours 2,326 per policy 1/2 = $1,263 hours

3. (initialed) Request payment for these hours at the rate of the employee's salary/hourly wage at time of the request. This option would be contingent upon funds available in the budget at the time of the request. If choose Option 3. Total amount $21,457.00 (This was Chosen)

Signed Hutcherson 1/14/08; Robert Townsend 1/14/08 and Pam Tomlinson 1/14/08

(At the bottom) NOTE: The execution of this form by the undersigned employee and the Town of White Springs, Florida does not vest/guarantee or entitle the Employee to compensation for any accrued sick leave. The employee will only be entitled to compensation for any accrued sick leave based on the manner of the employee's departure/termination with the town of White Springs, Florida. The employee's entitlement to compensation for any accrued sick leave will be determined by the applicable Standard Operating Procedures effective as of December 31, 2007.

Based upon 2,326 hours divided by .50% it means he had 1,163 hours of sick leave. or he would have 3.195 years of sick leave or 166.143 weeks of sick leave No other employee has been given such benefits and there is no record that the Town Council was aware of this.

In 2016 Kenny Hutcherson could no longer perform his job but he did not quit nor did the town replace him but continually gave him leave payments for over two years:

In accordance with the Town's Personnel file, Tomlinson, as The Town Clerk, was responsible for maintaining complete and accurate attendance and leave records. Stacy Tebo as Town Manager is responsible for forwarding all associated documentation of attendance and leave to the Tomlinson. It is then up to Tomlinson to assure that the timesheets reflect the actual time worked and the type of leave utilized; to bring the total to the regular working hours and to make certain the documents are signed by the employee.

Therein after, it was up to Tomlinson to issues the electronic payments, in the case of Employee Kenny Hutcherson, directly to Hutcherson's bank by wire transfer. Town Clerk/Finance Director Pam Tomlinson, allegedly in collusion with her Town Manager Stacy Tebo and Councilman and former Mayor Bullard provided payments to Hutcherson for the fiscal years 2016/2017 and 2017. The Town Council was unaware of the payments made.

What the Federal law says about Medical Leave

Under the FMLA, you are entitled to time away from your workplace for a serious health condition that makes you unable to perform your job. including time when you are out on short-term disability or Workers' Compensation. Although you are not entitled to receive your pay during this time of absence, your job is protected, and health insurance benefits must generally continue. One may continue health, life or supplemental insurance benefits during leave by paying one's portion of the monthly benefit premium regardless of whether one is on unpaid or paid leave status. Under the FMLA, you are entitled to take 12 weeks of unpaid leave during a twelve-month period.

In the case of White Springs, the Town would not have to comply with FMLA because the Town hires fewer than 50 employees. There is no mention of medical leave laws in either the Town Charter or the personnel manual.

Pam Tomlinson advised Joe Griffin that the Town was able to pay Kenneth Hutcherson that it is allowed in the personnel manual, yet the Personnel Manual does not state that more than 60 days total may be taken per year for both leaves-

Duration of leave – Annual leave may be accumulated but may not exceed thirty (30) days or two-hundred forty (240) hours unless approved in writing by the Town Manager.

Tebo and Tomlinson allegedly falsified leave reports, and employee time sheets, for Hutcherson, with fraudulent entries for Regular, Holiday, Annual Time, sick time and Comp time, which amounted to around $150,000 in payments to Hutcherson.

The Town's personnel policies provide annual vacation and sick leave benefits to employees, accrued vacation and sick leave vests with a maximum of 240 hours of each type of leave. The Town accrues unpaid vacation costs when earned by the employee and reports Compensated Absences due within one year and in more than one year, in the Statement of Net Position are reported in the Town's Annual Audit of Financial Statements.

During the year between the week of May 1, 2017, and the week of May 7, 2018 (for which time sheets have been provided by town staff), Hutcherson's purported (unsigned) time sheets report compensation for 1,355.25 hours of sick time, 442.5 hours of annual time and 119.75 hours of comp time, far in excess of the maximum annual vacation (240 hours) and sick leave benefits (240 hours) provided employees by the Town's personnel policies. The time sheets also report that 46.5 hours of Regular time and 96 hours of Holiday time were used to compensate Mr. Hutcherson.

Based on the Town's annual vacation and sick leave benefits policies, it is impossible that Mr. Hutcherson (who officially retired in May 2018) could have accrued vacation and sick leave benefits to justify being paid full-time compensation for the nearly two years during which time he did not report for work. Due to prior record keeping and supervision by Tebo, it is not known when Mr. Hutcherson actually stopped reporting to work.

Weekly payments to Mr. Hutcherson were made by direct deposit to his personal banking account. Hutcherson was a very capable employee and an artist with a backhoe. His tenure was the longest in White Springs history. Tebo could have placed the issue of compassionate income for Mr. Hutcherson on the council's agenda for public input and discussion, but they chose not to do so Employees who question or simply identify any management issues related to accountability, integrity and efficiency of the town operations are usually fired or offered the opportunity to resign.

From Helen Miller

to me, Joe

Did Pam provide Stacy's advance approval documentation? Let's see it. How would she know the length of the leave? Any leave over an extra month or so would exceed Stacy's financial limit re what she can approve on her own. I.e. the $2,500 limit. When she "knew" the leave would cost the town over $2,500, she needed to bring the issue to the council. Of course, it was never the intent to allow 1 yr, or 1 yr. paid leave since *the town has limits on annual leave and sick leave, defined by the 240-hour rule.*

Apparently. Ken Daniels, CPA, found the area where we had paid Kenny Hutcherson over $150,000 in funds while working on the fiscal audit. He stated that we can offer health insurance for a period of two years, but it is paid by the individual employee and the cost increases by a specific amount as determined by actuaries of the company. Of course, Hutcherson's name was not mentioned, and Daniels was discussing COBRA. Hutcherson should have gone under Medicare Disability and Social Security, and we should not have paid him for over two years from the Town's funds stating it was leave money, just to keep him afloat.

Hatton resigns

Attorney Karen Hatton submitted her resignation effective September 5, 2019, after she attempted to obtain, through a collection agency for the third time, money for Joe Griffin's judgments which were satisfied. I wrote to Ms. Hatton advising her of her lack of due diligence as an attorney which may have been biased since she also was the Assistant States Attorney who charged Griffin in the medals case. She apparently did not wish a complaint made to the Florida bar, since she swiftly wrote her letter of resignation, and the collection agency backed off after receiving the satisfactions of judgments by email. Since the judgments were no longer collectible due to the statute of limitations, this firm was hired to merely harass us for money.

Thereafter, Helen Miller asked that I contact Meagan Logan to apply to us as a Town Attorney. Meagan Logan was the attorney for Marks & Gray who won the case against Griffin and relates to the Civil Rights Case which went to the appellate court. $4,762 per "Bill of Costs" dated November 23, 2015, was the payment by us to FMIT, since the case was lost and the Town officials and staff received immunity. At mediation, our attorney's cost was more than $70,000 and we did not accept the $5,000 offered by FMIT to close the case. As such we could not consider that amount to be a win. It was our attorney's plan to only provide the town with information relating to public records and first amendment rights, but the Town brought in various statements relating to Griffin's prior behaviors and because Griffin was considered bi-polar at the time, the appellate judge ruled against us. I, however, did not have a problem with Ms. Logan and invited her to apply and contact Mayor Helen Miller.

> *It may be mentioned that Shirley Heath and Pam Tomlinson mentioned much hearsay which could not be verified but the animosity for Joe Griffin was monumental. After the aforementioned was discussed, the insurance under also refused the terms and offered only $5,000 for us to close the case. The appellate judge, however, made it clear that since Joe Griffin had a bi-polar medical condition, the Town and its officials were immune.*

Had it not been for Griffin's diagnosis in the Town's complaints of being Bi-Polar, the issues should have been in our favor. "The heart of the Reply is a weak refutation of our argument that the city was responding primarily to your blog posts and that retaliation for Internet postings is against clearly established law. The Town attempts to redirect attention to two items which it believes constituted cyberstalking: (1) Griffin's endless public records requests and (2) Griffin's efforts to contact City manager applicants."

Our Civil rights attorney 's email

"Here's what I think the evidence and law shows with respect to the two points emphasized by the Town:

- The Town repeatedly states that Griffin submitted documents other than public records requests and that

176

these comments somehow violated the law. You will note that there were no citations to the record in the Reply to support that claim. The few citations in the Town's original Motion for Summary Judgment were ludicrous: they were either completely innocuous ("I expect an immediate response to this request") or involved matters which occurred either long before or long after the police investigation (Griffin's hateful comments to the former City Manager).

- The Town never does refute our legal argument that the cyberstalking law could never apply to these activities for a few reasons, including the fact that **the Town is not a natural person and could not be a victim."**

"Once again, it should be obvious that Griffin's ceaseless public records requests and occasional snarky comments have nothing to do with Karin. So why did the Town complain about Karin to the police and why was Karin investigated? One must also ask why Karin is mentioned as a target in the mayor's infamous letter?

- There is no law against contacting applicants for public employment. In fact, that activity is constitutionally protected. Also, the only competent evidence on the subject came from Mr. Lawrence who characterized the contact as harmless and lawful.

"And, to beat a dead horse, Karin did not contact any of the applicants.

- The Town did a fair job addressing qualified immunity for the individual Defendants, but nothing really new came up in the Reply. As you know, I think that Tomlinson is probably protected by qualified immunity, Rodriquenz might be, and the mayor probably is not. That opinion does not change based on the Reply.

- I think the Town did nothing to advance the defense based on Monell policy making. The Town should have argued that it repudiated the mayor's actions and that Rodriquenz efforts to secure a warrant ultimately caused no harm to you because a warrant was never obtained. These were missed opportunities for the Town.
- The argument made is quite weak. The Town argues for Monell purposes that its action against your blog was confined in time and therefore not really an established policy. Of course, that argument concedes the main point that the Town acted against your blog and the actual evidence shows that the Town's machinations were not limited in time.?

"The Town's arguments concerning Karin as the invisible Plaintiff are pathetic. Apparently, the argument is that they included Karin in the criminal complaint because they did not know who was making the blog postings. The argument goes on to suggest that being made the subject of a criminal investigation is no big deal since she wasn't prosecuted. The shortcomings of that argument are obvious. The Reply unwisely emphasizes the fact that the Town targeted your blog. Also, the law is unequivocal that political postings on a blog are protected speech and cannot be prosecuted. Finally, it does nothing to refute the line of cases saying that police investigation can give rise to a First Amendment violation if it would deter a reasonable person from speaking (even a little).

- The section on defamation was well done. However, we couldn't care less about that add-on state claim.

In summary, the Reply Brief probably was not worth filing for the Town and might have even damaged their defense. They left some very good arguments lying on the table.

The case is now ripe for determination by Summary Judgment."

178

"I continue to believe that we presented a very solid case to the Court. The facts were well-documented in the record and the law was well-briefed. If the Judge is even slightly sympathetic to First Amendment claims, we should do well. On the other hand, if the Judge is hostile to civil rights cases, there is enough here (barely) for him to cobble together an order denying you relief. That would be a travesty, and I am not expecting that result. It is merely a possibility."

As it was, the Judge rushed his summary judgment over the holiday and stressed that Griffin being bi-polar was the problem. When an attorney does not have anything, they hit the table hard and that is what Ms. Logan did, and she won the case in favor of Town immunity.

<u>We were not the only citizens who had questions about the lack of transparency.</u>

A loyal blog reader stated the following:

A NOTE FROM A LOYAL READER.
POSTED ON JULY 21, 2018

"I still have questions that were not answered in the recent budget workshop.

1. Mowing the right-of-way of US 41 the money the town receives from DOT is it $11k a quarter as Ms. Rivers stated ($44k a year), or simply $11k a year as Stacy stated?

2. Since we have not had a DOC crew to mow the right-of-way in over a year, where did the money paid to the Town by DOT for this service go?

3. Regarding the spending of local option gas tax money, when did auditors start dictating how the Town spends money? Is it not up to the Council and a legal opinion of the Town Attorney as to how funds are spent? I am quite certain if any administrative salary money can legally be paid from the gas tax for anyone, it would only be the portion of their time spent working on "transportation" issues. Seems skewed to me that from what I heard 75% of the money is spent on support and only 25% are spent maintaining our roads. I believe what the auditor recommended was that the Town document what percentage of the gas tax is spent on what not dictates that the Town spend those percentages.

4. We didn't get to the Folk Festival but if the Park paid the Town $3,000 for EMS & Fire Protection during the event and the Town only paid Hamilton EMS $2,000 where did the other $1,000 go?

5. Stacey stated Andrew Green does not receive any salary for Code Enforcement. Does he receive a salary for Fire Marshal? How much is he actually paid by the Town and for what? Has he ever passed the State exam and gotten certified for his position operating the Town water system?

6. How long is the repair in front of the old Environmental Center going to take? That section of sidewalk that is ripped up leaving an open hole that is a safety hazard to the public and it's been weeks."

LOFT FUNDS MISAPPROPRIATED

The Town of White Springs had not retained a restrictive fund for Local Option Fuel Taxes in accordance with the Chapter 336 of the Florida Statutes. Neither the Town nor its CPA has complied with the requirement to spend such funds on Transportation. Instead, it has been placed in the General Fund and used for Legal Expenses, salaries, including a salary for an employee who was unable to work for two years prior to retirement.

The statute states that county and municipal governments shall use money received pursuant to this paragraph for transportation expenditures needed to meet the requirements of the capital improvements element of an adopted comprehensive plan or for expenditures needed to meet immediate local transportation problems and for other transportation-related expenditures that are critical for building comprehensive roadway networks by local governments. For purposes of this paragraph, expenditures for the construction of new roads, the reconstruction or resurfacing of existing paved roads, or the paving of existing graded roads shall be deemed to increase capacity, and such projects shall be included in the capital improvements element of an adopted comprehensive plan. Expenditures for purposes of this paragraph shall not include routine maintenance of roads.

(7)For the purposes of this section, "transportation ex-penditures" means expenditures by the local government

from local or state shared revenue sources, excluding expenditures of bond proceeds, for the following programs:

(a)Public transportation operations and maintenance.

(b)Roadway and right-of-way maintenance and equipment and structures used primarily for the storage and maintenance of such equipment.

(c)Roadway and right-of-way drainage. (d)Street lighting installation, operation, maintenance, and repair.

(e)Traffic signs, traffic engineering, signalization, and pavement markings, installation, operation, maintenance, and repair.

(f)Bridge maintenance and operation.

(g)Debt service and current expenditures for transportation capital projects in the foregoing program areas, including construction or reconstruction of roads and sidewalks.

CPA Ken Daniels revised the FY 2016-2017 Budget 136 days after the Final Audit was done using Local Option Fuel Taxes to pay an exceeded Legal Service Budget.

At the February 13, 2018, Council Meeting, Town Manager Stacy Tebo recommended that the Town Council approve "Resolution #18-02 – Amending the Budget for FY 2016/2017". Tebo states that "(T)he legal services budget was exceeded by $13,879 (in FY 2016/2017). Expenditure increased from $15,000 to $28,879. Expenditures were reduced in Roads & Streets Machinery and Equipment by $13,879 (in FY2016/2017)." The Council meeting took place 136 days following the end of the 2016/2017 fiscal year, far exceeding Florida Statute 166.241 Fiscal years, budgets and budget amendments.

The Florida Statute states:

(4) the government body of each municipality at any time within a fiscal year or within 60 days following the end of the fiscal year may amend a budget for that year as follows:

(1) Appropriations for expenditures within a fund may be decreased or increased by motion recorded in the minutes, if the total appropriation of the fund is not changed.

A Motion to adopt Resolution 18-02 (was made) by Councilman Willie Jefferson and seconded by Vice Mayor Tonja Brown". Also voting for the motion were Mayor Bullard and Councilman Spencer Lofton. Council member Walter McKenzie voted against the motion. It was carried by a 4/1 vote. Discussion of the motion included Council member McKenzie's concern that it was illegal to use the local option fuel tax money, which was the revenue source for Roads & Streets Machinery and Equipment, for legal services that were in no way related to any municipal transportation project. FS 336.025.2 clearly states "County and Municipal governments shall utilize money received pursuant to this paragraph only for transportation expenditures."

Our CPA also previously stated how these funds could be allocated and his famous statement *"you may lean on the LOGT (LOFT) hard due to the funding of the Roads and Streets from other sources in prior years."* What was allegedly meant at the time was that we received FEMA and other money, which the County was not paid for in a two-year period and we were to pretend we used those funds by taking it from the Local Option Fuel Tax (LOFT) funds.

The Town does not have timecards where an employee fills out the time spent for the work completed as I suggested to the

183

Council, which the Council rejected. This is necessary also for insurance audits.

Our CPA received a second opinion from Purvis Gray and Company of Ocala whereby he changed his statements that the Town was to spend LOFT for excavation, any allocations, budget Roads and Streets and budget it all on one line item.

When discussing the fiscal year audit, the CPA provided the following information:

In the past three years the Town's Net Operating position has been $214,000. If we divide the total expenditures by twelve months our operating expenses come to $127,000 a month. Our Town does not even have two months of operating expenses. By adding the $90,000 Grant for the Willie Guy Turner Park it comes to operating expense of 2.4 months, but the Town needs to have at least on the low side six (6) months of operating expense.

Daniels felt that it is a waste for Staff to collect accounts but rather than wasting staff resources, all such collections should be turned over to a collection agency

The General Fund's liquid Net worth is $148,900. In a full accrual Statement Recreation of $252,236 will appreciate but will drag the net down by depreciation. Grant Revenue goes out of the operating funds as well as the sale of Land.

It was suggested by Daniels that the Enterprise funds (Sewer and Water) are not removed and placed into the General Fund. Last year it was $44,000 and Stacy Tebo feels that it is fair to remove such money into the General Fund as she explained to Mayor Miller later in the meeting, Yvonne works on the billings and statements and there is no charge made in the Enterprise Fund. Mayor Miller felt the only deduction that should go into the General Fund would be the 10% Tax on the Town's Utility Services, since it is a Tax and Miller is correct in accordance with the ordinance. Yet Tebo stated that out of that money we must pay for Garbage removal, which in my opinion is not sewer and water and is separate and distinct and should not be part of the enterprise account whether it is on the same billing or not.

Ken Daniels stated that we had a $124,000 drain on the Boat Ramp when we had not received the funds immediately. Then we overbilled the customers for water and of those overcharged twenty out of 400 have been paid by ordinance. Apparently although everything was controlled by our Town Ordinance, the Statute did not allow such payments to the customer per Attorney Hatton

It was also mentioned that if the Town has a bond, it should pledge its revenues to cover those bonds. There must be a Debt Service Fund. Apparently, we can't call it a "Budget" if one looks at our Revenue position. We have many deficits because we didn't finish those grants for transportation and Roads. We were told not to spend LOFT funds. When it gets to May and June don't budget 100% change our Budget to a fraction like 80%. One has to move from informal deposits to restricted funds debt compliance. Right now, we are holding $14,000 from FEMA which has not been requested to be paid back from Tropical Storm Debbie. Our Water and Sewer revenues were $321,000, which has lowered to $262,000 in Water and Sewer revenues due to depressed billings when money had to be returned to the customer. This caused an Operating loss in the Enterprise fund of $224,000 while $44,000 was moved to the General Fund, making our operating for sewer and water far worse.

Daniels stated it is the Town's choice as to what they wish to do because it is the Council's right to determine how to treat the situation. Note Daniels apparently has found that his advice, especially in writing was not correct, so he is trying to remove all liability out of his court and into the Town's Court. Comments from our CPA included "Wish things were better. Get a handle on it." "No policy or Commitment to Pay. Liquidity Sucks-Crippling the ability to run the Town."

Department of State give a reason for LOFT not handled by the State

The attorney at the Department of State I had spoken with regarding LOFT stipulated that the State virtually protects its municipalities and will not go after these municipalities, and a reason was given. **The State believes that Municipal CPA's have a duty to guide municipalities into spending money in accordance with statutes.** Instead, our CPA did not guide our municipality but rather found a way for the Town to spend, spend, spend on such things as paying for the defense of Tebo to virtually sue one of our Councilors, now Mayor Miller, and remove her from her seat and let's not forget protecting Tebo from a claim of discrimination against Anita Rivers, all from LOFT funds. Later in the meeting, when Councilman Tom Moore was concerned about getting an attorney general's opinion because of his fear that the town would be charged for the $750,000 of LOFT previously misused. I likewise provided the information the attorney from the Department of State relayed.

McKenzie, not understanding basically stated that we were not going to blame the CPA. Didn't he understand that I was reiterating what was stated to Joe and I from the State Department.

Trying to be in compliance for late reporting

At the May 8, 2018, Council Meeting, Ken Daniels CPA, the Town Auditor, presented the Audit for Fiscal Year ending 9/30/2017/ Mr. Daniels reported, "The Town did not amend its budget post year end". Yet, in his verbal presentation, Mr. Daniels urged the Town Council to rescind "Resolution #18-02 – Amending the Budget for FY 2016/2017", pointing out that

Resolution #18-02 was passed much too late (136 days) to be considered in compliance with the state statute (within 60 days). In his Management Letter, a key element of the Audit, Mr. Daniels makes no mention of Tebo's and Council's efforts to amend the 2016/2017 budget post year end in the section on Current Year Findings, clearly anticipating that the Council would follow his admonition and rescind #18-02.

The Agenda for the June 12, 2018, Council Meeting included the item "Rescind Resolution #18-02 Amending the 2016/2017 Budget" as part of the Consent Docket. All items on the Consent Docket are considered by one motion unless removed from the Consent Docket by a member of the City Council.

Councilor Helen Miller requested that rescinding #18-02 be removed from the Consent Docket so that a discussion of the item could be conducted by the Town Council. After some discussion #18-02 was removed from the Consent Docket, but Mayor Lofton refused to permit discussion of #18-02, as a stand-alone agenda item. Mayor Lofton removed "Rescind Resolution #18-02 Amending the 2016/2017 Budget" from the agenda. At the July 10, 2018, council meeting, Rescinding "Resolution #1802, Amending the 2016/2017 Budget" was again removed from the agenda and #18-02 has not been rescinded. The fact that Tebo used Roads and Street funds to cover her shortfall in legal services is evidence of further official misconduct wherein she misused local option fuel tax revenue restricted to transportation expenditures in violation of state law.

How our CPA initially handled LOFT Prior to the Audit Review

July 13, 2018, at 5:01 PM

Pam:

To provide an example regarding the use of the Town's fuel tax, I offer the following. The proceeds that the Town receives will basically remain the same —It's the allocations among departments that must change.

In the past (I'm using round numbers for an example), the Town received $100,000 in revenues (including $25,000 in LOGT) and was expended among departments as follows Administrative $20,000; General Government $10,000; Police $34,000; Fire $25,000; Roads and Streets $5,000; Human Services $1,000; Recreation $5,000 (Total $100,000) You must now allocate costs differently using the same total revenue and expenditure: Administrative $10,000; General Government $5,000; Police $34,000.Fire $20,000; Roads and Streets $25,000; Human Services $1,000; Recreation $5,000 (Total $100,000) You may lean on the LOGT hard due to the funding of the Roads and Streets from other sources in prior years. If I can be of further assistance, contact me Kenneth M. Daniels, CPA,

Hamilton County, which has an interlocal agreement with White Springs, is very aware that White Springs does not spend such money on Road Repairs or within the perimeters of the Statute

I contacted various departments of the government to secure advice of what could be done regarding the misuse of Local Option Fuel Tax funds. The Home Rule protects municipalities even if they know that the Town misused local option fuel taxes. This allows officials of municipalities to violate the statutes continually because they know there will be no sanctions against them.

LETTER FROM THE ATTORNEY GENERAL DATED JAN 16 2019

Dear Mr. Griffin,

This is to follow up on your correspondence to the Florida Attorney General's Office regarding the alleged "misuse of over $700,000 in Local Option Fuel Taxes" by the Town of White Springs, Florida, and related concerns.

This office appreciates hearing from you. We are sorry that you have been unable to resolve your concerns through the law enforcement authorities and agencies you have contacted thus far. In regard to the Town's decisions or actions, the Attorney General's Office is not at liberty to provide legal opinions or statutory interpretations to private individuals. This office does not conduct investigations of the types of allegations raised in your correspondence. By law, the Attorney General represents the state and its officials in civil actions which affect the state's interests, and our "clients" are "all the state departments and agencies from all three branches of state government, including their individual officials and employees."

See http://myfloridalegal.com/pages.nsf/Main/610a9a5cb51 e569885256cc6005c4e3e.

If you are seeking a criminal investigation, I can only suggest that you continue to address the police or sheriff and state attorney's office. Requests for an outside investigation or concerns about alleged conflicts of interest or ethics involving public officials may be addressed to the Florida Commission on Ethics and the Governor's Office:

Florida Commission on Ethics Office of the Governor
Telephone: (850) 488-7864

Telephone:	*(850)922-6400*
Website:	*www.ethics.state.fl.us*
Website:	*www.flgov.com*

I note that you have also contacted the Governor's Office, the Joint Legislative Auditing Committee (JLAC) and Auditor General. You may also wish to contact your local legislative delegation as you continue to address those authorities. The JLAC's contact information is.........

Pam Tomlinson, Finance Director, said the reason Ken Daniels increased the amount which would be spent from the Local Option Fuel Tax for Roads and streets from 5% to 25% is because we needed to catch up.

To my knowledge, only an estimated $6000 was spent in 2018 to fix the roadway in front of Mayor Spencer Lofton's residence. All other potholes remain undone. AUGUST 2018: Stacy Tebo indicated besides the bottom of the hill being filled by Florida Fill and Grade, which was the worst, She has ordered 2,500 pounds of cold patch in 50-pound bags and has indicated that a 50-pound bag does not go that far.

BULLARD AND OUR TOWN ATTORNEY KAREN HATTON ADVISED IN THE JULY 2018 MEETING THAT DR. HELEN MILLER AND JOE GRIFFIN WERE WRONG AND THAT SUCH MONEY COULD BE SPENT ON ITEMS IN THE GENERAL FUND.

JOE GRIFFIN SENT TOWN CPA ADVISORY LEGAL OPINIONS which were ignored

From: Joe Griffin Date: Fri, Jul 20, 2018, at 10:36 AM

Subject: Re: fyi To: Ken Daniels

190

Advisory Legal Opinion – AGO 94-20

Section 336.025(1), Florida Statutes, authorizes a local option gas tax of one to six cents upon every gallon of motor fuel and special fuel sold in a county and taxed under the provisions of part I or part II of chapter 206, Florida Statutes.[1] The statute limits the use of such tax revenues by county and municipal governments "only for transportation expenditures.

CPA KEN DANIELS INITIALLY ADVISING TOWN HOW THE TOWN MAY SPEND LOFT RESTRICTED FUNDS:

———— Forwarded message ————-

From: Ken Daniels

Date: Thu, Jul 19, 2018 at 8:36 AM

Subject: RE: The Attorney last night said "follow the advice of the CPA"

To: Joe Griffin

cc: Stacy Tebo "Pam @ White Springs Town Hall"

Joe:

Of course, you can spend fuel tax funds on the salaries of Town officials.

Pam accounts for roads and street expenditures, she takes minutes of meetings in which road and streets are discussed (obviously), bills are received and paid relating to roads and streets. Ditto for the employee who patches a pothole. Stacy manages employees relating to roads and streets ("fix that pothole"). Council provides oversight/direction.

All costs that are directly or indirectly related to roads and streets are allowable costs. The above must be incurred to properly manage the roads and streets located within the Town of White Springs. (Direction by Council; employee management by Stacy; budgeting, bill pay, and accounting by Pam, actual maintenance by Town employees).

Many local governments allocate costs based on the portion of the budget that roads and streets represent when compared to the total (General Fund) budget.

Costs may be allocated to roads and streets, including salaries, as long as any reasonable method is used. The Town has not allocated costs in the past simply because funds were not available funded via general revenues. The Statutes that reference the use of the fuel taxes are at Florida Statutes Chapters 206 and 207. Ken

END OF EMAIL

From: Joe Griffin

Sent: Wednesday, July 18, 2018, 7:12 PM

To: Stacy Tebo; Pam Tomlinson; Ken Daniels.

Subject: The Attorney last night said "follow the advice of the CPA"

Therefore, I want to see every letter, email, notes of any conversation, etc. where Ken Daniels said it was okay to spend Local Option Fuel Tax revenues on salaries of town officials. Pam had one of them last night. I want to see all of them. If there are funds required to get these documents this week, please advise me Thursday and I will bring the funds to you, post haste.

For Ken, please tell me you didn't say that, PLEASE.

END OF EMAIL

During The July 10th Monthly Council Meeting our Town Attorney Karen Hatton who is an attorney with strength in Criminal, not Civil Law, and who must be able to read statutes, was asked what should. be done regarding the spending of restricted LOFT funds and she told us to listen to the Accountant's CPA) advice.

INTERPRETATION of LOFT MADE BY WHITE SPRINGS' CPA

On Fri, Jul 20, 2018, at 8:10 AM, Ken Daniels CPA wrote:

Mr. Griffin: Please see below:

Motor Fuel and Diesel Fuel Taxes

(Ninth Cent and Local Option Fuel Taxes)

Sections 206.41(1)(d) (i.e), 206.87(1)(b)-(c), 336.021, and 336.025,

Florida Statutes

Authorized Uses of Proceeds:

County and municipal governments may use the tax proceeds for

transportation expenditures as defined in s. 336.025(7), F.S.

Transportation expenditures are defined to include those

expenditures by the local government from local or state-shared

revenue sources, excluding expenditures of bond proceeds, for the

193

following programs.

1. Public transportation operations and maintenance.

2. Roadway and right-of-way maintenance and equipment and

structures used primarily for the storage and maintenance of such

equipment.

3. Roadway and right-of-way drainage.

4. Street lighting installation, operation, maintenance, and repair.

5. Traffic signs, traffic engineering, signalization, and pavement

markings installation, operation, maintenance, and repair.

6. Bridge maintenance and operation.

7. Debt service and current expenditures for transportation capital

projects in the foregoing program areas, including construction or

reconstruction of roads and sidewalks.

My interpretation of the above is that transportation does not exist in a vacuum. It requires oversight and direction. The term "operations" appears to be a very large umbrella and encompasses a broad range of services including management. I find no Attorney General Ruling to the contrary.

However, if there is any ambiguity in the term "operations", I would suggest that the Town's Attorney provide an opinion. Of course, I would defer to the legal interpretation.

Ken Daniels CPA

END OF EMAIL

JOE GRIFFIN ADVISES CPA THAT THE CPA USED THE WRONG STATUTE

From: Joe Griffin

Sent: Thursday, July 19, 2018 9:22 PM

To: Ken Daniels

Subject: fyi

Mr. Daniels bemused Statutes which require the payment of taxes to a State with the Taxes already received by the State for which the State allows a portion to each county and subsequently to a Municipality through an interlocal agreement with the county.

Florida Statute Chapter 336.025 explains each detail and is a restrictive fund statute. 206 and 207, County transportation system; levy of local option fuel tax on motor fuel and diesel fuel.—is not the correct statute;

PLEASE PROVE TO ME THAT I AM WRONG.

Joe Griffin

END OF EMAIL

The Town of Jennings and Hamilton County separates LOFT

In the Jasper News of September 2018, it was noted that Jennings, Florida's Budget Summary for the Fiscal Year 2018-2019 had THREE COLUMNS FOR ESTIMATED REVENUES AND THREE COLUMNS FOR EXPENDITURES/EXPENSES There was a General Fund Column; A special Revenue Fund and a Total In their Special Revenue fund they showed $35,300 Cash on hand, $4,700 Miscellaneous Revenues and a $18,000 "Transfer in"; but most importantly their $230,000 Local Option Fuel Tax is listed within that fund as Intergovernmental Revenue. In the Roads and Streets Special Revenue Fund column, they show $265,700 including the $230,000 of Intergovernmental LOFT.

Then there is Hamilton County Board of County Commissioner's Budget Summary for Fiscal Year 2018-2019. There are Four Columns: General Fund; Special Revenue Funds; Enterprise Funds and a Total Budget. Again, Hamilton County shows Intergovernmental Revenues of $12,701,949 under "intergovernmental Revenue of the Special Revenue Funds and shows Appropriated Expenditures/ Expenses of $13,200,716 listed as "Transportation".

JOE GRIFFIN's EMAILTO KEN DANIELS CPA is threatening

Maybe you can explain to me why Jennings and the County do things right with regard to the LOFT and White Springs is totally ignoring the law of uses for this "special funds" receipt, I'm looking at September 12th's Jasper News when it had both Jennings and the County's proposed budgets replete with legal uses of the LOFT. White Springs is blaming you for this mis-expenditure of special funds. Maybe the Attorney General and the Department of Transportation will solve this problem.

Your name and your emails have already been provided to each. Joe Griffin Citizen Activist

It may be mentioned that prior CPAs to the hiring of Ken Daniels for White Springs did not advise the Town to carry a special line item for LOFT.

Local Option Fuel Taxes

White Springs receives a 6.55 percentage of the 9 cent Local Option Fuel Tax revenue Hamilton County receives. This is in accordance with the interlocal agreement with Hamilton County. Although I have the figures for the years up to 2018-2019, I have made an estimate of what our Local Option Fuel Taxes should be for the 2019/2020 and 2020/2021 periods. Fuel Taxes have been reduced by reason of lower fuel costs as well as fewer trucks on the road, except of course during COVID-19 shutdowns. Based upon my estimate of $182,267 or $180,000, We cannot figure out where the money has gone.

White Springs		Hamilton County
FY 2013/14	$ 33.949	$ 76,607
FY 2014/	$ $ 89,246	$ 301,729
FY 2015/16	$ 118,653	$ 301,905
FY 2016/17	$ 165,231	$ 433,295
FY 2017/18	$ 225,490	$ 415,868
FY 2018/19	$ 210,738	$ 399,785
Estimated:		
FY 2019/20	$ 195,986	
FY 2020/21	$ 182,267	

Mayor Miller was the head of the administration for a period of one year, and in both the 2019-20 FY and the newly budgeted 2020-2021 FY, she has used Local Option Fuel Taxes

197

to float payrolls, insurance FICA etc. In 2019-20 FY $114,202.09 was spent under Street and Roads which most likely was all LOFT funds and is currently on the budget listed as restricted funds. None of these items for which LOFT funds were used followed the statute. In the 2020-21 FY, Mr. Whitehead did what was done before and placed $239,544.72 for Transportation expenses including payroll insurance, which doesn't qualify with the restrictions of the statute. That is more than the $180,000 anticipated as being paid by Hamilton County for our 6.55%. Of course, Helen Miller did what she complained other administrations did by transferring $50,000 as an interfund transfer from the Sewer Water Enterprise account to the General Fund.

I spoke with Helen Miller by phone to advise her that I noticed she also is using LOFT funds. Her answer was, we would not have had enough money to run the Town without it. The Town should be bankrupt, and we should have never bought the excavator but in the last year Helen Miller, as Mayor, apparently spent more LOFT money than in the other terms, knowing the State will not do anything about its misuse.

LOFT Funds were used for purchase of a MINI Excavator despite the Town owning a Backhoe

In August of 2018, the White Springs Council voted 3-2 to approve a 304 Echo II MINI Excavator at $47,000 plus a Trailer to be purchased from Local Option Fuel Taxes

Ray Vaughn said that he could use the excavator 50 hours a month because it is a lot quicker to dig ditches. He said he is not a rookie and worked with John Peeler's Mini excavator. He said the backhoe just can't straddle ditches. He said he can dig up unnecessary grown foliage; he can dig when there is flooding, around ditches, grass, tree limbs and trim near fences due to its versatility.

For years, I recall our budget utilizing the words "Public Works "since all our employees can do is to mow the grass essentially and clean ditches. The backhoe has not even been moved and when the excavator was used, a professional had to be hired (independent contractor). What the budget now states are "Street and Road" Construction. What the State of Florida did was change their landscape gardening classification to Street and Roads so if one unfamiliar with the Town of White Springs looked at our budgets, there would be no question for our spending LOFT funds for Street and Roads. Our people clean ditches, throw sand in potholes, and mow grass, except for one individual which also works with sewer and water. and he also has a consultant from Jasper assisting him in the sewer and water plants.

The Town's Budget for Total Roads and Streets Expense listed is $225,029. The Local Option Fuel Tax is estimated for the year at $210,738. However, Local Option Fuel Tax Funds are not being used for its intended purpose

The actual money for insurance for Roads/Streets was $13,804; $50,000 for Repairs and Maintenance; $15,000 Operating Supplies and $2,000 Road Materials and Supplies, Totals $80,804 In the "Roads and Streets Department, equipment, The new excavator is listed at an expenditure of $30,693 which is one-half of the cost, the total of which is payable in two years..

McKenzie was adamant about leasing an excavator, when necessary, rather than the Town purchasing an excavator. He was correct because, the first time the excavator was used, the Town had to hire an operator, and the excavator has not been used at all for months. Also, there were recommendations by council members to sell it.

The Council approved a Work Truck to be purchased with LOFT Funds

Instead of purchasing a used truck, the Town purchased a Chevrolet Silverado 2500HD 4WD double cab Work Truck. The Town budgeted $27,693 in Roads and Streets for the purchase of a new truck. Under the Sheriff's Association contract, the price is $27,533.55; this includes thee towing hitch needed for the trailer (for the Excavator which was purchased under Roads and Streets) and the tag. The truck is a double cab and will be able to transport four to five inmates. It hauls 14,400 pounds.

Although the Truck was purchased in part to transport inmates to mow grass on the berms, there is no longer an inmate program since Mr. Bell retired.

CHAPTER EIGHT – WHAT TRANSPIRED DURING JONE'S TENURE AS TOWN MANAGER.

Since Jones's conversations could not be understood, we elected to secure the Town Tape before reporting information on the blog.

We had no idea that Jones had a checkered past prior to his being hired but determined that when Joe Griffin advised Jones that he would need a background check and drug test, that is when all "Hell broke Loose" Nicole Williams, a relative of Jones sent out despicable blog and Facebook comments about Griffin and I for all to see. Jones started telling everyone that we were racists and that he did not need a background check because no one else had one, which was not true. Then we knew there was more, which somehow the Newspaper knew first. But of course, because Griffin wished to assist Jones, as did I, initially, he said Griffin's offer was bribery and spread all over that Griffin bribed him not knowing the elements of bribery. We had not offered him anything except our assistance.

Then on October 16th, at 8:21PM, Griffin drafted an email to Miller, Tomlinson and Town Attorney Logan asking whether the town or they personally had received information about Jones's fitness to be interim Town Manager, especially all criminal activity which Griffin was apprised of by a reliable source (Police records). The council made no response because a last-minute meeting for the next morning at 8:00 AM was scheduled.

The purpose of the October 17th Special Meeting per Mayor Miller was the "Discussion and appointment of interim town manager". Mayor Miller stated there was a Recommendation on Wednesday night by Rivers that Jones should be hired as town manager, because *"Jones is here – no other individual is here."*

The Mayor and Ms. Rivers not only violated the Sunshine Laws by not advertising or placing notice for others to apply but called a Special Meeting in less than 24 hours which was not CONSTRUED BY THE FLORIDA SUNSHINE LAWS an "emergency" since Ms. Tebo would not be leaving her position until November 8, 2019.

Council Member McKenzie stated that a good town manager needs to be resourceful. He stated that the area Jones must deal with, which he feels Jones will be good at is to bring people together. People take sides but a good town manager will not take sides and will find a solution, he stated. **McKenzie said that he hopes Jones takes the job, because he will get the people back together because we are on the same team. And if you have a good team, they will stand behind you. McKenzie said that in working with the staff here, one can say what they ought to do but we are a small town of 800 people, and we cannot just fire people. We must work with people because it is hard to get replacements.** He said, *"Jones will have to work with sta⁾ from a psychological, technical, and ..nancial standpoint"*.

Walter McKenzie also stated he hoped the feelings he has about Jones are correct because he feels this is a challenge that Jones step up to.

Rivers said the new software to protect our computers, according to Jones's suggestion will cost around $12,000 and Helen asked the Chief of Police whether we had any of the hardware. Jones stated we must control user access. Mayor Miller stated she does not want the same thing to happen to White Springs which happened to Lake City regarding ransom. Our system should be safeguarded, and Cyber security is important.

When Jones was interviewed by the Council, at the October 17th meeting, he mentioned his education with a 3.1 grade average at St. Thomas University for his MPA for which he did not receive a degree. At the time he indicated the Town of White Springs needs its own project software, milestones, and finances to capture everything that needs to be accomplished, but further stated he has no networking background. This means Jones has no education for conceiving, designing, and implementing computer networks for the Town of White Springs nor the ability to monitor computer system security and perform maintenance procedures. Jones stated he was good at database administration.

Jones likewise did not have Town Manager experience nor the financial expertise to assist our Town in bringing it back to the "black" since it is near bankruptcy. Jones only provided information about his work history and appeared eager to accept the Interim Town Manager position citing his MPA classes, which should help him as manager. However, since this was a rush to hire and neither Jones nor Mayor Miller stated that Jones had a checkered background. This hiring was devised in the "Darkness" without the Public's knowledge or providing the transparency needed so the public would be aware of Jones history without reading it in the newspaper or our blog.

Jones was hired as the interim town manager, with a unanimous council vote with remuneration of $25.00 per hour. He was told he could work from 10:00 am to 2:00 pm for a period of six months. Jones per one councilor was the person who would bring people together; thereby the council's vote was based on Jones' personality and that he was African American. This would assure the current officials would be re-elected in the upcoming April 2020 elections by the African American Vote.

Mayor Miller stressed Jones has had a 40-year career. (even if he had no Town Manager experience). Mayor Miller said that we need an interim town manager half time of 20 hours a week to begin the process. She then asked Jones about his commitments. Jones brought his dad up who he takes to adult day care. Jones stated he drops his dad off and his wife who works at HCP picks his dad up. He can be back in town at 9:30 a.m. The Council then decided that Jones's hours would be from 10:00 AM. to 2:00 PM five days a week.

Walter McKenzie told Jones that it is an exempt position. An exempt position is a role that is exempt from the overtime and minimum wage provisions of the Fair Labor Standards Act (FLSA). Exempt **employees** are usually paid a salary and perform professional services, while nonexempt employees are typically paid hourly and perform more manual or technical duties. *(EXEMPT POSITIONS REFER TO AN EMPLOYEE, NOT A CONSULTANT who may work what hours he chooses.)*

McKenzie said that Jones will be the bridge and become the interim manager. "And in time we may hire someone else, or Jones may love it so much that he will become the full-time manager." He stated, "we don't know where this is going and where it is going to end up, but Jones will span that bridge now." Jones indicated that he is making pretty good money with his full-time pension from Florida. Yet, when he spoke to Griffin and I before applying, he said he was willing to take on any job for extra cash. He was close to age 62.

At this special meeting when Jones was hired, Mayor Miller then gave instructions to Jones as to what he needed to do, since Jones, even though attending some meetings, had no idea what his duties would entail.

Ms. Tebo did not help Jones because it was not her position to do so. When she began as Town Manager, she managed everything from the beginning, without assistance.

The recorded Minutes of the meeting were cut off, when relating to the actual hiring of Jones as the Interim Town

Manager. The Notice of the Meeting was October 16, 2019, at approximately 9:00 pm, for a meeting to hire Jones on October 17, 2019, at 8:00 am, not giving sufficient opportunity or notice to the public.

When the Newspaper and others brought forth Jones' checkered past, there were various complaints among citizens including Griffin. Jones said Griffin was discriminatory and racist by reason of his telling Jones that the Town would need to secure a background check. But as a consultant he would not have to be subject to a full background check of his prior employment history nor would he have to take a random drug test even though he had a more current misdemeanor relating to cocaine.

Similarly, while retaining Jones as the Town's chief administrative officer on a part-time basis, the Council also retained Mr. Michael Whitehead through J&S Tax Consultants on a part-time, per hour basis to conduct a forensic analysis of the Town's accounting practices, procedures, and records. Mr. Walter Harry Davis was retained part-time, on a per hour basis for Water and Wastewater Plant Operations, and Attorney Logan herself is retained through her firm, Douglas & Carter, on a part-time, per hour basis.

At the October 30th special meeting, we finally received a verbal answer as to why Jones did not have to comply with an application, Attorney Logan confirmed that Jones was hired as a "Consultant", not as an employee.

After speaking with Ms. Logan after the meeting I sent her Florida's rulings by statute based upon an Employer's control, and nothing transpired. Attorney Logan appeared upset because of Griffin's complaints and gave us the following written response at the February Council Meeting to which Griffin's complaints had no validity of course, and for which former Vice

Mayor Brown became the victim of the council, after she wanted more time to review the information and did not vote.

My email to Attorney Logan regarding independent contractors vs employees.

Wed, Oct 30, 2019, 9:22 PM

From: Karin Griffin

to Attorney Logan

• *Florida uses a "right of control" test to determine whether a worker is an employee or independent contractor in most areas of the law. Florida courts have adopted a number of criteria to aid in making this determination. The criteria include:*

• *The extent of the right of control by the employer over the details of the work.*

• *Whether the person employed is engaged in a distinct occupation or business.*

• *The kind of occupation involved, and whether the work is done under the direction of the employer or by a specialist without supervision.*

• *The skill required in the particular occupation.*

• *Whether the employer supplies the instrumentalities, tools, and the place of work.*

• *The length of time the person is employed, and*

• *Whether the work is a part of the regular business of the employer.*

END OF EMAIL

THIS IS WHAT MILLER STATED:

When confronted with the need to secure a chief administrative officer after being given notice of Ms. Tebo's resignation, who at the time was the Town Manager, the Town Council acted to retain an interim town manager using a consulting contract with Mr. Jones, President and Owner of Countyline Design Business Services, Inc. Jones is a full-time resident of White Springs."

The contract which was issued was not a "Contract," but an "Agreement" and the "Agreement" made no mention that Jones was a consultant, nor did it state he was the President and Owner of Countyline Design Business Services Inc. The citizens had no adequate information from a Public Meeting about Jones checkered past, nor did they know he was a consultant until it was stated verbally, and it was not mentioned in the Article of the Jasper News nor was his firm "Countyline Design Business Services, Inc."

> *"Mayor Miller continued in her denial that the Council and the Town Attorney acted in good faith to identify and retain an interim Town Manager to administer the Town's affairs. She stated, the council and the Town Attorney had no corrupt intent, and did not secure special benefit for themselves, nor for Jones who was retained, under an agreement with his consulting firm, Countyline Design Business Services, Inc."*

Jones was given a contract per see, but a **"Memorandum of Agreement"** was issued on behalf of the town by the attorney.

"The Purpose of this agreement is stated as such:

> *"The Town of White Springs needs someone to serve as Town Manager on an interim basis until the Town determines the skills, experience and schedule it desires for a full time Town Manager and advertises and identifies*

an appropriate candidate to serve as the full time Town Manager. Jones has knowledge and work experience which makes him a logical fit for the position of Interim Town Manager. Accordingly, this MOA serves to outline the terms and conditions governing Mr. Jones's service as Interim Town Manager for the Town of White Springs.'

And then the Roles and Responsibilities stipulate Jones agrees to serve as Interim Town Manager for a period of six months, beginning October 17, 2019, up through and including April 17, 2019; that he works 20 hours per week, and accepts $25.00 per hour for all hours worked and authorizes. Jones to perform all duties and responsibilities afforded by the Charter to the employee ordinarily serving as Town Manager."

END OF AGREEMENT

Beverly Brazil volunteered for the town to assist Jones as of November 2019. Miller stated Brazil also assist the accountant with payroll and accounts payable as well as secretary at the Council Meetings. Although Miller indicated Brazil prepared the minutes for each meeting, those minutes in comparison with those done by previous staff were ridiculously non-transparent. Brazil would take an agenda sheet and just list brief explanations under each agenda item, and the sad part was the agenda did not contain full topics of what transpired at a council meeting. She was also the qualifying officer for the council election. Jones appointed Brazil as the Interim Town Clerk as a volunteer.

Miller stated in a letter, "The importance of Ms. Brazil's volunteering, and Interim Town Manager Jones' half-time status cannot be overstated as a cost savings to White Springs as we work toward an annual budget that is based on justifiable allocations of our various revenue sources. This is important for this fiscal year, since we are experiencing a number of unexpended expenditures, but also for future years since state revenue sharing / local option fuel taxes may decrease due to the impact of COVID 19 on tourism in Florida.

Helen Miller also stated that in November 2018 the Town Council retained an experienced municipal accountant to conduct an examination into the Town's finances. Due to limited time and availability as well as the Town's budget limitation he would devote two to three days a month to White Springs. The accountant said it could take 18 months or two years to complete the examination of the Town's financial records.

Miller said the accountant's first directive was the need to set up internal controls on all financial transactions by town staff. She mentioned internal controls have consistently been suggested by auditors and the state and disregarded by town staff over the years. She believed the Charter to be at blame for the conflict, which she said requires revision.

Town Business continued, at least at meetings:

Chief Pittman introduced a buyer for the old fire engine. Century made a Bid for the 1983 Fire Engine of $2,000. This was so Century could fix the old fire engine up and use it in the event an ambulance was not available. Mayor Miller asked Mr. Pittman if he recommended the sale, and he did. Consultant Jones endorsed the sale of the old fire engine which would be in the best interest of the fire department and White Springs. Tom Moore made a motion; Helen Miller seconded the motion; All agreed to sell the old engine 5-0. Mayor Miller thanked Chief Pittman for finding a buyer.

In December of 2020, Kellen Lindsey of Mittauer and Associate discussed the Mill Street Repaving project and has been working on it to get it ready to go, wrapping up the Kendrick Project. The town received approval from the Department of Transportation in July and Jones advertised the project for bids. The Town received three bids: Art Walker; Curts Construction and another high base Bid. Art Walker had the lowest bid of $221,224 which was over the construction amount of the grant of $170,000. or $51.224 over.

Mr. Lindsey said he would reach out to the district Department of Transportation (DOT), Kim Evans. What the district DOT will allow, since the project was funded with Florida Department of Transportation (FDOT), is uncertain. The town needed awards to pay $50.000 in additional expenses.

Tom Moore asked Mr. Lindsey to describe the project. Mr. Lindsay said the $221,224 was a bid for a DOT roadway improvement, submitted for Mill Street, County Road 136, or 3rd Street, to Willie Johnson, crossing the railroad. Demo and replacement of existing asphalt and making the road twenty feet wide, and with drainage, milling, and resurfacing. Also, proper drainage, signage, and safety striping at the Railroad. With the Sewer Project ongoing, Mill Street is not in it and only a small portion can get done through the Sewer rehabilitation project. There is not any major excavation on Mill Street to change anything on the bid.

DOT provides an additional $56K so we can begin the Kendrick Street Project which was posted on the blog on January 11,2020

The Council of the Town of White Springs, at the January 10th Special meeting, made a unanimous motion approving the Kendrick Street supplemental agreement to match the bid amount under 119.07.01.

We mentioned Kellen Lindsey, of Mittauer and Associates advised us that they ran into another problem with the Kendrick Street Project. Unfortunately, Art Walker Construction's bid was not the low bid, so we had to secure another contractor. The Kendrick Street Project is $250,000 and the low bid was

$310,000 and two others were over $400,000. Mittauer reached out to the Florida Department of Transportation to get additional funding bare bones.

Mittauer has spoken to Ken Evans of the Department of Transportation and managed to place together additional funding and timing of $46,000 and they are securing an additional $10,000 through The Department of Transportation Tallahassee.

Since we do not have the same contractor, it will be necessary to construct the sewer revitalization at Kendrick Street first so that the work is done.

Jones was asked as to what Funding may be left in the LOFT account, Miller also asked that he check with our attorney whether the LOFT funds could be applied toward fixing Mill Street.

Miller said we are over budget, and everyone needs to scale back if they can; It would be great to do the whole project; realistically with the Town, after it is found where DOT is and what funds are available.; *"We will work together. We don't want to send back $170,000."*

COVID 19 Resolution

There were definitions of COVID 19. Non-essential travel, essential travel, essential business, and non-essential businesses which were listed by the county, line by line. The Town considered posting it on the Website so people could get the executive orders Hamilton County has placed on as well as the Town Resolutions which may be discussed at the regularly scheduled meeting.

Jones was asked to input it on our website, but he stated that we do not have access to the Town's site, and we have to contact the site builder. It would take a day or two for the designer and maintenance person to place it on.

Vice Mayor Walter McKenzie suggested that we could place it on Facebook right away, but Town Clerk Beverly Brazil stated that there were too many pages for Facebook. It is hard to put eighteen pages up. Mayor Miller still wanted Jones to put it on the Town Website. We can just list the Title Number of Hamilton County's on the Town Website where all details will be acceptable by PDF link. (Hamilton County Website and Executive Orders.) It went on Facebook over the weekend.

Jones indicated that since the office was closed, he took ten payments, and took money, cash payments, with mask and gloves. He said, *"the last thing they want Is their water cut off."* There was a lot of cash being placed in the drop off. It is business as usual paying, in all forms, and he accommodated everyone, he told the council.

Mayor Miller asked Chief Pittman to coordinate with Manager Jones to secure the necessary kits even if one has to go to Australia. These suppliers of isolation kits are working overtime to distribute these supplies and there are many on back order as of now 90 days or more. A new vendor is donating many masks. Mayor Miller said we should have a good inventory of masks for the fire, police, visitors, and contractors who come into Town Hall. Mr. Jones has ordered masks as well as his having ordered local face coverings. He has ordered 500 3-ply masks and has contacted a local lady who is making one hundred masks which are washable and tie up, so we will have 600 masks. Mr. Jones has given some masks to our local businesses; Roosters; The Hardware Store; Whistling Dixie; Munchies; and American Canoe. **Initially Jones had forgotten Mayor Miller's prior request, so the ordering of masks was delayed by a month.**

Light Standard down at the Fylia residence

At the March 10th Meeting, we were told that of the $19,000 it will cost to repair the light standard, which was hit by a vehicle, landing on the Fylia residential property, that the

Town received $16,700 from the Florida Municipal Insurance Trust. Jones did not realize that there is depreciation involved for outside fixtures as well as deductibles. Now the Insurance Company will subrogate for its costs, and I do not know if FMIT will subrogate for the deductible to be returned to White Springs. As of now, the Town will be conducting much of the electrical installation through Ray Vaughn, It will cost $4,000 to stop traffic by the State. The Town will buy the pole and Ray Vaughn will install it. Farron Fylia waited months to have the lite standard erected.

APPRAISERS OFFICE CONFIRMS THAT THE CARVER PROPERTY IS OUTSIDE OF THE TOWN LIMITS and other issues of the December 2020 meeting.

The Community Center is still closed and further deteriorating. There are no funds or volunteers to renovate the Center.

The Excavator has not yet been sold as was intended before Stacy Tebo resigned.

The Old Jail was to have been sold per the Town council, after an appraisal was received of $27,000. Now consideration is being made to lease it. How much does our Risks of Direct Physical Loss Property Insurance with named Hurricane coverage cost? Has anyone at town hall figured out what we pay on that building property and liability insurance, what repairs need to be made or have been made, and has that amount been incorporated into the monthly fee for leasing the building? I am certain the answer is "No," so we will just continue bleeding money.

I inquired of Mayor Miller as to what the financial condition of the town is. She promised me an answer within two months, which never was resolved.

There also were issues with the road right of Way at Mill and Willie Johnson. When the Dollar General was built, the Store had to buy a right of way and certainly there would be considerable driving to a new community center. The Roadways are not wide enough nor large enough so that one could purchase a right-of-way. Mill Street has homes close to the road and one of the homes has a fence right next to the road, so the roadway is far too narrow for vehicles to travel. The Town needs adequate ingress and egress so that emergency vehicles may get through.

David Goolsby, Property Appraiser for Hamilton County was questioned about "in the town property" and "out of the town property." **When asked about the "big 5-acre lot just west of the Carver School Building he said, "that is land outside the town limits"** The Property Appraiser said Josephine Acosta spoke with Jones stating we need to rezone that property (The Carver Community Center proposed building and land) to "public service".

Arlen (Scott) Gay stated an RFP needs to be sent out to planning firms. It was recommended that the Council use Tracy Woodard's statement of work paperwork to make an RFP. Scott Gay made a motion to obtain a planner and to use Tracy Woodard's statement of work for the RFP. Ms. Dorothy Brown made a second. All were in favor. It was recommended a statement of work be sent to the council to engage a professional planner.

Financial disclosure is required of public officials and employees because it enables the public to evaluate potential conflicts of interest, deters corruption, and increases public confidence in government.

The Town's travesties

The Town Council allowed Jones to reconstruct the website on his own, eliminating the site builder. On the prior Town of White Springs website, all meetings, agendas, ordinances, resolutions, and workshops were on the site, from the year 2000. Since it was the habit of staff to attach any ordinances or resolutions to the meeting minutes, it made it difficult to find an ordinance or resolution, without having it on the website.

After Jones concluded his site with wasted space and only including s few event ads and photos of the council members and managers, I asked Jones whether the prior site builder had a backup that White Springs could purchase so that pertinent information such as ordinances especially would be on the Website. I received no answer and as such there was a void for all future managers of what was pending and discussed previously.

Another travesty was the fact that Mayor Miller required Attorney Meagan Logan to undertake much of Jones' assignments and managerial tasks. Logan had to write correspondence on his behalf, rewrite various portions of the employee manual for the Town as well as handling duties with respect to vendors and updating charter information.

Attorney Meagan Logan charged $225 an hour, including duplication. She also made a flat charge of $250 for attending a meeting and capped her salary to $2,500 a month. It may have been more than Attorney Koberlein's hourly rate of $140, but in each of the months she worked, her hours were well over the $2,500 cap of her billings. I saw a billing for one month where Ms. Logan doubled the hours, whereby in the real world, she would have charged more than $5,000. I realize this was Ms. Logan's first Municipal position as an attorney, but, I feel, Miller and the council did a real disservice to Ms. Logan who was not only an attorney but used as a secretary for Jones.

Mayor Miller recommended she would like to waive the $15 late-payment fee during COVID and go case by case for the people who ask for a late fee favor. In this way, there could be documentation of all decisions which affect the town.

A Grant from Ray and Kay Eckstein Charitable Trust for the Fire Department

Arlen (Scott) Gay has secured a grant from the **Ray & Kay Eckstein Charitable Trust** for the Fire Department. He stated he would like Chief Pittman and Ms. Brazil to manage the matter. The funds given to us by the trust, may only be used for its intended purpose, Mr. Gay stated. Mr. Gay warned the Town that the money must be used exactly as we are told to use it, instead of being combined with other checks the Town receives.

Mayor Miller assured Mr. Gay that this administration would never use the funds for other purposes. *"Current administration and staff are not doing that."* Fire Chief Kevin Pittman stated the money will be donated to the fire department for turnout gear for the firefighters that can help our department acquire personal protective equipment products, such as turnout suits, footwear, gloves, helmets, and hoods for structural fires. Chief Pittman said he has completed all the required information which was necessary to release the funds to the Fire Department.

Arlen (Scott) Gay had been working with Chief Pittman to assure that our Firefighters may have better protection when fighting fires. Mr. Gay was a partner of Ray Eckstein until the latter died. Mr. Gay asked that a "Thank you note "go out, as well. Mrs. Brazil stated she would call Mr. Gay as soon as the check was received. Unfortunately, Mrs. Brazil quit her volunteer appointment with White Springs shortly thereafter.

THE COMPLAINT AUTHORED BY GRIFFIN

This complaint is brought by reason that the Town Attorney, Mayor Miller and Councilwoman Rivers hired Jones as the "Interim Town Manager" and worked out the details of his said employment in the "darkness", even advising him that he would have the job, without advertising the position, without notice and subsequently calling a meeting in less than 24 hours to hire him as rapidly as possible, without other applicants being able to apply, even though our then Manager Tebo would be remaining as Manager until November 8, 2019.

At the October 30th workshop meeting, Attorney Logan stated that the public should not have any complaints because Jones is not an Employee under Contract but rather, he is a "Consultant". Jones subsequently has reminded the citizens that he is a "Consultant" as is referenced on his email to Griffin.

Town Attorney Logan then had the Town Manager Consultant Agreement completed for the November 12th monthly meeting and although the council was given just a brief time to review the Agreement, Councilman McKenzie mentioned that Jones's hours should not be fixed under the contract as 10:00am – 2:00 pm because his position is flexible.

Meagan's associate who functioned as town attorney in Logan's absence from the first part of the meeting stated that we can substitute the work Hours "COMMONLY" between 10:00 am and 2:00 pm. The Council then agreed unanimously to the contract as written.

The Town of White Springs did not advertise for a Town Manager as required by law after Tebo gave her thirty-day notice on October 9, 2016, at a Workshop held on October 16, 2019,

Mr. Jone's resume did not list one specific professional service, and he was not certified or licensed in any capacity.

The Council members were advised that Jones had committed **only one** felony years ago and **no** misdemeanors and Jones himself stated that he was having his record cleared by the Governor. **When checking with Governor DeSantis's office, there was no such record of that request. With more than one felony and arrests which required him to be incarcerated for** over a year, it would be of little hope that the governor would even consider removing Jones's record.

When advising the Council of the actual charges, the response was that Jones was doing such an excellent job for the council, in that anything which was asked of him, including management decisions by the council, was accomplished with their advice. It did not matter that Jones had more than one felony which required his imprisonment and a drug misdemeanor which was the most current charge.

It is hard to determine what was intentional and what is not. But from the standpoints of the Courts, what is in writing and what is in a contract, not an agreement, will stand up in court and not verbal innuendos or a written statement which does not follow the Agreement, nor which was indicated in any Public Meeting minutes.

When Jones came into the position at Town Hall, there was a large stack of bank statements on Tomlinson's desk, which apparently had not been reconciled. Jones complained about that. But when Griffin had asked about the Statement from the 29th of October through November 5th, Griffin was given copies of the checks from the statement before and after......eliminating any evidence that the "Jones employee" check had **been signed. Griffin complained and Jones stated it's all the bank sent. Apparently,** the Town was no longer reconciling its banking statements.

If the Town is worrying about benefits, by making Jones a consultant who would work only 20 hours a week there is no requirements the Town would have to pay benefits anyway. President Obama changed the full-time employee hours to 30, during his administration On January 8, 2014, a bill was passed by the house of representatives replacing Obamacare's definition of a full-time employee from someone who averages 30 hours per week to someone who averages 40. hours. When Obamacare came out with such high premiums, most larger employers, especially those of factories and with blue collar jobs could not afford to provide the high premium for full-time employee benefits so many chose to make their employees part-time and under 30 hours, so the employers no longer had to pay for benefits.

Town Attorney's response to Griffin's complaint that as an independent contractor Jones should have his own emails

To: Town Council From: Attorney Logan

Re: February 17, 2020, Citizen Complaint against Jones Date: March 3, 2020

"On February 17, 2020, citizen Griffin submitted a Citizen's Complaint against Interim Town Manager Jones alleging that Jones "is violating the law" when he creates the appearance of authority using his email address, phone number and office space to signify an apparent authority and an actual authority to bind the Town to contract provisions," when he is not an authority of the town as independent contractor. Although it is not clear what "law" Mr. Griffin was referring to, Mr. Griffin's complaints regarding Jones's status as a consultant or independent contractor appear to conflate principles of employment law with tort principles.

The status of an independent contractor, as distinguished from that of an employee, consists of a contractual relationship by one with another to perform something for him, but the one so engaged is not controlled or subjected to control of the other in the performance of the engagement, but only as to the result. Collins v. Federated Mut. Implement & Hardware Ins. Co., 247 So 2d 461, 463 (Fla. 4th DCA 1971).

Conversely, a principal in an employee-employer relationship retains the right to control the conduct of the employee with respect to the engagement entrusted to him. Id. The recognized distinction between an employee and an independent contractor is determined by whether the person is subject to or whether he is free from control about the details of the engagements. Id.

See also, Edwards v. Caulfield 560 So. 2d 364, 371-72 (Fla. 1st DCA 1990) (concluding that injured worker was an independent contractor and not an employee where worker had an "employment agreement" that allowed either party to terminate the relationship at any time, worker received no fringe benefits associated with an employer/employee relationship and had "complete control over the details of her work.")

In the present case, the Town of White Springs was clear in its intent that it desired a temporary arrangement with Jones without the formalities of an employment relationship, including a lengthy term of employment with the inability to terminate the relationship without cause, receipt and payment of fringe benefits and the continued expectation of employment. However, just because one is not deemed an employee does not mean the principal or entity utilizing a consultant or independent contractor will not be responsible for the actions of that individual under tort or agency principles. In contrast, under tort principles an entity utilizing an individual who is a consultant or independent contractor may be held responsible for that individual's tortuous actions (regardless of what that individual is called) even though the individual is not an employee. Although it is the general rule that one who hires an independent contractor is not liable for injuries caused by an independent contractor's negligence, there are exceptions recognized in the law of tort: Pope v. Winter Park

220

Healthcare Group, Ltd. 939 So 2d 185 (Fla. 5th DCA 2006) "

"Florida courts have previously recognized a ten-factor test for determining whether there is an employer or independent contractor relationship for purpose of tort liability. Keith v News & Sun Sentinel Co., 667 So. 2d 167, 170 n.1 (Fla 1995) (citing Restatement (Second of Agency, (1958)). These factors include.

(a) the extent of control which, by the agreement, the master may exercise over the details of the work

(b) whether or not the one employed is engaged in a distinct occupation or business

(c) the kind of occupation, with reference to whether, in the locality, the work is usually done under the direction of the employer or by a specialist without supervision.

(d) the skill required in the particular occupation.

(e) whether the employee or the workman supplies the instrumentalities, tools and the place of work for the person doing the work.

(f) the length of time for which the person is employed.

(g) the method of payment, whether by the time or by the job

(h) whether or not the work is part of the regular business of the employer

(i) whether or not the parties believe they are creating the relation of master and servant; and

(j) whether the principal is or is not in business. Id.

In determining whether the entity is or will be responsible for the individual's actions, courts will almost always look at how the outside world viewed the individual and whether the individual was cloaked with sufficient indicia of authority for the entity so that a reasonable person would believe the individual was acting as an employee or at the direction of the entity.

"While I do not believe the above factors as applied to Jones' relationship with the Town of White Springs would necessarily result in a finding that Jones is an employee for agency purposes, the Town's decision to allow Jones to utilize a Town of White Springs email address to conduct work on its behalf is only one factor (the employer supplying the instrumentalities and tools for the purpose of doing the work) of ten. (Likewise, in order to determine the existence of apparent agency, it must be determined that 1) There was a representation by the principal; 2) the injured party relied on that representation; and 3) the injured party changed position in reliance upon the representation and suffered detriment. Amstar Ins. Co. v Cadet, 862 So 2d 736, 742 (Fla. 5th DCA 2003). A principal may be liable for the acts of his or her apparent agent that are committed within the scope of the apparent agency. (citing Life Ins. Co of N. Am v. Del Aguila 417 So 2d 651 (Fla 1981)) Id

"IT APPEARS THAT THE TOWN CHOSE TO MAKE JONES A CONSULTANT FOR EMPLOY-MENT PURPOSES FOR VARIOUS REASONS, ALL OF WHICH WERE BENEFICIAL TO THE TOWN, INCLUDING NON-PAYMENT OF EM-PLOYMENT BENEFITS SUCH AS RETIREMENT, HEALTH INSURANCE, ETC. AS WELL AS THE BENEFIT OF HAVING A SHORT-TERM AGREEMENT DURING WHICH IT COULD EVALUATE ITS NEEDS AND TERMINATE THE AGREEMENT QUICKLY, IF NECESSARY, WITH NO FURTHER OBLIGATIONS TO JONES.

*AT THE TIME, IT MADE JONES A CONSULT-
ANT, IT DOES NOT APPEAR, THE TOWN WAS
EVER ATTEMPTING TO DISAVOW HIS
AGENCY STATUS OR RESPONSIBILITY FOR
HIM AS AN AGENT OF THE TOWN OF WHITE
SPRINGS. RATHER, THE TOWN'S SOLE CON-
SIDERATION IN MAKING JONES A CONSULT-
ANT FOR EMPLOYMENT PURPOSES (AND NOT
TORT OR AGENCY PURPOSES) WAS THE
FREEDOM ASSOCIATED WITH THE ABILITY
TO TERMINATE THE RELATIONSHIP
QUICKLY AND CONCRETELY WITH NO
STRINGS ATTACHED AND NO RESULTING
CLAIMS BY EITHER PARTY. AN INDIVIDUAL
CAN BE AN INDEPENDENT CONTRACTOR
FOR EMPLOYMENT PURPOSES AND YET STILL
THE RESPONSIBILITY OF AN ENTITY UNDER
TORT OR AGENCY PRINCIPLES.*

*JONES HAS NOT VIOLATED ANY LAW BY US-
ING AN EMAIL ADDRESS ASSOCIATED WITH
THE TOWN. RATHER, HIS USE OF A TOWN
EMAIL ADDRESS IS ONE FACTOR TO BE CON-
SIDERED AMONG MANY IN DETERMINING IF
HE WILL BE FOUND TO BE AN EMPLOYEE OR
AGENT OF THE TOWN. GIVEN THAT THE
TOWN HAS AUTHORIZED THIS USE AND HAS
NEVER DISAVOWED JONES'S' AUTHORITY TO
ACT ON ITS BEHALF EVEN IF DOING SO MAY
RESULT IN HIM BEING FOUND TO BE AN
AGENT OF THE TOWN. MR. GRIFFIN'S
COMPLAINT IS WITHOUT MERIT AND
SHOULD BE DISMISSED."*

END OF LETTER

February 27, 2020, meeting - committee problems

A Special Meeting of the Council was set on February 27, 2020, with all Council Members Attending.

Although the prior meeting was a workshop where council members could not vote, this meeting gave the committee an opportunity for the members to attend the council meeting. **The motion at the end of the meeting was to continue with the Azalea Festival even though there were continual comments by Councilor Anita Rivers that White Springs does not have the money**. The following is a discussion of how the council arrived at their decision.

Ms. Sonja Small had been the President of the Special Events Committee since January of 2020, taking over the presidency from Ms. Paige Bullard who had worked with the Special Events committee since Tom and Madeline Moore resigned.

Mr. McKenzie stated that that No one knows what is going on.

Ms. Small stated that she was new to the Council but that in the February 6th meeting four people were present and at that time approved the duck races, vendors, and the bands which were $500 each.

Vice Mayor McKenzie stated there have been no regular reports of what was conducted at the meetings and there have been no notifications of when the meetings are held so that the public may attend.

There apparently is a binder where the information is placed as to the meetings and the minutes which are sent in to the Town Manager. When Stacy Tebo was town manager, because all the committee members have other jobs, she managed the meeting minutes from the notes the committee gave her. **Mr. Jones, our current consultant/town manager, stated he will not be managing the minutes of the committee's meetings and that it is up to the committee themselves.** The notes are sent to Yvonne Bryant, our Administrative Assistant, who then provides them to Mr. Jones. **Ms. Small commented that, since Mr. Jones has not overseen his voice mail for months, in her opinion this job is too overwhelming for him, and I am certain any information passed over to him is just ignored.**

I know everyone points their fingers at Ms. Bryant but, even the meeting notices and agendas are not placed on the bulletin boards, because they are held up on Mr. Jones desk for some reason. And since there has been no problem in receiving timely notices, until the Council breaks the rules, it does not appear Ms. Bryant is at fault, only the delays of our manager, in providing that information to her.

Vice Mayor McKenzie reminded the committees that they had to follow the Sunshine ample notifications so members of the public and the council could attend committee meetings, whether it is the fault of our manager, or the Council not providing ample notice. Although three days' notice is required, everyone was provided only a two-day notice. In fact, the workshop only had a one-day notice.

The problem is that there is no organizational guidelines for a new committee president to follow.

Sonja Small received no instruction and had no idea where the checks from the Town came from. Paige Bullard so kindly joined the 2020 committee and stated that checks were issued by the Town so the vendors providing the merchandise would receive remittance at the time of sale with invoices provided later. This was based on estimates, and Pam Tomlinson had overseen it, Mrs. Beverly Brazil said that if she receives an invoice, she will try to make certain they have a check within the day, approved by the council, and she then will give the check to the committee member so they can pay the retailer immediately at the time of pickup.

Ms. Small stated that no one from the council ever contacted her or the committee members until the recent communication with Tom Moore. She said that it was not because she did not attempt connecting with council members. She stated that she introduced herself at the Dr. Martin Luther King, Jr. event. She said since she became president, she has been busting to get things done even though she works, like the other volunteers who also have jobs.

The most difficult problem has been her inability to commit to vendors or bands because the committee had a lack of information from the Council or the Town as to whether there was a commitment. She stated that people have seen on media that the Wild Azalea Festival was canceled, which made it more difficult. I admitted to placing the information on the White Springs journal where the council decided at the workshop that the festival would not happen. **Vice Mayor McKenzie stated he had no confidence in the festival continuing and Mayor Miller stated it was a "rebuilding year" but it could not be voted on by the council, until the next meeting.**

After the MLK event, Ms. Small was told Jones was the Town Manager and that she would have to work with Mr. Jones. Mr. Jones then sent her an email REQUIRING Ms. Small to attend the Council meetings to report like other committee members, when she works. She was upset that Mr. Jones REQUIRED her to come to meetings and at that time, information was provided to Council Member Tonja Brown. Ms. Brown provided what information she had, but the actual information as to the meeting minutes was given to Mr. Jones who did not relay the information, it appears. Yet Ms. Brown was blamed for not providing information or giving the council misinformation.

Ms. Brown was also blamed for saying that there was no information relating to the Christmas Parade, but I remember Ms. Brown offering to assist with not only the Parade, advising the Santa Suit was missing and working with the breakfast for Santa committee event. At the time, a suit was going to be secured from the park and Council Member Tonja assisted with not only the breakfast but with the parade, as Spencer Lofton had done the previous year when he was Mayor. Council Member Brown even assisted with the preparation of food for Breakfast with Santa, and it sounded like the Committee also paid for things out of pocket because they could not depend on our Town Council for assistance.

The Town paid for the hot dogs and drinks and Yvonne Bryant. and the committee provided the pancake mix and syrup.

It was mentioned that the Town did not assist the Committee with the Veterans Day' luncheon and program so that the money came out of the individual pockets of the committee because the Committee feels our veterans are important and the committee and Ms. Small would not let them down Ms. Small also contacted Arlen (Scott) Gay for the $500 donation, he had provided for the MLK *event (which the Town had no money for)* and inquired as to what it may be spent for. Mr. Gay of course appreciated her call and advised what it could go for. Ms. Small has done everything correctly from what I have seen. The committee has always needed the decisions of the council but to date have not received anything from the Council or Manager.

Ms. Small because of work asked the Churches also for help through committee members. Ms. Small stated she does not take things lightly if she puts her name on the line and in the case of the Azalea festival, if the Council changes something mid-stream, she is out of the money personally. That is why she could not commit until such time as the council decided if the Committee would receive money or whether the Council would not provide money and cancel. Then the money she received from vendors had to be returned and how would the Council wish for her to do so?

Tracy Gotlib, a member of the committee, stated that part of the Committee must do everything at the last minute. The Band will cost $500 and that was the cost for any band but the Devil Jacks of last year is the band of choice, but the committee could not commit, even for local bands which would cost less because the Committee had no idea what the Council would allow in the way of money. She said that although the Budget states a specific amount, the committee has always tried to keep the costs down. Tracy Gotlib worked with Page Bullard prior to Ms. Small's presidency and is a valuable committee member. Griffin and I know her personally and she is also a very industrious worker and will do what she can to make certain everything runs smoothly.

Although former Mayor Bullard was aware of the Budget listing $5,000 as the line item for the Azalea festival, Tom Moore asked Mr. Jones to provide him with a copy of the budget to review. This was after Council Member Anita Rivers kept saying that our Town does not have the money and after so many comments of that sort, Bullard donated $1,000 personally. He stated that the only council members attending the Azalea festival previously were Tom Moore and Tonja Brown.

Ms. Small stated that when she became president, she never received any directions, just clippings and a few notes and no agenda was provided. Anyone can receive the committee's records. One can find the minutes book up front at Town Hall and Stacy Tebo took care of everything.

Anita Rivers stated she received no accurate minutes from the committee, from September on. There were no Minutes for October, November, and December. She also blamed Ms. Bryant, our Administrative Assistant, for not sending the agenda to the Council Members and the public. Yet, previously Stacy Tebo managed all that information for the Committees and Mr. Jones made it clear that he would not be responsible for handling that information. Ms. Rivers then stated that *"we are not being notified."*

Last year, it was stated that the Council and the Azalea Committee worked alongside Mayor Lofton, who was involved. Spencer Lofton knew what was going on and assisted with going to the Hamilton County Tourist Development Council (TDC) which yearly was providing $1,500 for Advertising. Vice Mayor McKenzie advised he is on the committee of the TDC. Yet TDC never received copies of checks and receipts from Pam Tomlinson and as a result if TDC provides anything at all it will be only $500 because no request went out. This was something Mayor Lofton managed when he was Mayor. As Ms. Small stated, she works and has a badge and a gun and cannot take time off work to manage everything.

My question is this. If Vice Mayor McKenzie was on the board of the TDC, why was he unaware that the Town had not provided receipts and where the TDC money was spent. if he was on the Committee. Why did not Mayor McKenzie, after obviously learning we had not provided such to the TDC either contact a Committee Member or Pam Tomlinson for the information and give it to the TDC. **From what I overheard is that when one of the committee members contacted Walter McKenzie to see whether he would donate some food to the "Taste of White Springs" he chastised the committee member so badly for asking, that they, the committee will never ask him again**. Many condemned the prior administration but obviously members of that administration worked with the committees, except for Vice Mayor McKenzie.

Sonja Small was never aware of the TDC grant but she filled out an application. She could not visit the TDC because of her business hours. She said she cannot do the shopping and Mr. Jones stated he cannot go shopping and do his job.

The Tourist Development Council (TDC) Grants Program is responsive on a quarterly basis to organizations/events which promote the County's appeal as a tourist destination by sponsoring tourist-oriented sports events, cultural, and special events.

Tom Moore stated that when he was on the committee, everyone had an assignment. The money was provided the vendors when receipts were submitted. Paige Bullard also indicated that she paid for all the awards, not the Town.

Vice Mayor McKenzie said he appreciates the efforts of the Committee.

McKenzie then summarized the discussions so far.

- There have been no reports to the Council which has not been properly informed.
- There have been no Public Notices
- The budget is as far as the money goes. it would be great if we raised thousands of dollars, but the budget is our concern.
- Communications are bad on both sides and not as good as wished.
- The TDC grant if any is a problem.
- The Council has a fiscal responsibility to the Citizens. The festival is in three weeks and all we have are bills. $310 for the Bounce house, $800 for the Azaleas from Nobles, and nothing for the porta potties at the Ballfield.

McKenzie stated that "if you saw a problem, you should have asked. It is the responsible thing with money." It was serious enough that Anita Rivers called a meeting.

It was questioned why the Azalea festival is being held at the Ballfield when we have an Eco Center so that Porta Potties would not have to be purchased and where people can go to the downtown businesses. In fact, the Hardware store is willing for us to use their area. Paige Bullard said that someone was almost hit by a car and that there is space only for three to four vendors.

There is also the problem of the Car Wash across the street (Which the EPA would have a fit over because the oil grease and dirty water goes right into the aquifer since it is not a regulated car wash facility). The new renter of the property on Woodard land can include anyone for free without paying the fees that the actual vendors pay to the Town. And the person renting the car wash can do whatever he does for his own business. Vendors would not come back if they did not make money. And the park includes more people so many vendors can come. There were 20 some vendors but it has been said that the Council cancelled the Azalea Festival, so they have not committed.

There is money in the Budget, but the Town of White Springs needs a return to profitability. They need to stop the outflow of Money. The Administrative Assistant was blamed for not sending things out when in fact since Jones has become manager, he has not provided our Administrative Assistant with the information. Nicole Williams asked why she did not receive notices. The reason she did not receive notices was because Ms. Williams had not attended a committee meeting for 18 months.

Council Member Rivers stated if we lose money on the festival, we cannot do it. It was stated that with no money, the festival cannot host events. Paige Bullard mentioned that the Festival Cost $5,800 and the revenue received was $4,800. After consideration of the TDC Grant, there was a profit of $2,500.

The council then questioned why we were securing a sound system for $800 from Donald Johnson. The Park always provided the Trailer and Sound System for free. The response was that now the sound system must be provided by Donald Johnson. That the Town's sound system is not adequate for a live band and then there was a complaint that the Band should have their own sound system.

A complaint was made to the committee that they must be accountable to the town with proper notice. McKenzie stated we have the money but cannot spend any more money than we receive. Anita Rivers said that "You do not spend everything in your bank account. A member of the audience explained White Springs is on the State Event calendar. Events are determined in advance. The Two major events bringing more tourists in are the Bicyclists and the Florida Folk Festival.

The most profound statement made at the meeting was by a man in the audience. He said that the Town does very little for the Citizens so the least it can continue with the Azalea festival. Finally, the council agreed on a price. Vice Mayor McKenzie made a motion for the budget not to exceed $4,000 and the additional donation made by Bullard of $1,000 would go directly toward the event plus what TDC offered, if anything, for advertising. Anita Rivers then seconded the motion, but the Council would not provide the $5,000 in the budget.

Why Council Member Rivers kept complaining that we did not have the money to spend on the festival various times throughout the meeting is a mystery to me. Our council should be collaborating with their committees and the public. And furthermore, with McKenzie on the committee for the TDC it just shows he is not interested enough in the Town to have advised Pam Tomlinson at the time that the TDC did not have receipts which Paige had previously provided Tomlinson. He could have helped but like Jones he must not think it was his job.

JONES retaliates against GRIFFIN

Griffin's Testimoney to Karin and in writing when he returned home FROM TOWN HALL

"Jones claimed on May 15,2020 at our bruhaha at town hall that I tried to hit him in the head. I was supposed to lean into the counter, stick my arm out and whack him in the head through the plexiglass and the iron bars. The truth is I pushed a stack of paper at him.

I got news for the Council. I will continue to ask for public documents as long as we have Sunshine Laws and Public Records Laws, I will continue to seek information from the town which has to do with how the Town conducts the people's (mine) business. I have the Supreme Court on my side. See Curry vs. State in the Government in the Sunshine Manual.

Beverly Brazil is complicit in this denial of Public Records because she is the Custodian of Public Records. Lawsuits, which I am close to filing, will be against Uncle Tom-mie Boy and Beverly Brazil. See how the Council likes them apples. Provide the documents requested NOW. from 15 October 2019 until 15 November 2019."

The police were called, and the initial complaints to the police differed from those which were taken on depositions. Griffin has suffered palsy because of taking prescribed Ambilify for his bi-polar condition so his hand often shakes, and he wears a ring. Also, the front counter which Griffin was behind is bar height over which there are iron bars and plexiglass Not having the statement of charges made, Mayor Miller demanded them at a meeting so that Griffin would be charged for something soon. In fact, Griffin left the building and waited for law enforcement which he hoped would be the sheriff's department. But instead, it was Police Chief Tracy and police officer Marsh, the latter who at one time man-handled Griffin at a meeting by turning him around abruptly. Pam Tomlinson originally provided Griffin with an actual first check which was not directly deposited, and Griffin lost it because his paperwork always landed on the floor of the office and was then thrown in the refuse container.

The depositions:

BEVERLY BRAZIL

In Ms. Brazil's deposition, she indicated that the nature of the dispute between Mr. Griffin and Jones was that Griffin received incorrect paperwork from Town Hall, still looking for a check made out to Jones in lieu of Jones' business. The reason there was no check was because the payment in question was directly deposited

Since the records of direct deposits are on QuickBooks, the attorney asked Brazil why Griffin was not provided with that. She believed he was.

Attorney Slanker asked Brazil to clarify her opinions from what she knew, was guessing and what she knew for a fact, since Brazil was prior law enforcement. Brazil stated that he wanted the check to prove that Jones was not a consultant but an employee of the Town.

Brazil stated Griffin basically walked up and directly asked for Mr. Jones at the counter. She then stated that once she got Mr. Jones and he was talking to Griffin, that Brazil headed back to her office and that is when she heard a loud bang. She said she did not see what caused the bang because her back was turned. She confirmed that it was just one bang she heard.

She turned around after hearing the bang to see what was going on, but she did not see a stack of papers had fallen on the ground because the counter was too high for her to

234

see. After that Jones asked if y'all saw that? He said, "Did you see that?" The attorney asked Brazil. Brazil said she heard it but did not see it. She further stated that Mr. Griffin never threatened anyone. The only thing he repeated to Jones was "Go lay down by your bowl."

CYNETHIA WILLIAMS

On Thursday, which was May 14th, Mr. Griffin came into Town Hall to pick up a 119 request that he requested from the city. At that time Cynethia thought she gave him the envelope at the time, and he went through it, and took out the paperwork. He kept the disc and pushed the paperwork back through the window stating "This is not what. I want. I've told them so many times that this is what I want, that I want, and I want that. and I want that."

Cynethia said Griffin was asking for a cancelled check and the cancelled check was for the employee, Mr. Jones. And Ms. Brazil came, and Ms. Brazil told him that, "Mr. Griffin, I have nothing else to give you, this is all I have, this is all I could produce, the bank does not have a cancelled check. The employees' payroll is a direct deposit, and I cannot provide anything else to you. I don't know what you want, but I cannot provide anything else for you."

When asked whether the Town keeps a record of the direct deposits, Cynethia said they gave him the information of the direct deposit. I did not look at the content. that was in envelope, but they told me it was a content that showed that he had direct deposit. She just gave him the envelope and she had not prepared the contents of the envelope. Mrs. Brazil did, and Cynethia said she was just in the front and was the one to give it to him when he comes in and she collects the fee for the 119.

Cynethia said "No, I was just fixing to say, and then the next day he returned he had copies of like checks, and this is what he came in and he presented it to them. This is what I want right here. I need to speak to Mr. Jones and Ms. Brazil. 'So, Mr. Jones and Ms. Brazil came out of their office spontaneously about the same time. And he--- Well, the first--- Let me back up. Thursday when he got the paperwork he took the disc out, but he shoved the paper back through the window and said

he didn't want that.

"So, Friday when he came in, he had a photocopy of something showing what he wanted. But Mr. Jones and Ms. Brazil both came out and said," "We don't have. anything else. We've given you everything we could give you. The bank has given you everything we could give you. We have nothing else." So, then he took--- He said, "But I want this know, kind of like hitting the counter, and I know y'all can get this for me. I want---." "I want this, You and I know you can get this. for me, and this is what I want." Cynethia advised Attorney. Slanker that he never took back the paperwork he had shoved through on Thursday. He only took the disc.

"Friday when he came, he had his own paperwork, and Friday he pushed the paperwork he had into Ms. Brazil and Mr. Jones. Ms. Brazil and Mr. Jones looked at it and they say, "Well, Mr. Griffin we do not have anything like this. We cannot provide you anything like this. So. Mr. Jones talked to him for a few minutes about it, and then.

Mr. Jones pushed the paperwork back through the window to him. Mr. Griffin say, "Well, y'all can get it, you can get it. You keep telling me you can't, so I'm gonna. have my lawyer, I'm gonna get everybody involved, I'm gonna, you know, I want this. and I want what I want." So. then he went to push the paperwork *back, but when he did. He shoved it through there, but he hit the window, and the window made a loud noise. So, the banging on the Plexiglas that was alluded to in the report was when he shoved the paperwork, and she was a witness.*

"From my knowledge he went to do this, throw the paper back--- It was from him putting the paperwork-- --but it hit the window." ATTORNEY. SLANKER: "We're recording this, so I just want to--- You are taking your hand and like directing it in like a straight motion like--- Like throw the paperwork back." "Well, yeah, because he was standing up, and I think it was this hand more. And he went like this if I'm not mistaken. I'm not sure which hand."

ATTORNEY. SLANKER: So, he wasn't just like slapping on the glass to make noise? "No. No." Cynethia said. "Well, I got nervous. I kind of stepped back. And I didn't know exactly, you know, I saw him do this, and then I heard the bang. So, I can't say that he didn't, you know, intentionally hit it. But all I could see is he went like this. I walked away." "He's been requesting this information of Mr. Jones for the longest. As of even today he's still requesting it."

At the time of the disposition, Cynethia mentioned that Jones had resigned. When she was asked about some sort of scandal leading to that she said she heard talk, but it was just talk and she couldn't elaborate on that because she really didn't know. "But the thing is that this has been ongoing, and he's still right now today he's called the new city manager requesting the same thing. And I don't know what he needs it for, or why he want it, I have no idea."

"He was making legal requests, he asks for the requests, but there's no way to produce that request because even

the new city manage right now has gone to the bank, inquired from the bank, and there's no way to get a cancelled check, there is no cancelled check." "And I think the new city manager herself has also like right now. given him the same information, but he said he doesn't want that information. Okay. So, he's very, you know, stern about that."

Cynethia did not hear Griffin threaten anyone "No more than, no more than he, "I'm gonna get my lawyer, and I'm gonna--- I want what I want. You guys can give it to me. . His voice was just--- angry. All I know is he said, "I'm gonna get my lawyer and I'm gonna get what I want, because I want what I want." Cynethia did not recall Griffin saying some variation of the phrase, "Go lay by your dish or go lay by your bowl."

"So, you didn't really hear much of the conversation between him and Mr. Jones?" "In the end I know Mr. Jones say--- I do know Mr. Jones said to him, "Sir, are you threatening me?" "And Mr. Griffin, if I'm not mistaken, say, "Well, you know what, whatever you say, I'm saying to you that I want what I want." And then that's when Mr. Griffin said to him, "Call the police like you always do. Get me removed. You're good at that. Call the police and get me out of here." "Griffin was speaking loudly but not screaming but portions got a little louder. And that's when Mr.--- After Mr. Griffin said that to him, Mr. Jones said--- he asked Ms. Brazil to call 911 and have someone come and remove him."

"So, you didn't really hear much of the conversation between him and Mr. Jones?" "In the end I know Mr. Jones say--- I do know Mr. Jones said to him, "Sir, are you threatening me?" "And Mr. Griffin, if I'm not mistaken, say, "Well, you know what, whatever you say, I'm saying to you that I want what I want." And then

that's when Mr. Griffin said to him, "Call the police like you always do. Get me removed. You're good at that. Call the police and get me out of here." "Griffin was speaking loudly but not screaming but portions got a little louder. And that's when Mr.--- After Mr. Griffin said that to him, Mr. Jones said--- he asked Ms. Brazil to call 911 and have someone come and remove him."

Cynethia mentioned this was a distraction which caused her to discontinue working and everything got resolved and calmed down when Jones asked Brazil to make a call. Griffin left the office. (He waited for the police standing next to his vehicle.)

"And Mr. Griffin, I like Mr. Griffin, you know. Nothing, you know, he's not--- He's not his self. He's, you know--- Yeah. But yeah, he has this condition you know." Attorney. Holmes asked Cynethia whether Griffins actions would be considered criminal, and she replied "I'm being honest with you, I don't know. "That's a fair answer," Holmes replied.

Attorney. Holmes then inquired "Let's just--- I don't want to get into too much speculation, but you mentioned earlier that there were some rumors involving Mr. Jones and is leaving A bank loan of some sort that might have been--- he may have been seeking that may have had some connection to his no longer working there." No, I don't know anything about a bank loan" Cynethia said.

'That's fine. Do you know anything about the circumstances of his departure from working there?' Holmes said. Cynethia said the only thing she knew is that. "he was tired of the aggravation, you know, from Mr. Griffin. And it just ---he said he resigned."

"And I know Mr. Griffin have a blog, and Mr. Griffin talks about people on his blog. And I know Jones has been

on his blog from day one. I don't know. Listen, I was not working there at the time, I was volunteering. I was a volunteer. I had just started, so I don't know what the whole issue was. I think I started April the 20th,

so this happened right after I started. So, I don't know. Ms. Brazil asked me, she heard that I was a good worker, would I come up and volunteer. And I came up to help out."

"No, ma'am. The Town Manager right now had the financial person to contact the bank and get everything pertaining to that check, or whatever he's asking about, and she has information from the bank, she gave Mr. Griffin the same thing. Mr. Griffin told her that's not what he wanted. So. it's exactly, it's still going on as of today."

"Well, see, actually, when he calls the request supposed to come in to me or the new lady that we have hired too. And it's just that, "I'm calling, I want my I--- I'm still looking for my 119. I want the check." "We don't have it. We don't have a check. There is no check. Believe me, if I could make one for him I'd give it to him. Because he wants it, you know."

TOMMIE JEROME JONES

The deposition was produced telephonically, and after being first duly sworn was examined and testified as follows:

Attorney. Holmes asked Jones to describe the nature of the dispute that Mr. Griffin had that day. "The nature of the dispute. Well, Mr. Griffin, he requests a lot of what we call public record requests" Jones said. "And I was in my office that day and that particular incident in involving a check, I believe, a check he said I had, and I was not giving it to him."

"And, when he came into the office, we had already prepared that information for him, and it was at the desk where he had in an envelope marked "refused" by Beverly Brazil.

He had refused it. It was what he asked for, it was what we had to give him. That's all we had to give him." Jones stated he had never received a check in the name of Jones. "It was two payments direct deposited, which was totally incorrect, because I was never, because I was never an employee for the town, I worked through my company. That was corrected when the accountant. David Michael Whitehead came in. I had a contract with White Springs. I was never an employee of White Springs. "We kept telling him there's no check made out to Jones." He said "Yes, it is." They told him "No. there never was a check made out to Jones." Jones admitted there were a couple of direct deposits which were mistakes and when asked if there was a record "Well, the person that did it was Pam Thomas. She was the town clerk at the time. Yeah, I mean, she sent it over yes." Jones said that was all included which was given to Mr. Griffin. "He wants a check and feels I am withholding it from him. I had no checks to give him. "When the attorney alluded to the Town being annoyed, Jones said "Not being annoyed, we just kept giving him. the same thing that we had to give him; we couldn't give him anything else. He was annoyed, we wasn't annoyed."

When the attorney mentioned Jones wrote that he had turned around walking back, he heard something crash violently to the floor, Jones was asked what the cause of that sound was. He said, "I don't know what it was because my back was turned, but evidently when I turned around and asked the front desk assistant what that was, evidently, he had taken that paper and reached through the pass-thru and I guess something was was on The counter and when he pushed the papers back toward, you know, through the pass-thru, whatever was there fell to the ground. You know, I don't know what it was. ""I don't know if he threw anything. But he startled the people, you know, the ladies in the office, and I just had to correct him, I had to stop him from doing that. "Jones said the sound that was a violent crash to the floor was something solid, something solid

"No, he was hitting the plexiglass with his hands. It was a minimum of at least three times. When I saw the last one, I heard the first one first one. When I turned around, he was steady up there slamming on the plexiglass when I turned around. No, he was hitting that glass intentionally." He was angry, he was angry. I know he smacked the glass. I saw him smack the glass. (In his original statement Jones stated that Griffin's body was gyrating)

The attorney asked whether Jones was familiar enough with Mr. Griffin to know that he has some sort of medical condition that makes his limbs shake to which Jones said "No." Jones said he had never seen him in a casual situation where his arm is kind of shaking a bit. Jones said that when he hit the glass, he screamed, "I want it now" Jones said that was a demand; that was a loud demand. "I want it now was a literal scream at the top of his lungs."

At that point, Jones turned around and walked back to him and asked whether he was threatening him. "He was, I mean, he had, had rage in his eyes. And I looked at him and he was demanding that, I mean, like it was a demand, it was a violent demand, and he wanted it right now! And I said "look that's all, he was looking at me, have to give you. The town has nothing else for you. And I asked him, was he threatening me because the way he was looking and the way----his posture, you, if that glass wasn't there, I think there would have been a confrontation in that office.

The attorney asked whether Jones told the officer that Griffin tried to hit Jones at any point. Jones said "He tried to hit me. He was trying to get to me, but he couldn't get to me. Yeah, he told me, you know "Just shut up and go back to your dish, whatever that means? I guess he was trying to call me some animal or something." Jones felt that line was threatening. "A verbal threat, you know, and with those actions of his leading up to that statement.

Jones said he was 63 and stated he doesn't work there. He resigned one week before being there one year. He said he got everything in order for them and left. "I couldn't

take it anymore" My biggest problem there was Mr. Griffin. Constantly, every day, emails, name calling, accusing me of things I did not do. "I have emails to all those things.

He accused me of changing the Town's employee application for my own benefit and I didn't touch it. The Town Attorney did that, and she verified that. He defamed me

for that kind of stuff. I have all this stuff in writing. Jones said "Well, I was contracted just like the Town attorney and the Town accountant. We had the same contract."

When cross examined by the prosecutor, he said "three girls, three women were called the "N" word. Yeah, he used derogatory terms calling me you just another black nigger, something like that. I retired up here in 2015, you know, after working 33 years with Broward County Transportation Department as an IT analyst manager, and somehow these people found out about me, you know, they needed somebody up here to do, you know, I guess with skills to do what needed to be done as the Town Manager. He recruited me, he and his wife, to fill in. And I think the mayor asked some people on. He came to my house one day and recruited me for that job I told him, I don't want to do the job.

I don't want it .I came up here to retire. And so, one day I went to a Town Meeting and what's her name, Stacy Tebo, she was the manager, and she had resigned, and they was

looking for someone, you know, the council do you know of anyone who can, you know, that you would recommend for this position, and people recommended me He was

there also (referring to Griffin). Yeah, we had a decent relationship until I was hired.

You know what happened when I was hired? This man was so corrupt, he came to me and asked me, "Okay, now, good, now you the Town Manager, now you and I can

become co-managers? What do you mean, co-managers? He stated Griffin said, "I have everything you know, everything, you know, we can run this town together. I said "No, man, I am not doing that and after that everything was downhill.

Jones further said, "He promotes this intimidating provoking persona. And I have been told by other people that you know he has actually made physical contact with people

you know, demanding things from them. One of the members on the board told me that he cornered her, you know, and grabbed her and physically accosted her. Yeah, at that particular time, yes, you know. You know, we're there to do the business of the Town and this guy is coming in there with all this loud noise, you know, talking, you

244

know talking the talk he talks, and acting you know uncivilized if- The way I put it.

Well, I called his bluff. You know, he told me to do that and when we did, he took off. Ms. Brazil called. She called. He found out what she was doing that he took off in his car, and they caught him out there in his car. Took off to his car. It was a bluff. Okay, if it is a trial, like I say, I have lot of information, even from calls he made to the previous Town Manager. There's some defamation of character, nasty, vile things he say to people. A lot of it' is there but I have actually –Yeah, some of its there and also, I have recordings on the phone too and emails.

Yes, I could have done some great things for that town and I did you know, to keep 'em from going under, but this guy was just ---He called himself a citizen activist. He's a citizen antagonist. Let me tell you one other thing he did, Ms. Slanker. The town is lacking, you know for money, revenue. We have very little revenue. So, the previous Town Manager went out and applied for some grants and they received the grants. But see, they wasn't thinking out front you know. Because some of those grants, you know you can pay them back with reimbursements and some of them you can pay the back with what they call advance pay. Once the contractor does the job, the contractor gets paid but reimbursement the town has to pay. So, we had, we had a $168,000 request from one of the contractors and we didn't have that in the bank. We didn't have that kind of money. So, we had to get a loan from First Federal.

And on the application, I completed it and it asked the question about any other ---it was a question about any other liens of judgments against the Town and the Town had been sued by one of the previous firefighters. Wut when I answered the question, I was thinking primarily about, you know, loans that the town had requested you know. And he called the bank and told the bank that's not true because the Town is being sued by a firefighter.

And what happened, he interfered with the Town's business and because of that one question, I think they still got the loan, but he called the bank and told them about that. And that was irrelevant because the Town wasn't responsible for that suit, the insurance company paid for that suit. Whatever, but these are the kinds of things he did. He took care of the Town business. He was angry and he was acting like an angry person. Because this wasn't the first tie, he was under the impression that I was withholding information from him. And, he had tried everything he know and that was all the information we had to give him. That was it. Was not withholding anything. It was direct deposit. No checks made out to Jones. He said there is. There isn't. There wasn't.

"*And what happened he interfered with the Town's business and cause of that one question I think they still got the loan, but he called the bank and told them about that. And that was irrelevant, because the Town wasn't responsible for that suit, the insurance company paid for that suit. Whatever. But these are the kinds of things he did. He took care of the Town business. A He was angry, and he was acting like an angry an angry person. Because this wasn't the first time. He was under the impression that I was withholding information from him. And he had tried everything he know, and that was all the information we had to give him. That was it. Was not withholding anything. It was direct deposit. No checks made out to Jones Jones. He said there is. There isn't. There wasn't.*"

KARIN'S STATEMENT REGARDING THE CHARGE AGAINST GRIFFIN

White Springs Police Department Report Number WSPD20200068 05/15/2020 1 2:00 PM OFFICER MICHAEL B. MARSH WS2 – Deposition Assessment

With respect to the dispositions relating to Griffin's action at Town Hall on May 15, 2020, there are some points Griffin wished for me to point out. Contrary to Ms. Cynethia Williams stating in her INITIAL COMPLAINT that I, Karin Griffin, came into Townhall with Griffin two days in a row, I was not there nor a witness. In fact, because of COVID 19, I could not be in the office at the same time. Only one person may be in Town Hall at any given time.

Griffin had asked for a copy of the public record from Jones all year long. And according to Mr. Jones, the same information was provided to Griffin previously. Ms. Brazil in her deposition felt the information was provided to Griffin. If that check was issued by mistake, and another was issued, that could have been explained prior. Because no explanation was given to us, Griffin continued his search because he lost the copy Pam Tomlinson gave him.

"Mr. Jones stated, "That was corrected when the accountant, Mr. David, Michael Whitehead came in. I had a contract with White Springs I was never an employee of White Springs." Initially, Finance Director Pam Tomlinson did not know Mr. Jones was not an employee and the citizens did not know he was not an employee for a month after he became Town Manager. I am certain the reason he became a consultant was because of his felonies and two first degree misdemeanors which

would not have constituted him filling out an application in accordance with White Springs' requirements. Mr. Jones stated he had a contract, but he was only under an agreement. He did not have a contract drawn for the Town, whereby the Town agreed to its terms but rather, the Town dictated not only his pay, his hours, and where he worked in an "Agreement." He also did not take on additional clients but worked solely for the town.

We, however, did received what Griffin Requested from the new Town Manager, two days after she began her new position with the Town. It showed a correction by Mr. Whitehead to Countyline Design Business Services in which FICA was taken out and there was another per Mr. Jones' testimony on the deposition. A first check with the intent to have direct deposit is usually a paper check. Secondly, no citizen knew. until the newspaper mentioned Mr. Jones' checkered back-ground, he was to be an independent contractor. I had asked Griffin many times to drop the matter because after his complaint, the check Pam Tomlinson provided him was changed to Jones' company.

For the record, when Mr. Jones came up to the front desk to speak with Griffin about the incorrect paperwork given to him, he NEVER had his back to Griffin but stood in front of Griffin trying to antagonize him by first stating "Are you trying to hit me?" when Mr. Griffin was behind the bars and Plexiglas where customers stand. Then Mr. Jones asked, "Did you see that?" and everyone said "yes." Much of what Jones stated in his deposition was fabricated. i.e. Griffin never laid a hand on three women and the everything Jones stated regarding the loan at the bank was his version, again which was wrong.

Yet Cynethia Williams was closest to the barred Plexiglas area because her desk is right next to the counter so that she can respond to citizens making utility payments and inquiries. Although Ms. Williams stated she walked away, Ms. Williams remained at her desk the entire time. The only time she moved from her chair was when the papers Mr. Griffin shoved through the slot fell on the floor, she picked them up and gave them back to Mr. Griffin.

Although Ms. Williams stated both Mr. Jones and Mrs. Brazil came simultaneously to the front where Griffin was, Mrs. Brazil did not arrive to the front until later.

Cynethia is the first cousin of Jones and worked for him as a volunteer but because of the Florida statute regarding nepotism, she was unable to be paid and said she left for that reason.

In her deposition, Ms. Williams indicated Jones shoved the paperwork back at Griffin. "So, then he (Griffin) went to push the paperwork back but when he did, he hit the window, (possibly with his wedding ring since the slot is small) and the window made a loud noise." Ms. Williams solidified the pushing of the paperwork which caused the noise. The attorney said "So he wasn't just like slapping on the glass to make noise? "Ms. Williams responded, "No. No" Yet Ms. Williams stated that she had walked away when she remained at her desk. If that were not the case, how did Ms. Williams know that Mrs. Brazil contacted the police, and that Mr. Griffin left on his own accord? She would have had to have been at her desk the entire time.

Ms. Williams said she did not remember threats except "he (Griffin) was gonna get his lawyer." She also did not remember hearing Mr. Griffin state to Mr. Jones that "he should lay by his dish," which Mr. Griffin did state. What Ms. Williams could not have heard is Mr. Griffin stating he should be removed or to call the police "like you always do," because he has not been removed previously. His voice is naturally loud. She said at time his voice was getting louder, but he was not "screaming" as Jones stated because even I, Karin, have never heard him scream even when he has hurt himself badly.

Since Jones was facing Griffin the entire time, the only sound that may have been made was Griffin pushing the paperwork through the slot. Jones had not walked away. It is possible, Griffin's ring hit the plastic opening which was the noise everyone heard because of his palsy. Again Mr. Jones stood in front of Griffin the entire time and never turned his back on Griffin. There was nothing solid on the counter and Mr. Jones would have noted it if there was since he was facing Griffin the entire time. Jones knew Griffin did not hit his hand three times against the Plexiglas since he was facing him.

Furthermore, the entire time Jones was attempting to antagonize Griffin and Griffin knowing Mr. Jones was lying, kept telling him to go lay by his dish. Mr. Jones continually lies, and he did not see such a thing from Griffin and no one else heard Griffin hitting the Plexiglas except for one loud bang. Why would Griffin hit the glass intentionally when it was Griffin who wished the County Sheriff's Department to witness the actions of the Town Staff and Jones. Griffin has never trusted the White Springs' Police, who are political and now neither officer works for the Town.

To solidify the antagonistic attitude against Griffin by Jones after the May 15th incident, Griffin contacted Mr. Jones to see whether we could take a photograph of the Town Hall because Griffin wished to prove there was no way he would attempt or could hit Jones. Furthermore, the police report was written up 45 days after the incident, so we thought the former was the reason. When Griffin and I arrived, Jones had locked the door.

250

However, because I had a camera with a lens, I could photo-graph the inside through the window-panes. In some photos you would see Jones holding a camera directed at me taking photos. Thereafter, Griffin said "Enough" and told Jones to open the door, and he then did. Jones then put Venetian Blinds across the window of the entry door.

At the time of this incident, the rage in his eyes we found was a serious UTI in which I took him to the VA in the middle of the night. He also never assaulted a person, even though he was assaulted. That is until he became mentally ill after an incident in Town Hall with Vanessa George and took out his anger on me, his wife. He also was treated for cancer in one of his eyes, which left one eye smaller than the other.

Griffin does not hit anyone but speaks to them verbally and one of our Councilmen (McKenzie) did not like what Griffin said and hit him in the jaw. And another Citizen (Harris) came up to the porch and started punching him. Griffin did not hit back.

Mr. Jones problem was himself and his inability to perform his job as Town manager. Checks had not been deposited for a month at one time. If you look at his resignation letter the complaints, he made were about Mayor Helen Miller. Also, he stated "During my tenure, I have been steadfast at helping the town to recover from systemic narcissism schemes from within its own govern-ing body." We have a copy of his resignation letter. The problem Mr. Jones and the Town Attorney and council had with both Griffin and I, Karin Griffin, is that we stated Mr. Jones, to be a Town Manager, must be an employee and not an independent contractor/consultant. We also had information that no government agency would hire someone with armed robbery and burglary convictions to oversee financial matters. Plus Mr. Jones, it was obvious, could not perform his duties. And as one can see from the statements made in the deposition, he did not have a professional vernacular and that is why Attorney Logan wrote all correspondence.

Jones continually called Griffin Names among which were being a racist, and a drunk when Griffin rarely has a drink and many of these were in writing. I asked Griffin if he used the "N" word, and Griffin did not recall ever using it but he said with the names he was called, he may have done so but never remembered. It would be usual if any such reference were made to call Jones an Uncle Tom, but he did not recall either reference. This changed later after the incident at town hall, where his narcissistic tendencies took over and Griffin was heard calling people the" N" word to their face and when I intervened, he felt I was sticking up for the Town, which I was.

Jones said he was 33 years with Broward County, but his previous resume stated 23 years. Helen Miller stated he had 40 years' experience.

Initially Jones s stated when he was in prison, he received his Certificates for Water and Wastewater. Since Griffin had his certificates but never worked at a site, Griffin felt Jones could easily get his certifications back, provided Jones with at least three new books, two old books and notes on passing the test. We thought he would assist our Town, and he said it would be easy to pass, but he never tried to study, to our knowledge. We found later that he never had the certifications but was assisting those at the prison who had.

The first time Mr. Jones came to our home, he asked for a job trimming trees and lawn work for extra money. He did not sound like a man with a great retirement. We had discussed Jones with Mayor Miller but from the standpoint of Sewer and Water handling but did mention Jones did the coursework for an MPA but never received a degree.

Griffin wished to assist Jones until he was familiar with government issues, and it was not because Jow wanted to be a town manager. I, Karin, with a diverse background, also offered to assist Mr. Jones as a volunteer with finance and clerical if needed. But that all stopped when he lied about us and said we were committing bribery, but we had nothing to bribe him with. Nor did we ever bribe him or consider bribing him. Our intent was to assist but his cousins, three of which are on the council, were overjoyed to have a "Black" Man as Town Manager, whether he had experience. And one of the councilor cousins smeared our Facebook pages saying nasty comments about us as a result and how it was important to have a Black Man as our Town Manager with a Black Council.

Including driving time that day, Griffin was away from our home and at town hall for a period of twenty minutes. When asked about the time Griffin was at Town Hall, Officer Michael Brandon Marsh stated three…five or seven minutes at Town Hall. Griffin disrupted no one, any more than other individuals who were upset with the incorrect billing of their water, and a friend of ours when the Town would not allow electricity to be connected after his house burned.

In the original statements by the police officer Michael Brandon Marsh and Cynethia Williams, there was never a mention of shaking. That was something new to Mr. Jones who appeared to clarify that Ms. Williams shook her head. I must state that Griffin would have noticed because Ms. Williams desk is that near to the counter.

Our question raised is how that would be the case in the depositions unless they were trying to get more on Griffin?

But look at the Statement made about Ms. Williams by Jones: "She was shaking. She was shaking. She was shaking her head, and she was quiet. And she became very reserved for a moment there, you know quiet, you know." Cynethia Williams is older and indicated she was once a teacher, so I am certain she was not shocked about angst between Jones and Griffin.

Someone needed to tell Jones about the Florida Laws regarding recordings where the other party did not consent to. And Ms. Tebo took all of Griffin's comments when he had not received information from her to the State's Attorney's office. States Attorney Sigmeister and his assistant could not find anything construed to be criminal or defamatory plus someone needs to read the definition of "defamatory" before making such accusations and what it constitutes.

There was a meeting where a special resolution was required before the acceptance of the "Line of Credit". In that meeting, no terms were provided to the citizens relating to interest, our initial payment, etc. The next day, since we banked at First Federal, Griffin called the loan officer, Lucrecia Barber, to secure that information. Ms. Barber told Mr. Griffin that she could not provide that information to him, since he was not an employee. Griffin stated that neither was Jones an employee. But an adviser. Ms. Barber then asked what Mr. Jones was and Mr. Griffin responded that Mr. Jones was a consultant. Ms. Barber then said she would be calling the Town Attorney. I was a witness to that conversation as Griffin had it on speaker phone. It was, thereafter, the Bank pulled its loan. It had nothing to do about the firefighter suit.

The next day, Jones provided the loan application to us, and I am not certain why or if Griffin had asked for it before calling Ms. Barber. In the loan application, I, Karin Griffin, reviewed it and noticed that Jones did not include any litigation against the Town. I, Karin Griffin, was the one who provided the paperwork by email to Ms. Barber at the Bank. It was alleged that Mr. Jones contacted Mr. Preuter, the Fire Chief, while he was away on Military Drill, and told him to come back to White Springs to fight a fire.

Mr. Jones and Councilman Walter McKenzie met with Mr. Preuter thereafter Preuter's return and terminated his employment as Fire Chief. Originally Preuter asked for $30,000 plus attorney's fees. Yet, the case settled for only $30,000 because no one could prove it was or was not retaliation. FMIT denied any wrongdoing in the paperwork received from the courts but paid Mr. Preuter $30,000 for alleged retaliation. Yes, someone would not sue White Springs, unless White Springs was involved and in this case a council member and a consultant for White Springs were involved, whether the phone call could admissible with Florida law.

Jones felt if the insurance company would pay the judgment, it was not against the Town. Yet, with the many suits and judgments the Town has incurred, the town's premiums have been increased. There is also fear that someday the insurer will drop the insurance.

Shortly thereafter Jones resigned leaving many bills unpaid as he had previously mismanaged, even with benefits like Health Insurance. Mayor Miller then contacted us and told me, Karin, that she did not know what we had done with the bank, but she thanked us. She had created a monster in which he could no longer be managed because Jones had turned on her and we had gone through several meetings where the three cousins and he tried to defame her and stated she was unfair in her dealings with Jones. These dealings pertained to laws which were required to be followed and against all our advice and laws reiterated regarding independent contractors, she gave this man an opportunity she should not have, as she stated, "to save the Town Money." Yet, the cousins were ignorant of employment laws and felt Jones should have received benefits such as an employee would receive.

END OF STATEMENT

Griffin and I had to appear before Judge Sonny Scaff various times and Judge Scaff allegedly may have realized that the Town was persecuting Griffin, with the various disorderly conduct cases as well as injunctions. The Judge, knowing that I always provided research, called me his "second attorney." Judge Scaff had an ability I had never seen among judges. He would listen to testimony and know exactly who was fabricating a story and who was telling the truth. It was a sad day for Hamilton County when this great judge retired. He was the fairest, law abiding, of all judges I had ever met.

When Griffin and I appeared in Court on the disorderly conduct matter, it was determined that we would be going to trial. Instead, I came forward with a check book and asked if the matter could be dropped because it was a ridiculous matter to go to trial when all Jones would do is lie. After paying more than three-hundred dollars, Judge Scaff said he wanted the second attorney (me) to confirm that the case was being dropped. **To the prosecutor's dismay, Judge Scaff stipulated the charges to be nolo contendere** *(a plea by which a defendant in a criminal prosecution accepts conviction as though a guilty plea had been entered but does not admit guilt):* **The prosecutor still kept asking what the scandal was, and our public defender said he did not know.**

The Town required a loan from a bank to pay a contractor off, so the town could seek reimbursement. Other banks had high interest rates but First Federal, the Town's bank, offered **a Line of Credit** with lower interest rates. Jones omitted items on the application to First Federal but that was not the main problem. After Griffin's conversation with Ms. Barber and Ms. Barber's conversation with the Town Attorney, the bank withdrew its line of credit. **What I had been telling the council and the attorney was correct. An independent contractor/consultant cannot manage or oversee finances for the Town. Of course, if the bank had only known of Jones's checkered past, they would have never collaborated with him even as an employee of the town. There are no internal controls in White Springs.**

First Federal would have provided us with a wonderful opportunity of a line of credit to pay a contractor at least a portion of what the contractor was owed, (1/3) while the Town awaited reimbursement from the state. The Contractor completed the entire project, and the amount owed was over $300,000. It was with gratitude from the citizens of White Springs for such a great offering of a line of credit, **but the application also stated there was no debt and such does not show on our budget for 2020-21**. But we were advised, in a meeting relating to the Line of Credit provided by First Federal, that we owed another contractor $6,000 (Jordan and Sons from April 2020) and we owed money to Mittauer and Associates for work with an unknown amount.

The lawsuit by David Prueter stipulated that he is in a protected class due to his military status and obligations to perform service in the Armed Services. Jones and one of our council members met with Preuter after **Stacy Tebo would not follow the Council's request to re-hire Kevin Pittman as fire Chief. Instead, Ms. Tebo hired David Preuter as the fire chief.**

My understanding also was that the Town council members were going to request Mr. Preuter to resign his position as Fire Chief because firstly, he did not have any firefighters locally to serve with him. Stacy Tebo hired Preuter as the Fire Chief against the Council's orders. The council said he could join the Fire department under Chief Pittman, but he needed to resign as Fire chief. Ms. Tebo. In the meantime, left, and Jones was to oversee the matter for the council.

Manager Jones' comments about having a friendly conversation and requesting a resignation may not have allegedly happened. Mr. Prueter stipulated in his Jury Demanded Case in the Circuit Court for the Third Judicial Circuit in and for Hamilton County, that on November 16, 2019, **he was in Clearwater Florida with his Reserve Unit participating in active duty drills pursuant to his employment with and obligations to serve in the United States Army Reserve.**

On November 16th, a fire/emergency occurred near or in White Springs. Despite Mr. Preuter participating in military drills, someone at the town phoned him and demanded he leave his military unit to be present at the fire/emergency. This of course was impossible for him and secondly, who in White Springs would have dared to tell Mr. Preuter to leave his military unit? This does not make sense because everyone knows Employers cannot deny promo-tions, seniority or other benefits because of military obligations, and a Military person cannot be fired from his or her civilian job, for any reason other than misconduct or cause in retaliation for seeking re-employment.

But this is what Mr. Preuter alleged: "As a result of his inability to leave his active-duty drill assignment, the Defendant terminated Mr. Preuter's employment. He is stating that the Town not only discriminated against him but is claiming retaliation based on his military Status."

Jones had relayed to us at public meetings that he was going to speak with Mr. Preuter to ask him to resign. That did not happen, and all council members DID NOT speak to Preuter, telling him to leave his military post to fight a fire, so it allegedly had to be Jones or Walter McKenzie, the latter which I doubt. The case was settled in court at $30,000.

Mr. Jones had no liability, only the Town for what he may have said or not said to Mr. Preuter, because Mr. Jones is not an employee but a consultant. When asked about the termination of Mr. Preuter, he told two different stories so we are unsure what the truth may be.

Problems relating to communications and Jones' abilities.

When asked a question by the Council Members, a quick answer is given stating something has been done; **'it has been handled"** to find out it has not been contended with.

When asked why something had not been accomplished, there seems to be abundant excuses so one is not certain whether it will be done. There have been times when our mayor has asked him to **"please handle it now"**.

When we received $20,000 from Nutrien, $10,000 was to go for the down payment of the Fire Engine. Despite Jones being told that the remaining $10,000 was to be used for additional equipment needed. Jones paid the entire $20,000 to the Lender, leaving the Fire Department to barter for additional equipment despite Jones being told how the funds were to be managed. I believe one of the employees was blamed for not managing the funds because she left her employment.

We had learned through the Hamilton County Sheriff's office and County Staff that the officials and administration of Hamilton County were refusing to work with Mr. Jones, unless it was absolutely necessary, and as such they avoided all phone calls and person-to-person communications because they felt they could not trust Mr. Jones to give them an honest answer. This was a tricky situation since the town must work with Hamilton County and it is in partnership with the County.

It was difficult for the Citizens of White Springs to understand Mr. Jones' conversations at meetings, because he does not articulate clearly so that one may be able to understand him. It may also be that he uses an African American dialect of which Caucasians have difficulty understanding in mumbled tones. In today's world, one should be able to articulate the English Language if one was born in the United States.

The Town attorney did more work than Jones

Our Town Attorney has had to complete the Town Applications, the Personnel Manual, as well as writing letters of termination such as the letters sent to Yvonne Bryant, for which Mr. Jones should have had the ability to manage and research but obviously has no Human Resource experience. Jones terminated Ms. Bryant's employment after he found that she had stated she had a bachelor's degree, and she had none. This, however, was after Ms. Bryant went to her doctor to find that the Town (Mr. Jones) **had failed to pay for the employees' health. Insurance and had not done so for a year.** Retaliation is at its finest. Ms. Bryant had worked for the Town for years and could have assisted Jones but for the fact that Jones had not renewed the health insurance on any of the employees.

Jones dropped health insurance due to non-payment

Life and Health Insurance had an actual projection of $2,301.84 and Mr. Jones said there was a 10% increase in health insurance, so it was budgeted at $33,340.44 from the projected $10,359 for the prior fiscal year. Mayor Miller questioned the discrepancy in what was projected previously as compared to the current projections as being well over 10% and no answer could be given (*5 e answer, however, is that Mr. Jones had failed to pay the health insurance premiums from the time he had started as Town Manager, and it was not found until Yvonne Bryant sought a doctor's appointment and found she did not have insurance*). Jones was not in a hurry to contact the insurance company and stated he was going to secure more quotes. Someone must have finally told him of the urgencies since no employee had insurance, because he accepted the insurer's terms.

Your excrement was taxed

Also discussed at the September 15th workshop was the fact that the sewer utility was taxed by 10%, as a new commodity being purchased, for years. This means, the citizens' own waste was taxed. One of the major items related to the $16,000 in Sewer Tax which was needed to be recaptured in the budget by the Town. Initially because Jones did not understand the budget, Michael Whitehead added the $16,000 deficit to the Ad Valorem Taxes which only 16% of the citizens who own homes worth more than $25,000 pay. As a result, our Town Manager consultant Jones said that the Ad Valorem Tax of 6,00 should remain. Mayor Helen Miller was adamant that the Town should remain at the current rate of 4.39030. The latter was voted upon by a quorum of three, Miller, Rivers, and Nicole Williams.

It was determined the $16,000 deficit would be listed as an increase in the Enterprise Account. When asked whether the taxes would be returned to the citizens, Attorney Meagan Logan said "The Town doesn't have to pay you back a dime for the Sewer Tax which was illegally charged and that is because you did not know enough to complain about the tax and secondly since you did not complain the statute of limitations which starts at the time of your complaint in FL for debt collection, the four years have passed and the Town owes you nothing."

Every man is supposed to know the law, and if he voluntarily makes a payment which the law would not compel him to make, he cannot afterwards assign his ignorance of the law as a reason why the state should furnish him with legal remedies to recover it. Ignorance or mistake of the law by one who voluntarily pays tax illegally assessed furnishes no grounds for recovery.

The Town also never understood that their municipal insurance, like business insurance, does not cover consultants but employees and volunteers for liability due to negligence. That is because consultants must carry their own general liability and professional liability insurance.

Amanda Bruce given tasks which should have been handled by the Manager or Mayor.

Mr. Jones hired a young lady by the name of Amanda Bruce when he was allegedly feigning COVID-19. Ms. Bruce had no idea what to do and was given the task of attempting to secure a loan from First Federal among many other projects, because a contractor required payment of a $310,000 job for which the Town would be reimbursed for by the FDOT. Mr. Jones did not consider assisting Bruce, even by telephone. With assignments beyond her scope of knowledge, which the town manager or council member should have managed, instead of her. Beverly Brazil quit working for Jones after the charges were made against Griffin as did his cousin Cynethia Williams-McKire. He would no longer let Mrs. Brazil into the office and Mrs. Brazil not only had some experience in general accounting and clerking but is a retired Law Enforcement officer. Mrs. Brazil had to ask the council if she had permission to help Ms. Bruce, which the council approved.

When Mrs. Brazil was helping Ms. Bruce, checks from the Town's utility customers were found everywhere, but which had not been deposited in the bank.

262

Jones decided what he will or won't do

Although our former manager collaborated with various committees, Mr. Jones made it clear that he would not entertain duties for volunteers, such as putting the meeting minutes together as the former manager had previously done.

Jones stated that having to be the Public Records custodian, having the sudden resignation of the incumbent Town Manager, and a twelve-week FMLA leave of the Town Clerk (Tomlinson), forced him to be in an unfavorable position of performing the duties of Town Manager, Finance Director and Bookkeeper Jones blamed Mayor Miller for not providing options; however, it was the duty of Mr. Jones acting as town manager to hire the employees he so required and should have had sufficient insight to go through the financial records and stacks of paper of the prior manager to assure everything was done'

Finances are one of the most important duties relating to the administration of the Town and it shall be the duty of the town Manager to review such reports and reconcile bank accounts. Bank Accounts were unreconciled, by Jones and prior managers or the finance director. Although we have a forensic analyst on staff, **it was not Mr. Whitehead's duty to formulate a budget for 2020-2021. It was Mr. Jones duty**. When asked questions about the budget, Mr. Jones could not provide the answers and as a result Councilman Rivers requested Mr. Whitehead attend the budget meeting. The only council member to understand or question the idiosyncrasies was Mayor Miller.

The fact that Mr. Jones did not see fit-to-deposit utility checks for a month is not a good indication of a professional Manager. Mr. Jones did not pay bills, including Duke Energy, which provides electricity to our town and the office, during the time in which he had not deposited the checks.

Mr. Jones **did not check whether the employee's check had deductions for other benefits** such as the health insurance that had not been paid for months. Jones gave a reason for the significant increase in health insurance from $10,359 to $33,340.44 as a 10% increase which did not compute. Mr. Jones did not feel disposed to check what benefits and other requirements for payments were due during the year, which may have caused the increase, nor did he secure options. Instead, he kept working on computers and security. He may not have paid premiums since the time he started as the consultant/manager.

Mr. Jones did not act prudently and when the health insurance Underwriter decided to offer a reinstatement if the Town would pay the past due premiums. Jones did not understand he was given special consideration. Instead, he did nothing for over a week or two and stated, there are other insurance companies, which is not the attitude one should take in a pinch. He obviously had no experience with the health insurance issues which caused problems nationwide.

Since benefits were part of the employees' benefit packet, but not given to the employees by error and omission, the Town would have to pay for an accident or health incident as a result. Jones did not understand that. It may have been that the insurance company elected to reinstate coverage if the Insurer received the back premiums as a one-time deal, due to COVID 19.

Mr. Jones uses words that he thinks will sound good when answering the Council or Public (i.e. Mr. Jones stated the Town needed a bank letter of credit, when a short-term loan or a line of credit was required). A bank letter of credit is primarily used in international shipping and is a financial instrument that guarantees a buyer's payment to a seller is received on time and in full, if the seller meets certain conditions. If the buyer cannot pay, the bank will cover the remaining balance. The bank charges a fee to the buyer based on a percentage of the cost.

He also brought up a program pertaining to the County Appraisers determination of property values which would never be used by the Town, to show that he had expertise in determining Ad Valorem Taxes. And when we arrived at that point of discussion on the agenda, he quickly stated it was already discussed to not bring attention to the fact he did not know what he was talking about.

When the Mayor requested that the Street and Road employees fill out time sheets as to what they do in the time frame of a day, and a week. Mr. Jones said it was not necessary, he said he knew what they did, and finally some months later he stated prior to the budget he had employees fill out the necessary forms.

Although Mr. Jones hiring was based upon his computer expertise and skills, he was not a programmer and even had to have someone assist him on the new White Springs Website he placed together. However, the problem **with the new site is that there is no transparency; it does not include minutes of meetings, agendas, ordinances, the charter and all like information which our former site had**. There was wasted space and in comparison, to the County and other Cities providing no actual information. Subsequently one would have to contact the Town by Public Records requests to secure a copy of the meeting minutes, but Mr. Jones feels it is not his job to be the public records custodian so therefore, no transparency.

Because the new Town of white Springs website no longer has ordinances, agendas, or meeting minutes, this has caused havoc for predecessors. This is because no one kept physical records in a logical manner. (I.e., keeping the ordinance stapled to the meeting minutes, but not making a copy for an ordinance book or area). The sad part is that he never checked whether a backup of the site had been made, nor did he manage his own backup so it again could be placed online for the Citizens. The site only has photos of who is who and items on events in White Springs.

Mr. Jones did not need to work on the White Springs site with the budget problems we had at the time, but he allegedly felt Mr. Whitehead, another consultant who does not have a degree and is not a CPA, could render the budget. At the budget workshop Mayor Miller placed both in shame because they did not know what they were doing and had not even conferred with each other.

Mayor Miller attended the Suwannee League of Cities Dinner Meeting in January and secured a quotation from TrueChoice Technology out of Sanford. All departments in White Springs have had telecommunication problems with phones, high tech internet and safety, The Town's provider was Windstream. TrueChoice Technology provided a quote of $500 as compared to Windstream at $750 a month.

Jones as a Consultant/Manager was employed, to serve the council and the community and was to bring the benefits of his training and experience in administering municipal or county projects and programs. Yet, **Mr. Jones does not have the necessary training and experience and as a result lacked the communication skills which hinder the County from collaborating with us.**

The manager prepares a budget for the council's consideration, but Mr. Jones did not understand the budget process, the statutory requirements or the laws governing what must be done and **has passed on that responsibility to our forensic accountant/consultant who now is libel for any possible errors or omissions in the budget. Fortunately for him, the council has the last say to accept or deny the budget.**

Appointed managers serve at the pleasure of the governing body, but Mr. Jones would rather argue that the Council interferes with his job when he has not accomplished the job which the Charter Requires. By the time the Town Council realized the errors of their ways, they were fearful that Jones would sue them. He is African American and brought up the word "discrimination" various times. In fact, once Jones quit because of the bank loan fiasco, where the bank would not collaborate with a consultant, Mayor Miller contacted me and expressed how happy that he was resigning. This was after her inquiring about how Griffin managed to place Jones in a bind with the bank.

To confirm that Jones did not know his role. These are the following complaints he made against Helen Miller

Town of White Springs Town Manager Complaint Against Mayor Helen Miller Jones Complainant 7/12/2020

Complaint 1:

White Springs Mayor Helen Miller during the Towns regular council meeting by not presenting a motion to other council members for a vote violated the following section of the Charter. She made a unilateral decision in the presence of other council members with disregard of: Section 2.05 Procedures (3) Voting. Except when roll call is requested, voting shall be by the ayes and nays and shall be recorded in the minutes. A majority of the Council shall constitute a quorum, but smaller number may adjourn from time to time and may compel the attendance of absent members in the manner and subject to the penalties prescribed by the rules of the council. No action of the council, except as otherwise provided in the preceding sentence and in Sections 2.06 and 2.07, shall be valid or binding unless adopted by the affirmative vote of the majority of all members of the Council.

Mayor Helen Miller did in fact at the council meeting, in an act of indebtedness or subjugation granted Mr. Griffin a request without holding a vote, by making the "Complainant" Jones, the Public Records custodian. Due to the sudden resignation of the incumbent Town Manager and a 12-week FMLA leave of the Town Clerk, Mr. Jones was forced into an unfavorable position of performing the duties of the Town Manager, Finance Director, and Bookkeeper. Mayor Helen stated in the meeting, and I quote "When we hired Jones, we didn't' know he would be the Finance Director too." Instead of offering alternative remedies to compensate for the long-term absence of a Town Clerk (e.g. obtain another sourcetoprepare119requests), The Mayor made a knee jerk reaction to citizen Griffin's question of who the Public Records Custodian is.

Furthermore, Mayor Miller has intimate knowledge of Mr. Griffin's unyielding dogmatic style of making an abundance of public records requests. She has used Mr. Griffin as a tactical ally to debilitate the honest daily operations of her political foes with monetary stipends for records request. In the words taken from the Griffin's Blog, "The White Springs Journal" "In fact she (Helen Miller) was turning over many a $50 bill to us after we paid for those records or at the time she made her requests." Mayor Helen Miller knowingly and wantonly accommodated a verbal request from Mr. Griffin blatantly ignoring voting procedures on actions during a council meeting. Her act of Malfeasance during the council meeting has caused harm to Mr. Jones' job performance and severely hindered his office's ability to respond to records request with no staff to assist in responding to those requests. The mayor knew the outcome of such a vicious onslaught of requests from Mr. Griffin.

A custodian of public records in Florida is an elected or appointed state, county, or municipal officer who is responsible for maintaining an office that holds public records. A custodian may also designate another officer or employee to permit the inspection and copying of public records. The custodian must disclose the identity of the designee to the person requesting the records

Town of White Springs Town Manager Complaint Against Mayor Helen Miller Jones Complainant 7/12/2020

Complaint 2:

On June 17th, 2020, Mayor Helen Miller violated Section VIII of the Town of White Springs Administrative Manual Standard Operating Guidelines when she on her own accord made a telephone call to the editor of the Suwannee Democrat Mr. Jaime Wacther to place a press release regarding a mother alligator and baby alligators.

During the June 17th food giveaway, I heard Chief Tracy Rodriquenz vigorously explaining to someone during a telephone conversation that she does not make statements about Town affairs without conferring and going through the Town Manager. After Chief Rodriquenz finished her conversation, I asked her "who was she on the phone with?" She said Kara Compo, a news reporter. Ms. Compo wanted to know more about an alligator in the pond at the Black Bay seafood company. Ms. Compo's editor Jaime Wacther had given her an assignment called in by Helen Miller. I confirmed with Jaime Wacther the call was made to him by Helen Miller, and it was not an emergency, which would have been the only acceptable reason for not going through the Town Manager.

White Springs Standard Operating Procedures clearly states elected officials are to channel all reports to Newspapers, Television, and the sort through the Town Manager. This was a total disrespect of the policy and should not be overlooked as trivial.

The White Springs Charter states: Section 2.06 Powers and Duties of the Mayor and Council. (2) Official Head. The mayor shall be recognized, as the official head of the Town by the courts, by the Governor for the exercise of military law and for all ceremonial services.

Further defined: Mayors in council-manager communities (or chairpersons in counties) are key political leaders and policy developers. In the case of the council, the mayor is responsible for soliciting citizen views in forming these policies and interpreting them to the public. The mayor presides at council meetings, serves as a spokesperson for the community, facilitates communication and understanding between elected and appointed officials, assists the council in setting goals and advocating policy decisions, and serves as a promoter and defender of the community. In addition, the mayor serves as a key representative in intergovernmental relations. The mayor, council, and manager constitute a policy-development and management team.

Town of White Springs Town Manager Complaint Against Mayor Helen Miller Jones Complainant 7/12/2020

Complaint 3

The mayor has repeatedly tried to get me to terminate Mr. Vaughn for incompetency just on her words. Listed in the Town Charter, under Article III, Item 1 there are guidelines on the behavior of the Council or any Council Member. It states, Neither the Council nor any Council Member shall interfere with the conduct of any department head, officer, or an employee in the discharge of his or her duties.

The mayor blatantly during the May 12, 2020, council meeting interfered with the conduct of the Town's Utilities Department Director's duties which are solely under the preview of the Town Manager. The mayor gave directives to the Utilities Director on the supervision of his staff. She told him to implement a form to capture each employee's time spent out in the field. This was an effort to discredit the Town Manager's supervision of town staff. Council member Anita Rivers informed Mayor Miller that the mayor was getting into personnel issues governed by the manager. She was overcome with asserting authority for which her ceremonial title does not possess and continued her assault on the Ray Vaughn.

She went to the point of telling the Director how to design and when to start a work assignment log Again, this is not trivial but another blatant act by this individual to operate this government in a strong Mayor form of government. She has walked into the manager's office uninvited and told him of Mr. Benjamin's Fry unverified infidelity. She stated he only sits at boat ramp every morning meeting various woman, during work hours. During the April 2020 regular council meeting, the Town Manager requested the council to set a pay rate for newly hired Beverly Brazil. The mayor responded that is a personnel matter under the review of the Town manager. Now, how can this be a personnel matter not under the council's oversight and directing the activities of the director is not a personnel matter?

> By not placing time spent in work assignment logs, one does not know if the worker managed street and roads, mowed grass, worked in the sewer water facilities or in the office. Completed logs would assist in the classifications which are required also under Workers' Compen-sation' audits and Millers' guidance was necessary since Jones was unfamiliar with much of his duties.

Complaint 4: Beverly Brazil's Resignation

On June 3, 2020, at 10:12 AM, I received a call from Mayor Miller requesting a one-hour meeting in the Manager's office. Upon her arrival around 2:00 pm, she started in soft about Mrs. Brazil resignation trying to disguise a request to create a position for Mrs. Brazil. I informed her previously I was not going to create any new positions. She stated she felt bad because she brought Mrs. Brazil to me. I stated, "Yes you did." but that was Mrs. Brazil's decision to resign. Afterwards she started asking about the relationship between me and Cynethia Williams. She stated people are concerned about who is supervising Ms. Williams and I told her the Town Clerk will be the supervisor. She replied, "Oh that is your answer?" I replied "Yes, meeting over."

"Subject: Resignation"

Date: Wed, 15 Jul 2020 19:06:25 +0000 (UTC)

From: Manager

Please accept this email as my official notification to the town of white Springs council of severing all ties and responsibilities as Town Manager. All signature authority and credit cards have been shredded. I will contact Chrissy Cribbs of First Federal to confirm the termination of all my access to every financial account for which I had signing authority.

I choose not to work in such a polarizing environment of individuals.

May peace be with all of you.

Kindest Regards,

Jones Interim Manager

10363 Bridge Street

White Springs, Florida 32096"

END OF EMAIL

From: tjones@whitespringsfl.us >

Sent: Thursday, July 16, 2020 9:07 AM

Subject: Rescind Resignation

After listening to concerned minds for the ultimate wellbeing and continued uninterrupted operation of Town Business. I have been asked to rescind my resignation submitted yesterday. Hereby this email, I am rescinding the resignation.

I will not allow anyone to interfere with the duties of the Town Manager as granted by the Charter. All of the council members, urging me to reconsider, must hold any and every one, accountable for violations of the Charter. I will immediately place the person on notice, and I am holding my previous complaints as evidence of real violations.

Kindest Regards,
Jones Interim Town Manager
10363 Bridge Street
White Springs, Florida 32096"

END OF EMAIL

(Did Jones actually shred his credit cards? It is usual to return them to the council; and someone calls the credit card company to take Jones' name off as a user.)

The three African American Council Women Cousins had begged Jones to come back and Tom Moore who said there was no use fighting it, also did likewise. Jones wanted a Contract like the Former Managers who were employees. Jones wished for such things as severance for 13 weeks and a multitude of other benefits which he could not have without being an employee. **The African American cousins blamed the Attorney and Helen Miller who they contended were conspiring against Jones to not give him what he should have**. Council member Nicole Williams and Anita Rivers thereafter continually bashed our Attorney as well as Mayor Miller at every meeting. **Yet these cousins did not understand that Jones could NOT receive that which prior employee town managers were provided under contract. He was a consultant.**

Permanent Town Manager Interviews

Interviews were held on June 24th for the Town to hire a permanent Town Manager; The reason one candidate withdrew prior to the interview date was because our Town has had so many lawsuits. and of course, there is the matter of our blog according to Mayor Helen Miller

The interviews were a "cluster%&#*." Upon Mayor Miller entering the premises at the Women's Community Center, Council Member Rivers began her attack. First, Rivers demanded to know who decided on the Women's Club for interviews to which Mayor Miller responded that she did. Then Rivers went on and on about how the recorder not working, how the interviews could have been scheduled on a Thursday so Cynethia Williams could have run the recorder at Town Hall. Mayor Miller had orchestrated the connecting all of the applicants in day and time slots and on her behalf, *"You can't demand that all interviewees can come on a specific day."*

All this time, the Candidate with the most experience was sitting in the room awaiting his interview. However, the verbal hostility at the front of the room did not seem to bother him. Yet, he verbally stated he was annoyed because all the candidates, including Jones and Griffin, could listen to his interview.

Next Anita Rivers asked who made up the evaluation sheet to which Mayor Miller replied that she had. The arguments continued about what was wrong with the evaluation sheet. It seemed like it was too cumbersome for the councilors, and that each of the councilors had their own ideas of what they wished to ask. One of the council members said the form was for an evaluation of an employee who was already working for the Town. Anita Rivers made a motion to remove the evaluation form and Councilman Tom Moore seconded it only for the reason of having a discussion.

Mayor Miller explained that we have always had evaluations and after discussing numerous topics, Council member Moore said the first ten questions could assist him and everyone else to know what they are seeking. He tried to work the form in as a guideline, but council member Rivers would not budge. Instead, she stated she wished it to be removed.

Mayor Miller said the reason there was consideration for evaluation sheets was because we have three new councilors and that we have always used evaluation. Then Council member Nikki Williams piped up and said, *"Well where is that evaluation?"* Of course, the information was not there. And the council women complained that they had no input, and that Mayor Miller did it on her own.

Then there were comments about how none of the councilors had seen the form prior to just at this interview. Nikki Williams said she did not know if we were at a meeting or an interview.

The most amazing comments made were two by Interim Town Manager/Consultant, Jones.

First, he said that the form should not be used because it favored him. Then he stated that Mayor Miller had given him the evaluation a couple of months ago *(We also know this because Jones said he worked up the evaluation, then took that statement back, while Mayor Miller covered it up)*. Mayor Miller asked why he did not give copies to the other councilors. He said based on him being a consultant, that it was up to Mayor Miller and her attorney. And I, Karin, said, he is a consultant and should not be making decisions anyway. Then Nikki Williams said *"Mrs. Griffin, if you do not remain silent, you will be removed."*

The motion went through that the evaluation form would not be used in the interview process. Prior year's evaluations used a number system to rate the candidates which is a perfect example for government rather than just random' deciding one person may be the best and finding out they are not. But that numbering system determined who the best hire would be, but of course Anita Rivers and Nikki Williams know more than those who have had prior experience. You only need to ask them. Our new Council Member said that one of the candidates did not have prior experience referring to Griffin,

Mr. Emrich was the first candidate to stand up for his interview. He was upset that Jones and Griffin would be able to listen to this interview. Yet Griffin felt Emrich would be good for the Town and told him so. Griffin said he was there just to make things honest, and he really did not wish to be town manager. Emrich withdrew his application for Town Manager on the basis that allowing all candidates to listen to other candidates being very unprofessional and it has not happened to him in the last 30 years of interviews, and he walked out. Emrich later wrote me on Facebook advising me how wrong I was, when it was not my decision for this type of interview in the first place. All one can do in those cases is shine more intellectually and he may not have been prepared to do so.

Mayor Miller has done everything for Anita Rivers to help her to achieve a seat on the council and support her with the information needed. Miller stood up for Nikki Williams and Anita Rivers even though they put her in the Be Faithful debacle which cost our town money, and she has worked for them to have prime positions throughout. Miller also held Jone's hand and now he is slapping the hand that fed him.

Griffin withdrew his application. He was hoping that Emrich would have allowed an interview and would have been hired by the council, but he knew that Jones was the shoe-in. He decided that Helen Miller deserved her council and Jones. I felt badly for Emrich because he traveled a great distance for the interview, and he would never be hired because he was not African-American.

Jones quit and the Millers tried to have him shut down

Jones quit after he became the Town Manager. Because he was still remotely using our computers the last time he quit, Miller and another councilor were concerned. Jones used Town stationery for his "termination" letter. We believe he quit again so he could get the contract he wanted providing employee benefits not applicable for a consultant.

Miller, and her husband came into Town hall with our computer professional David for the purpose of David shutting down all the computers. Shonda Werts, who works one day a week in another position outside the office, had been helping Jones and was at Town Hall. Someone contacted Nicole Williams or the cameras in Town Hall were reporting the Millers were in town hall to someone remotely. Jones was paranoid and had all kinds of safety security features for his security.

Jones gave Werts instructions to not to allow Helen Miller or anyone else to have the passwords to the computer nor to allow them to be in Town Hall. Shortly thereafter, Nicole

Williams arrived. She was extremely nasty to them, telling the Millers they had no right to be in Town Hall. She further mentioned that Jones needed to finish some things, so they had no right to shut down the computers. David called the Security Computer people and had them remove Jones' access code. Part of this interaction was videoed on Nicole William's Facebook but only her friends could see it. I am not a friend after her disparaging remarks about us, so I asked a neighbor who is her friend on Facebook to show it to me and I was able to see it. Unfortunately, the manager's office was locked securely, and Helen's husband had a hammer in his hands ready to break the lock when Nicole arrived.

Helen Miller and Tom Moore resign from the council

In the meantime, Anita Rivers, and Nicole Williams verbally assaulted Mayor Miller at the October 10th meeting, bringing up the prior night's events. I tried to tell them that Jones is a third-party contractor, and third-party contractors must be removed immediately when he did not have a contract with the Town and was a non-employee, The council told me twice I would be removed if I was not silent.

An Activist from Lake City, Sylvester Warren III stated that Helen Miller should be ashamed of herself and although she may have done good things for the Town previously and she did, Miller needed to resign, inferring Miller treated a "Black" man differently than white people. Anita Rivers called Miller a racist and the attacks continued of Mayor Miller even though Miller throughout her last 10 years befriended Anita Rivers and Nicole Williams helping them with so many things as well as the town no matter what color one's skin was. Although the Saturday night October 10th Special meeting was to recite Jones resignation which pummeled Helen Miller for calling in the Sheriff's office, it was something I had never seen, and citizens attending the meeting were in shock. Rivers told Shonda Werts that she would be managing the office alone even though she did not have the experience. Tom Moore asked about her background, and it was slight. But she would be in control temporarily.

At our October 13th meeting, Helen Miller presented her resignation as of October 31, 2020. On October 14th, Tom Moore resigned from his position as council member. Sylvester Warren also verbally attacked Attorney Meagan Logan in the October 10th meeting so she may have considered giving her resignation, but Logan may not just resign without giving proper notice.

Jones, on Town Stationery. Gave his final resignation on October 9th, 2020.

"Dear Council Members: This is my official notice of "Termination" to the Town of White Springs. During my tenure, I have been steadfast in helping the town to recover from systemic narcissistic schemes from within its own governing body.

Having said that, I am appreciative to have been given the opportunity to serve the citizens of White Springs. The mixture of soft and hard skills I have acquired throughout my work life provided a buffer to the onslaught of biases I had to navigate every day. The town residents ought to have grown-up support from its electoral body. Instead, adolescent tactics prevail and dominate the order of the day.

Today Helen Miller came to Town- Hall and demanded keys to the front and side doors. I denied her request. She also pretended to have an urgent request about the "Agenda Package" for the upcoming council meeting on October 13, 2020. I informed her today (10/09/2020) will be my last day providing services to the town. She seemed to be surprised at my answer. She continued by questioning me about my intentions on attending the meeting for which I answered, "No". She pushed the issue and asked, "where would I be?" I replied "home." She continued by asking would I be submitting written notification. I answered, "I will". She wanted to know if I would be providing usernames and passwords. I answered "No." I was not going to jeopardize or compromise the security of those accounts.

As I proceeded to prepare pertinent instructions for all the access to numerous accounts, my network access was interrupted. I could not finish. Mrs. Miller had contacted David White of TrueChoice Technologies who then contacted the Town Attorney who informed Mr. White, it was okay to reach out to innovative networks to have the account associated with my login disabled. This is normal protocol, but not for an elective official unilaterally meddling in the daily operations of the Town Manager.

My resignation actions were peaceful with no intentions whatsoever to malign, destroy, disrupt, or coverup. Mrs. Miller proceeded to contact the Hamilton County Sheriff's office and accused me of removing town property, which is a bold face falsehood. The officer I spoke with name is P.J. Fouraker. I have provided training to Shonda Werts for all the front desk cashiering responsibilities. She is highly adept at the end of day closing and using the IMS billing software. Mr. Whitehead is aware. I will defend myself and take action regarding any and all untruths."

Instead of bringing forth instructions relating to what critical issues and finances would be necessary immediately and, in the future, Jones, in his letter, he gave the following instructions:

1. Complete the ongoing FY 2018-2019 Audit Sexton & Scholl CPAs
2. Employee Payroll.
3. Properly enter bills
4. Pay Bills
5. Blue Cross

CHAPTER NINE – WHAT TRANSPIRED DURING GEORGE'S TENURE AS TOWN MANAGER

After the October 2020 meeting, Vanessa George was hired as the interim Town Manager. She started her position at the end of November 2020.

The council appointed two Black Women to replace the two seats which opened by resignations. Anita Rivers became the mayor. The Town now had an all African American/Black Council and all staff employees were Black.

Sylvester Warren, although an activist, was a close friend of Vanessa George who also was an activist in Lake City. The Warren Family previously peddled illegal drugs to the tune of over $3,000,000, and each family member served time.

Vanessa George is a realtor with various businesses ties. She is a director of her own Daycare Facility, Lollipop, but has ties with NPI Profile, she is an MD Counselor and called "Doctor" and is involved with Twenty-eight fourteen LLC.

Since 2005, Vanessa George has been a licensed realtor. George is a native of Lake City, she attended and graduated from both Columbia High School and Lake City Community College (Florida Gateway College). Vanessa went on to Florida State University where she earned two Bachelor of Science Degrees in Political Science and Criminology. To further her education, Vanessa earned her master's degree in history which she used daily to educate students in the Columbia County school system, from a non-accredited university; George is a member of the Lake City Realtor and The National Association of Realtors; she has a vast amount of experience in the residential marketplace. George is "Dedicated to Results."

Our Vice Mayor said that Vanessa George has done more in a week's time than Tommie Jones did in a year.

Having no clear information on the Town's Website and organization by the former town manager, Jones, I elected to send Ms. George as much information as I could by email. I had full notes on most items and if I included personalized comments, Cynethia eliminated them, as agreed..

In a two-month period as interim manager, Vanessa accomplished various crises. took stock of what bills the Town needed to pay yet and what income may be anticipated (expense and income). When she brought it up to the meeting, White Springs had only $12,000 left. As of January 12, 2020, Ms. George advised the town of White Springs paid out $640,944.73, from which $575,801.13 went to past due bills for Mittauer & Associates, Art Walker Construction and Curt's Construction, leaving $65,143.60 to pay bills for which she provided a check register.

When Ms. George undertook the interim Town Manager position, Mrs. Brazil agreed to undertake the Financial Director position at a rate of $15.50 an hour on a part-time basis. After issuing 3 to 4 incorrect payroll checks payable to Vanessa George and having them returned by Ms. George for correction, Mrs. Brazil again quit. Ms. George then did what a smart manager would do and that is to hire the "FIRM" of J & S Accounting, not just Mr. Whitehead. By hiring J & S Accounting, Ms. George was saving White Springs some $25,000 in benefits and insurance. It was a win-win for everyone.

Prior to January 2021 and the termination of Attorney Logan, GEORGE, never notified the town council in advance of a proposed hiring, unless outside of the sunshine, She solicited her school mate and friend to be the White Springs Town Attorney. No other candidates applied even though FOREMAN stated the job should be advertised and it was.

GEORGE's Contract

It was my desire to assist Vanessa George and the staff as much as I could until, the meeting discussing her contract. The fact that the council had never received an advanced copy to go over and the fact that Vanessa essentially dictated her own contract, seemed as though she was fleecing our small town. She was familiar with larger cities like Lake City which could afford her types of demands. But as a Town Manager with no previous experience in a town which was in financial crisis, what was everyone thinking? To make matters worse, knowing our financial situation, I could not believe how much money she requested. No one that has worked in White Springs as a Town Manager ever made that type of salary and some had previous municipal experience which Vanessa did not. And none were given computers at their residence so they could work at home and a vehicle for their use for town business.

Per Section 3.01 of our Charter, the Town Council enters into a mutually acceptable written agreement for the services of the proposed Town Manager. This agreement may specify the term, conditions and benefits of the appointment. The Town Manager shall be appointed solely based on executive and administrative qualifications. This does not mean a proposed manager should give the Council an ultimatum which is what happened. in the case of Ms. George. The council was unable to review the proposed manager's contract in advance; instead, excerpts were read by the attorney which were decided upon by Ms. George. The only condition the council could vote on was giving Ms. George compensation of $65.000 if they agreed to a one-year contract or $60,000 for year one of five years with an increase of three percent each year.

Under her contract she was given twenty (20) weeks' severance including twenty (20) weeks of health benefits. What was not told to the Council or known, is that since the Town of White Springs does not have 20 or more employees, the town does not have to provide health and life insurance benefits once her employment terminated. Moreover, those with employers with 20 or more employees, the employee is offered COBRA and must pay for their benefits not the employer. Yet, the council did not review or understand certain laws but signed a valid contract allowing everything Ms. George desires.

I understand the staff were given sizeable salaries and the council, after the audit, required raises. A small town does not have the departments and activities or employees of a larger municipality and thus far less money. So, if one chooses to work in a small town, one cannot expect municipality pay for a large town. The only ones benefiting are the officials and staff with the citizens receiving nothing.

Since the agreement was not negotiated or read in full at a public meeting, and voted on by the council, before the mayor signed it, the Council has created a legal obligation to satisfy those terms of the contract. All severance, salary and benefits paid to Ms. George are required to be paid in one lump sum which makes it difficult to terminate her employment until the five years of her contract is up or until White springs files bankruptcy.

The Town requires that the applicant chosen must be willing and able to accept the terms and conditions of such employment including the salary and benefits which may be offered, including the completion of the Town's employment application and submission to a drug test. Further the applicant must be willing to enter into a written employment agreement and follow the conditions of the personnel manual of the Town. This did not happen and for the fact that the Council was fleeced. *The COUNCIL DID NOT OFFER THE TERMS OR THE SALARY AND BENEFITS.*

Vanessa George had a challenging time as a manager. I could provide information initially to her, but thereafter without a forensic report on the finances, along with no prior information of meeting minutes, ordinances. and workshops, she had a tough time, when records were not instituted, by the former manager, Jones. It may have been that part of her problems stemmed from the fact that she did not spend all her time in the office but kept her activist role in Lake City plus managing her various businesses besides being a real estate agent. In a Town Manager position, I believe one must have an accounting and finance education, as well as great organizational skills. Unfortunately, a Town differs from a business, because transparency is necessary, not only to the State of Florida but to the Town's Constituents. It was not just Vanessa George who was to blame for the financial problems the <u>Town</u> had, but all the Town Council members who refused suggestions from the previous managers. Other than for the town charter and employee manual, no internal controls, or procedures on which one could rely were available.

For at least two decades, we have had to suffer the old guard as councilors where nothing would change, and laws were not adhered to The Town appointed and elected new younger Black Councilors without the appropriate education to serve the Town of White Springs, under Vanessa George's appointment as Town Manager. Prior Council Members chose managers who were among their friends or acquaintances, not considering educated staff that could have assisted the Town. The Town posted such jobs but, the interview process was entirely a waste because most people in White Springs were elected or hired by the town, based upon friendships or the color of their skin and decisions were made, outside of the Sunshine Laws. George desired an all-Black Council. Sometimes one must be careful of what they wish for.

Vanessa George took on the position of Interim Town Manager running. Mayor Miller and Walter McKenzie's choice of Tommie Jerome Jones almost placed our Town into bankruptcy. Acting Mayor Anita Rivers appointed Ms. George with Council approval and although she had not previously held a position of Town Manager, she seemed better educated than any we had interviewed or hired in the past, except for Lawrence and Tebo. We needed someone who would take the "bull by the horns" and this young lady did, in the very beginning.

These are the things Ms. George accomplished in a short three months.

- Finances and budgetary items were finally being handled as they should be with Ms. George ascertaining that the public were aware of White Springs' financial situation on a monthly basis.

- Past due Construction projects were reviewed immediately, and Ms. George has worked with the various government agencies to assure payments were made

- An outstanding balance for the Mill Street Project was being managed where Jones dropped the ball.

- Ms. George had been working with Hamilton County on items of public concern, but specifically she was attempting to have the Hamilton County Sheriff's office police our area. Our Police Force was not serving our community and the Sheriff's office had already been providing 80% of the coverage.

- Our former Town Manager and Financial Director Clerk who worked part-time could not seem to get a grip on why the County did not pay the Fire Department under its contract for its services rendered to Hamilton County. Ms. George immediately worked with the County and although the County refused to pay for what services had been provided because the fire fighters did not adhere to their obligations under the contract, Ms. George negotiated with Hamilton

County; had reviewed the various contracts and apprised the Fire Department of what was necessary and was currently getting the last quarter of money. Plus, she worked with the County for a new contract.

- Where First Federal would not provide us with a line of credit because Jones was a consultant and frankly lied by omission, on the applications which were completed correctly and re-submitted by Acting Mayor Rivers and Ms. George.

- Where we have lost money on our Water Bills and Waste Pro, Ms. George conducted an audit with our finance department J & S.

- Ms. George hired J & S Accounting, rather than an employee, to manage our bookkeeping and accounting so that we are not paying out benefits and salaries, which I believe she mentioned would save us some $25,000 a year by having J & S as a consultant.

- Where the Town of White Springs has never followed their ordinances for Code Enforcement, because the old guard did not wish to hurt their friends, only those they did not like, Ms. George has suggested the Town Council act as judicial body for code enforcement and there would be a workshop with the Town's attorney. The Town should be securing revenue from those who do not wish to comply with ordinances.

- Ms. George has been working with Kimerly-Horn, our planner regarding Environmentally Sensitive Lands and with respect to the new Community Center, which was abandoned, for lack of funds, by our Town Councilors since 2017. The Town Council has elected to go forward with the Community Center by securing an extension of time on the CDBG from Tallahassee through the Department of Economic Opportunity.

- Ms. George has met with the engineering firm as well as providing information regarding the limitations of utilizing the current site for the new Community Center/hurricane shelter.
- Bills are now paid on time after one year of leaving checks sitting on desks and not being deposited.

Ms. George secured $50,000 for the Town of White Springs through the Coronavirus Aid, Relief, and Economic Security Act., (AKA CARES Act)

- Working with Town Staff, since Jones ruined our Town's internet site, all meeting minutes, ordinances, resolutions are being organized and placed in binders. All paperwork are evaluated and managed.
- Transparency was brought forward to the public, from Town Hall for the first time in decades. Agendas are being prepared. The White Springs Journal was provided manager's notes and paperwork on items for the first few months, so the citizens may be aware of what is happening at Town Hall. The old guard never wished to be transparent and never allowed the public to know what was going on.
- Ms. George had our Town Attorney. Foreman conduct a workshop on the Charter Review. The Griffins signed up to serve on the Charter Review committee and have currently reviewed the charter with changes, which Griffin suggested the Council review prior to having the Attorney make any suggested changes. (THE CHARTER BINDER WAS COMPLETED BY ME IN TWO WEEKS AND A COPY GIVEN TO ATTORNEY FOREMAN, PLUS ONE TO TONJA BROWN. NOTHING WAS DONE BY STAFF TO MY KNOWLEDGE.)
- Attorney Foreman, at Ms. George's request, met with Ray Vaughn who was familiar with all the properties of

the Town. This was to determine what Surplus the Town may have. It was time to have this surplus sold or eliminated and Ms. George was also working on all inventory, with Mr. Vaughn consisting of Town equipment and property.

There were areas which Ms. George had not handled

It was disappointing to realize Vanessa George could not handle an inventory of property without the assistance of the Town Attorney, costing the Town $660 in attorney expense. She could have worked with Ray Vaughn on the inventory.

Tom Brazil's workers compensation claim was almost two years old. Tommie Jones didn't know how to handle it but Vanessa George who has business experience should have rectified the matter and paid the collection agency to clear Mr. Brazil's name.

Never has Ms. George per item (h) Submitted to the Town Council and make available to the public a complete report on the finances and administrative activities of the Town as of the end of each fiscal year.

Ms. George has not (j) Keep the Town Council fully advised as to the financial condition and future needs of the Town by providing a financial and budget progress report at each regular Council Meeting.

Our Agenda packets do not include old or new business, whether we will be selling surplus, what the status of certain contracts are with an internet site, the sheriff's department etc.

Although she may be the purchasing agent of the Town, for the purchase of all supplies and equipment in accordance with the approved Town Budget, To date she **has not conducted all sales of surplus Town owned, seized or forfeited personal property** which this and the previous Town Council has authorized to be sold. No advertisements for bids have been done and she doesn't even make reports. It has also not been carried as old business on the agenda nor has it been discussed in meetings.

Ms. George, the Town Clerk nor the Council have taken the **required four-hour Ethics and Public Records training.**

Section 6.03 Budget Compilation by the Town manager is required and should start as of July 1st. She has not conferred with the attorney as to what may be done about LOFT funds, and she should be allocating funds for special projects including restrictive funds and having workshops. Other municipalities have a separate and distinct restrictive fund for LOFT.

Per the Charter. It shall be the duty of the Town Manager to **review financial reports with the department heads** and to advise or be advised of any allotment which is in danger of being exceeded. This budget report review must take place at least once each quarter and never has been done.

Nevertheless, the contract for Ms. George did not reiterate the Manager's Duties of the Charter, and although I sent them to her, who would expect her to comply, when none of the managers complied and Lawrence was silenced by Mayor Miller. The Auditor General's Report was what was necessary for the Town to awaken. Griffin threatened an audit but the only way in which higher government will comply is if a Council Member makes the complaint.

In Attorney Foreman's "April 6, 2021, letter, providing public records information, without doing due diligence, he blamed Griffin for sexual harassment.

"I am in receipt of numerous complaints relating to your behavior at Town Hall, including incidents that may constitute inappropriate sexual comments made to Town staff. Be advised that moving forward you are not to

further harass Town Staff in connection with your public records requests or any other business you have with the Town. Town Hall is not a public forum but is for conducting the Town's business. The Town's employees are not obligated to permit your conduct towards them, particularly when it becomes threatening or sexual, and they will contact law enforcement to have you removed from the premises in the event you choose to continue."

It is unbelievable to receive a **blank agenda** like the one we now receive. Before we would receive many items on an agenda, and it included payables. Vanessa George does not provide payables with the agenda as in the past. Also, it is Ms. Georges duty to advise the council and the public what funds we currently have and what bills need to be paid against those funds.

Unlike when she began as town manager, she rarely has a report but has a bundle of excuses if someone dares to complain. What we did hear at the end of the meeting is that the Town owes a net $37,000 dollars which must be paid immediately with respect to our portion due of three different grants, for which she seemed heated. She mentioned that it had not been taken care of by the prior administrations. She may be right because our prior manager had no experience at all and didn't even deposit the utility checks into the bank for a month. But the council loved him because of the color of his skin.

And wouldn't it be nice if Vanessa George explained to the Public and the Council what happened with the First Federal Line of Credit that was to have been offered again? The last we heard at a meeting was that Ms. George and Anita Rivers were to sign the paperwork. Thereafter everything went silent. Wouldn't it be nice to have that line of credit to pay of unexpected bills similar to a credit card? All we were told was that the Bank Line of Credit wasn't needed, but it makes me wonder if the bank removed their offer again due to the Town's financial situation. After all the Town was broke prior to Ms.

George starting so where did we now get the Money? Is Ms. George taking from Peter to pay Paul? The council never asked or explained this to the public.

Now the following was not on the agenda nor was it added but Kellen Lindsey Senior Project Manager at Mittauer & Associates, Inc, Jacksonville Florida requested that the Town sign and accept Change Order Number 10. He was unable to attend the meeting, so Ray Vaughn was provided the information and Mr. Vaughn turned it over to our Town Manager. This is in regard to the Sewer revitalization project.

Apparently, Windstream placed some kind of equipment in a pipe which is under concrete. This Change order allows the contractors to remove the concrete in the FDOT roadway which needs to be excavated, and the equipment removed. FDOT approved its removal, and the cost will be $19,930 which Mr. Lindsay stated was very reasonable in his conversation with Mr. Vaughn.

Town Manager negotiates without Council approval

Although, to my knowledge, the Town Council in a public meeting, did not allow the Town Manager to negotiate with the Hamilton County Sheriff's office, Ms. George did. She brought in the Sheriff's office representatives to a meeting, where it was decided upon, that the Sheriff could provide a deputy for thirteen hours each day. At the time, the Sheriff's deputies were already in charge of 80% of the calls in White Springs because our police department was political as well as lackadaisical and did not respond to those calls. This was an excellent decision made by Ms. George, even though she did not have the permission of the Council to negotiate on their behalf. This is something Griffin kept telling the prior Council Members to do, but it was not something that interested them, because the Town police were easier to control, whereas there would be no control or bias with the Sheriff's Department.

Although the Town Charter states we must have a Police Officer which is a Town Employee, Attorney Foreman brought forth that portion of the charter. which the Council elected to delete. This was not voted on by the citizenry.

Internet Cafes

The Town had an ordinance prohibiting Internet Cafes within the Town of White Springs. One had started near White Springs, but the building was in Columbia County so it could not be banned from operating, by the town council. Although Mayor Rivers was adamant against internet cafes, that all changed. The Town Council introduced Ordinance, 2022- on July 5, 2022, allowing the re-entry of internet cafes on June 14th with a second reading on June 28th. Of the 26 individuals who were present there were less than five registered voters who were in favor of the re-entry of internet cafes. Sheriff Harrel Reid opposed the ordinance *"It is gambling and illegal and brings a criminal atmosphere into White Springs."* Ms. George stated it would provide the Town some $96,000 a year if they operated more than five gambling devices. If they operate less than five gambling devices, internet cafes would be forced to pay a tax of $5,000 a year. And the Town needed the money desperately. There were no guarantees in the ordinance, and it would be up to the Town or FDLE to regulate the cafes.

The public was concerned with the additional crime associated with internet cafes and there was at least one lawsuit plus references by a church that one of the cafes was too close in proximity to the church, in accordance with statutes. One of the council members, who he other council members forced to resign, alleged stated that each of the council members, except her, received $5,000 in cash to allow the internet cafes to operate in White Springs.

Dr. Roger Greene lawsuit regarding the internet cafes refers to an ordinance passed by the town alleging the Town did not place a public notice advertising the meeting in advance, and the ordinance was not on the meeting agenda. Despite the opposition of twenty-three citizens, the ordinance was still approved by the council. The lawsuit alleged the council members violated Sunshine Law by meeting privately and allowing gambling devices within the town limits, which violates Florida law.

Griffin then drafted a lawsuit against the Town Clerk and the Town Manager, seeking the highest possible punishment for violating the Sunshine law, and cited an audit performed by Auditor General Sherrill Norman which states that thirty or more public records requests were not responded to or acknowledged. This lawsuit was dismissed by the court. Again, Griffin was acting pro se.

The third lawsuit filed was from BBL Management Services against the Town Council. The lawsuit was filed for their deferred applications which were not addressed during several council meetings. BBL Management Services requested to have zoning changes on their properties at the October 11, 2022, June 13, 2023, and the August 15, 2023, meetings. The suit alleged the council acted illegally as the planning and zoning board, by ignoring the requested changes instead of providing an answer.

The Riverbend news stated, "These lawsuits, along with the recent operational audit, reveals significant problems with White Springs' government."

Any money received by the Town of White Springs ceased when the Florida Gaming Control Commission's Division of Gaming Enforcement, with assistance from the Florida Highway Patrol's Rapid Response Team and the Hamilton County Sheriff's office had search warrants for the two internet cafes on Highway 41 (Springs Street). On April 10, 2024, the state raid made five arrests for possession of slot machines and keeping a gambling house. confiscated 179 suspected illegal gambling devices, computers, ATMs and an undetermined amount of cash. The State of Florida regulates slot machines which are only legal in eight pari-mutuel facilities in Miami Dade and Broward counties and facilities operated by the Seminole Tribe of Florida.

Finally, a more lucrative Fire Services Agreement

On October 18, 2022, the Board of Hamilton County Commissioners discussed fire services with Ms. George and Fire Chief Steve Stith. Ms. George stated that it would take approximately $275,000 to provide 24-hour coverage with a guaranteed response from two certified firefighters. The Board discussed offering $137,500. Which would be half of the amount needed to provide a 24-hour response. Fire Coordinator Henry Land discussed the language proposed in the agreement, versus the language in the current Fire Services Agreement. After a lengthy discussion, Commissioner Ogborn made a motion allowing legal counsel to draft an agreement for fire services between the Town of White Springs and the county in the amount of $137.500 which would be paid after the town of White Springs submits fire services expenses. A second to the motion was made by Commissioner Murphy and the motion was carried by a unanimous vote.

GRIFFIN Was excoriated for his public records and threats

The Sheriff's Department nor the State's Attorney would assist Griffin even though there are specific Statutes, and the Sunshine Laws which prevail. The SHERIFF's deputies would not assist GRIFFIN in an investigation of the Town because they feared they would lose their jobs at the Sheriff's department. Officer Martinez, who offered his assistance with an investigation of the town, told the Griffins, he could not help them. However, once he heard his job would be in jeopardy, he told GRIFFIN he could not assist because he could not afford to lose his job. The "Home Rule" applied and the Rudd Act, so there would be no penalties against the officials or management within a municipality. Law Enforcement could not investigate a municipality, but one could take suit against the town for damages only if an attorney were willing and able to sue the town and with Griffin's record it would be difficult. I tried with Morgan and Morgan and was denied any assistance

The Infamous July 13, 2021, Meeting

The Griffin's' blog WAS known as the "White Springs Journal" which was shut down after the TOWN OF WHITE SPRINGS TOWN MANAGER, Vanessa George Assaulted GRIFFIN during a Town Hall Meeting on July 13, 2021, by crawling over the Town Council Table while threatening and screaming in an inaudible tone at GRIFFIN. This was an attempt to stop GRIFFIN from leaving the meeting premises and in retaliation for his criticism of how the public officials were draining the Town of funds and the lack of Transparency.

Griffin was physically challenged but could walk on a limited basis prior to the July 13, 2021, meeting. The fear of GEORGES ANGER and what she could physically do to him, caused him to lose his balance when attempting to flee. As a result, Griffin fell backwards with the back of his head hitting the metal chair which had fallen with him on the concrete floor. He lay on the floor, unable to speak, motionless and eyes open, pupils dilated in shock.

Since this transpired at a council meeting, Attorney Foreman, the Council, the Town Manager, and the public all were in attendance of Vanessa George's verbal and threatened physical assault. Yet not a one rejected the Town Manager's actions of Civil Disturbance and Assault but apparently allowed a disciplining of a citizen by a verbal threat and attempted attack as being acceptable.

GEORGE's reasoning to Assault Griffin was due to GRIFFIN calling GEORGE a *"Dirty lying dog"* after GEORGE's and the Town Clerk AUDRE' WASHINGTON RUISE's continual excuses and denials of following Chapter 119 of the Florida Statutes as well as not allowing or answering Complaints allowing GRIFFIN to redress his Grievances by GEORGE's refusal to abide by the Florida Sunshine laws.

This threat or attempt to inflict offensive physical contact or bodily harm on a person who is in his Mid- 70's and who was physically handicapped/challenged was beyond the pale. His hips were held together with a metal chain since his pelvis was shattered in or about 2009. This placed GRIFFIN in immediate eminent danger of or in apprehension of a thirty some year-old female Town Manager. VAUGHN subsequently physically removed GEORGE off the council table and out of the council room and two DEPUTY SHERIFFs helped GRIFFIN off the floor. The two deputies then assisted GRIFFIN to his vehicle so I could drive him home.

Because of GRIFFIN's activism, most public figures did not like his complaints and requests for them to follow the laws of the US and Florida Constitutions, the Public Records and Sunshine Laws of the State of Florida. Many officials and staff attempted to have him arrested for civil and criminal charges. At times, the complaints were fabricated by town managers, staff, certain White Springs police officers and council members so that GRIFFIN would be charged with civil and criminal crimes. Subsequently GRIFFIN was arrested for his activism. The public officials made certain that GRIFFIN would not have a seat on the council, nor would GRIFFIN have an opportunity to serve as Town Manager. Yet NEVER, prior to GEORGE's assault did GRIFFIN ever feel he was in imminent danger until GEORGE crawled over the council room table, screaming in inaudible tones, and threatening him.

After July 13, 2021, GRIFFIN continually has dizzy spells. He could not stand or walk without assistance which continued to his death. GRIFFIN had lost his short-term memory which did not allow him to recall specific conversations, computer functions nor could he speak distinctively. He had lost a total of 150 pounds, because of his difficulty in swallowing any solid food. Later, because of his weight loss, in order for him to receive nourishment, a feeding tube was surgically implanted at the VA. His sight had been impaired due to the concussion he suffered so he no longer could operate a vehicle proficiently and had difficulty reading at certain times in the day.

GRIFFIN had and continued to have subsequent falls, one of which broke his nose. The broken nose caused a drainage problem for over two years until his death, despite a Jones Tube surgically implanted after his bout with eye cancer. Because of his frailty, he was subject to various infections which had rendered him hospitalized twice PLUS constant Emergency Room Visits, EMT and Ambulatory assistance which had cost him thousands of dollars. The doctors of the Veterans Administration could not understand why he was in this state since he did not have a stroke, and he kept seeing specialists at Lake City and Gainesville with no remedy.

His initial concussion on July 13, 2021, however, was severe and the bump on the back of his head remained for almost six months and damaged his motor skills. He was told by doctors that he would be confined to a wheelchair with no ability to walk again because of the assault. This caused GRIFFIN great depression and EXTREME frustration especially when he tried to verbally request something and was told he was NOT understood. At the time, his speech was horrific, and he sounded like he was drunk because he could not enunciate. No one could understand him, so I became his interpreter, which angered him.

It was when Griffin started drinking vodka that his speech became normal. When he ran out of vodka, he drank a bottle of scotch even though he always said he could not understand how anyone could drink it.

The July 13,2021. Incident with Vanessa George eradicated Joe Griffin's ability to use any form of good judgment. Other people noticed his Narcissistic tendencies throughout our eleven-year marriage. Yet, his actions did not affect me or anyone else as badly, until his fall at Town Hall, after Ms. George threatened him.

The VA (Veteran's Administration) initially provided physical therapy and subsequently home nursing through two firms; both of which stopped caring for him, because he was abusive, during their visits. He was upset that one nurse was Black, and she was told to not come back. He fired a seasoned registered nurse because she spoke to me. When taking him to the VA, should a doctor or nurse, or even his psychologist speak to me about his condition, he would not go back to them again. In fact, he would rudely tell them that they were not allowed to speak to me about his condition.

Despite going to neurologists and other doctors at the Veterans Administration Hospital (VA) in Lake City, Griffin was in poor mental condition. He was diagnosed as being bi-polar in 2009 but had refused his medications for over two and one-half years.

Although he normally was not OUTRIGHTLY abusive, that changed, and he became not only verbally abusive but physically as well on occasion. One day, when angered at something I said, he gave me a couple of arm punches when I was driving the vehicle. He never did it again when I mentioned that if I lost control, we would both be dead. He would periodically kick me, or attempt to kick me, and it did not seem to bother him that there were witnesses, but at our home, I had the ability to move away from him quickly. He kept telling me to "Get the Hell out of his house" and I planned to.

He blamed me for taking him to the dentist he chose as well as all work which was done on his teeth. If I suggested anything relating to his health or welfare, he felt it was a criticism. But if he wanted something, I had to respond to him immediately or he would go into a rage that was like that of a two-year old child, throwing a tantrum because he was not getting his way. This happened when he experienced cognitive dissonance when reality did not match up with his internal beliefs. He became extremely vindictive and seemed to lack a moral compass. Although he previously talked about being a racist, after the fall, he outrightly called Black people the N word and he was angry that I dared to speak to the White Springs staff members who were Black.

GRIFFIN would not eat and lost a total of 159 lbs. down from 280 to 121. His blood pressure was low, so he was dizzy. We kept having him checked at the VA Emergency Room. He kept getting Urinary Tract infections (UTIs) where at one time I had the ambulance take him to the VA hospital. I could not move him from the couch and feared he would die. The doctor tried to blame me because he was malnourished but later found out I was not the problem. After feeling better, Griffin checked himself out of the hospital. This was after he had an argument with the doctor and told her she could not hold him, or he would charge her with kidnapping.

He constantly started fights. He had to control me and everyone else, in every way possible and the fear of him coming after me and hitting me with his wheelchair, caused me to lock my bedroom door.

GRIFFIN tried to get the Department of Children and Families (DCF) to remove me from the premises or have me incarcerated, by calling the health department, who referred him to DCF. I was the one who assisted him despite his anger toward me. He contended that I was stealing all his money, that I was allowing him to starve, and that I was abusing him. After showing the DCF representative my financials as well as his and showing I no longer was on his account but set up monthly budgets for him, the representative then secured statements from the neighbors. The neighbors had difficulty with GRIFFIN's constant yelling at me and for being so abusive, so it turned on Griffin that his claims were unsubstantiated. The DCF could see his multiple bags of Cheetos and the various cans of soup which I placed in a blender before giving it to him. I learned his intent for contacting DCF was to frighten me so that I would "behave" because the DCF gave him options initially on how to have me removed and he refused.

if I asked him to change his clothing, he became angered and told me not to yell at him. He felt he had to be and was perfect and by my comments that made him less than perfect, so his anger caused tantrums. He had a habit of throwing things off the porch and into the yard when he was angry.

After he received his dentures, he had pain because Aspen Dental had not repaired or removed six problem areas. We went to another dentist in Lake City who took X-rays and wrote the problem areas on a sheet of paper but did not include his Dental name and the dentist did not wish to serve Griffin further. The corporate office of Aspen Dental refused to allow GRIFFIN to have dental work done, at any of their facilities because of his derogatory speech, calling everyone on the phone names and spewing threats, at their corporate office. A lawsuit was taken against Aspen Dental by GRIFFIN but was lost because GRIFFIN also was rude to the judge, the dentist that x-rayed Griffin did not sign his name to the evidence of the six problem areas and GRIFFIN would not allow me to correct some statements which he made which made no sense, I did not interject because I would have suffered for it. GRIFFIN sitting at the plaintiff's table threw paper on the floor and said a few angry words but did not swear thankfully. The Judge had to warn him twice about his anger. He at least was happy with the initial facts I laid out and this is something I have done many times. He allowed me to speak about the case on the way home and then I no longer was allowed to speak to him. This type of behavior never existed prior to the fall, and it was difficult getting used to it. He also threatened Sheriffs, Judges and the officials and staff at White Springs.

He treated the nursing staff poorly and his reputation of being rude and crude, caused two different doctors to offer their specific procedure to provide him a feeding tube and get him out of the hospital. He even tried kicking me from his bed which the head nurse chastised him for, but that did not help the situation. The staff at the VA Hospital in Gainesville baker Acted him while he was still receiving medical care. It was usual for him to feign helplessness and the "poor Me's", indicating his life did not matter and he wished to do away with himself. This was only an act because he very much wished to live but needed the attention. Yet there was no one who would assist him except for me. He was even rude with his friend, and only friend, Jim Smith.

A nurse trained me on how to use the feeding tube and how to clean the area and place bandages on Griffin daily. Griffin initially allowed me to feed him two bricks (that is what the protein packs are called) in the morning, but that was not without problems., there was not only black mold in the tube but also in the top part where the apparatus attaches to the tube. I was concerned but a visiting nurse told me that coke would clean out the tube. I knew the top part was removable and could be cleansed with a brush. Of course, I used bleach in the cleaning process. This happened various times as well as his contacting parasites which ate the flesh around his feeding tube which I handled. The problem with feeding tubes is that if GRIFFIN became angry if something would not go through the tube, the louder he became, the more food and bile would shoot out of the tube and on to the floor.

It was not long thereafter when Griffin did not allow me to change his bandages or feed him through the feeding tube. I continued placing food in a blender so he could drink such proteins and soup by mouth or with a large straw. He refused, and I would find it on the floor of the family room, sometimes with insects in it. The carpet was saturated in his TV room with coke, tomato or V-8 juice and vodka, soup. and Cheetos. He threw everything on the floor, and I could not clean the TV room unless I was able to get in the room before he did so I was usually up early. I continually changed pads which were full of urine and that was daily for both his bed and TV room couch. Griffin had not taken a shower for over two years and the only time he was in water was a pool at a motel we stayed at. He rarely allowed me to hand bathe him.

The psychologist at the VA, in my first visit with Griffin, indicated that Griffin was mentally ill. He has been Baker acted three times before I moved to White Springs. Even the Gainesville doctors' Baker acted him at the hospital because he feigns, he is dying or wants to die for sympathy. He no longer goes to the Neurologist nor the psychologist. The VA psychologist is African American, and he called her the N word, even calling other African American nurses names at the VA. He had not seen his psychologist for at least 1.5 years since she made the mistake of telling me about his prognosis after the fall in Town Hall.

But Griffin did not wish anyone to be aware of his Medical Records. In a suit against Sheriff J. Harrell Reid (Case 2023-CA-102) Griffin state "A VA staff member talked to the Sheriff or one of his Deputies and gave the Sheriff or the Deputy some of Joe's Medical Records from two years ago. Joe's doctor/patient confidentially was destroyed, and he planned on bringing Legal Action against him as well.

I noticed Griffin walking around circles with his hands curved up as if he were someone from the living dead with an abundance of people surrounding him, at Flagler Beach. I had previously had him seated in the car. Griffin needed attention and got out of the car to make a scene. I finally got Griffin in the vehicle, and we were off to the motel. I helped him walk to the pool and he seemed happy for the first time that day. Griffin wished for a strawberry sundae. He wanted to go inside the building, but his wheelchair would not go over the small step. I had never been at the Waffle Cone establishment before and did not know there was a handicap door on the other side of the building. There were people sitting outdoors enjoying their ice-cream when Griffin went into a tantrum calling me every name in the book. Although embarrassed, I alone went inside and got him a great strawberry sundae. I believe the young man who assisted me made it a special sundae because he also heard the ruckus.

The VA doctors wished me luck because Griffin once feeling better discharged himself against doctors' orders. Griffin told me if he is unconscious, then I can call an ambulance. He cites "kidnapping or being held against his will" if police or EMT's were called. Yet he has held me hostage, keeping me away from any other relationship, was verbally abusive and I had been his slave for 12 years because he refused, to do things for himself. And the latter is a lie because I have seen he could do things for himself, but he refused.

He wanted me to continually serve him, and he had mentioned frequently that I deserve his abuse for chattering. Yet I barely talked to him

When he entered the Aspire dental office, he was loud and started condemning the doctor and staff because of what he paid, and they would not prescribe further drugs. He had no logic, so he refused to understand an evaluation needed to be done first. You don't just prescribe narcotics. The receptionist/nurse said he could not scare the other patients by being so loud and abusive. Fortunately, Griffin had a young surgeon from the Jaguars who accepted him.

I realized GRIFFIN required an analysis of his Mental Condition and I then did what former police officers suggested and decided to have GRIFFIN committed for an involuntary mental check.

The Clerk of Court for Hamilton County forwarded me the forms for an ex parte. After I completed the form, I returned it to Hamilton County. Jamie L. Tyndal Acting Circuit Judge checked the following boxes on the Ex Parte Order:

- Mental Illness: There is reason to believe that the Respondent is mentally ill as defined by Chapter 3944.455 (3) Florida Statutes
- Refused Voluntary Examination: The Respondent has refused voluntary mental examination, after conscientious explanation and disclosure of the purpose of the examination.
- Inability to Make Self-Determination: The respondent is unable to make a self determination as to whether a mental examination is necessary.
- Present Threat of Substantial Harm. Without care or treatment, the Respondent is likely to suffer from neglect or refuse to provide self-care. Such neglect or refusal poses a real and present threat of substantial harm to the Respondent's well-being. It is not apparent that such harm can or will be avoided through the help

of willing family members or friends or through the provision of other services.

- Ex Parte Order for Involuntary Mental Examination: All and singular, the Sheriffs of the State of Florida, their duly authorized Deputies and all other law enforcement officers are hereby commanded to take into custody, the above-named Respondent and deliver, or arrange for delivery, of the said Respondent to the nearest licensed facility for involuntary mental examination pursuant to the Order. A copy of this Order shall be made a part of the Respondent's clinical record.

Chapter 394 of the Florida Statutes, known as "The Baker Act," governs mental-health services, including voluntary admissions section 394.4625), involuntary-examination (section 394.463), and involuntary placement (section 394.467). In Florida , the Involuntary Commitment law is referred to as the Baker Act. If someone you know has been involuntarily committed, you have the right to be fully informed about the step-by-step procedure of involuntary commitment, as well as your rights and the rights of the person who was, or is being, committed.

In the afternoon of October 30th, GRIFFIN had me drive him to Town Hall, where he told me that I was not to go in with him but rather stay in the vehicle. I noticed he had excrement and urine on his clothing and asked him to change before we left. He refused. We then arrived home after his business was complete at Town Hall. He still did not change his clothing.

Four Sheriff's deputies and two EMTs arrived at our residence on October 30, 2023, at 16:44. All were tall and muscular. GRIFFIN argued with the deputies that he did not have to go with them, and he was provided a copy of the ex parte signed by the judge. He laughed and said he would be out in three days, and he called me a bitch, while they were loading him onto the gurney. He told Deputy Persell Fouracre that he would rather go in the police car than the ambulance and was told "no", especially when his hygiene was so poor. All the deputies and EMTs wore gloves when handling GRIFFIN.

Griffin was attempting to get out of the psych ward and go home. I received a call from the VA Advocate wherein Griffin told her that I gave the VA a copy of the Judge's order Baker Acting him, instead of the police Baker Acting him due to the order made by the judge. The Advocate explained that his admission to the VA had nothing to do with the Baker Act. He was evaluated Lake City Hospital and sent to the VA for another purpose other than the Baker Act. She did not know whether it was because of lack of nourishment, and of course, she admitted the psychiatrist had seen him. He told her he needed outside Cheetos, Coke, or V-8. The hospital gives him what he needs but she said I could provide them to him when I arrived. The advocate only followed up on Griffin's statement to her that I, Karin, provided the VA with the Baker Act Ex Parte paperwork, which I did not. I told her I do not want his information; that I do not wish to see him or hear from him because he has made it clear he wants me out of his life.

That was why Griffin said he would be out of the hospital Thursday because with a Baker Act it is usually a three-day evaluation. When he was transferred from The Lake City Hospital to the VA, however, it was due to his lack of ability to care for himself and lack of nourishment so the VA had him transferred to the psych ward to treat him in Gainesville, since he obviously could not care for himself.

The Baker Act exams were not over; the treatment remained; he could not check himself out of the psych ward and the psychiatrist had the power since GRIFFIN was not well. GRIFFIN called Jim Smith also and requested Cheetos and cokes to be delivered to him at the hospital.:

307

When it was time to release GRIFFIN from the hospital, the doctor I had spoken with previously told me Griffin was very angry that I placed him there and said GRIFFIN was diagnosed as having a "personality disorder" which they cannot treat. In other words, GRIFFIN was found to be manipulative and a narcissist, but they cannot treat narcissism because it is not considered a mental illness. The doctor advised they will be notifying the police about his narcissistic condition and his anger. She advised that if I had a restraining order, I would have been able to have him go elsewhere......but since I do not, he is coming home and that I should leave for my safety.

I phoned my daughter and told her I would be moving to her home on the 9th of November Because Griffin did not have keys to get into the house, I would wait for his arrival before I left. While GRIFFIN was hospitalized, I moved my personal items into storage Tamara drove to White Springs and arrived at 8:00 AM. We searched for the items I may have forgotten and included the clothing I had and miscellaneous items in our vehicles. Some items went to storage, and some were moving to her home in Ocala. I left everything which was his and a few of my items in the house and we took photos as proof.

When the van with two nurses pulled up, you could hear their concern of how I would react to him. Tamara and I had the indication that he said awful things about me to them. He was acting so nicely when they put him in his wheelchair, but as he started going up the ramp, the wheelchair caught on something, and he started swearing. The two ladies seemed shocked at his anger. When he again started up the ramp, I told him I waited for him because I wished to make certain he could get in the house. All his keys were inside. Then he told me he was going to sue me. Tamara and I then left for her home in Ocala.

There were witnesses to what transpired at the meeting of July 13, 2021; yet when GRIFFIN asked Deputy Major John Davis of the Sheriff's department for a report which his

Deputies, should have written up, at least in the form of an incident, GRIFFIN's request was disregarded. Major Davis indicated over the telephone to GRIFFIN that the Deputies advised him of the incident, but that is all. In fact, no written report was made. even after Griffin's complaint to Major Davis, which is contrary to Florida Law and procedures when becoming a Law enforcement officer. In fact, Lieutenant McKire of the Sheriff's Department stated there was no report and the Sheriff advised Griffin to no longer contact the Sheriff's department.

More Griffin Problems at meetings

Yet another Sheriff's Deputy, Bradley A Meeks the May 9, 2023, meeting completed a FIBRS Incident report. "At the end of the meeting, the council remembered Griffin had asked to speak to the Council. GRIFFIN was called-up to the front podium to make his statement."

Once GRIFFIN finished speaking, he told THE COUNCIL to "have a nice day" and began to exit the council table. in HIS WHEELCHAIR. As Griffin was leaving Council woman Jacqueline T. Williams made a comment to GRIFFIN. The comment Williams made **was _"one red blood cell a way from death"._** Griffin asked if she was threatening to kill him. At this point, the council meeting had been adjourned. Griffin approached me to request a report from the police, due to him feeling threatened. It raises the question why the two deputies at the July 13, 2021, meeting did not make a report in writing. Does one have to ask the Sheriff Deputies to make reports if one feels threatened or injured? Or should the Deputies just do their job? Yet, if it is Griffin, obviously the laws which govern law enforcement do not apply, despite multiple witnesses at that July meeting.

GRIFFIN continued his plight to secure public records and answers from the Sheriff's Department and from the Hamilton County Board of Commissioners which provided no responses to his inquiries. He showed so much anger that he made some of the clerical staff weep. Only the Clerk of Court tried to assist GRIFFIN, but his loyalties were to Hamilton County, his employer, lest he be fired too. The Sheriff's Department told Griffin he will no longer be provided public records and any such requests from GRIFFIN would be ignored. The Sheriff's department continually had stated they do not have to comply with the Sunshine laws, specifically pertaining to public records. This is not unusual because the Town of White Springs at one time made ordinances which applied to GRIFFIN only and different ordinances regarding the same subject to all other citizens.

When records were provided to Griffin, by the Hamilton County Attorney, the answers seemed to conflict with the Florida Statutes. Chapter 30, Section 15 of the 2019 Florida Statute which states the specific powers, duties, and obligations of the Sheriff. The Sheriff has a duty to enforce both the Florida Constitution and Florida state laws, and such laws were to be executed through the delivery of law enforcement services, the operation of the county Jail, and the provision of court security.

On October 27, 2022, after not receiving meeting minutes requested from the town clerk, The Sheriff's Department nor the State's Attorney would assist GRIFFIN even though there are specific Statutes, and the Sunshine Laws which prevail. The SHERIFF's deputies would not assist GRIFFIN in an investigation of the Town because they feared they would lose their jobs at the Sheriff's department. Officer Martinez, who offered his assistance with an investigation of the town, told the GRIFFINs, he could not help them. He was afraid his job would be in jeopardy

Prior to Jones, minutes or meetings. were readily available to the public on the Town Site. That no longer being the case, GRIFFIN went to Town Hall to ask for the latest minutes. Cynethia Williams said she could not provide them or a note as to why, because the Town Clerk was out of the office. Then in frustration, GRIFFIN made more than one racial slur. First Ray Vaughn, the Utility director, was called by Cynethia Williams and Vaughn also explained that meeting minutes could not be provided without the clerk's okay. Although I explained in a civil manner that his statement was inaccurate, Griffin kept calling everyone the N word and telling Vaughn that he was not a custodian and had no right to tell him that the document would not be available. I. in the meantime, shut the power off to GRIFFIN's wheelchair, and pushed him out the door to the vehicle. That incident did not go well with the Administrative Assistant, who is Black, and she and Vaughn reported it to the Hamilton County Sheriff's office who took a report and charged Griffin with a notice of Trespass.

No one spoke to GRIFFIN. Attorney Foreman advised the Town Council in a meeting that "Trespass" was a method in which to stop someone from harassing staff and these may not have been his exact words, but we received the message. The attorney said there would be no continuous requests for records. The Attorney was specifically addressing Griffin despite not naming him.

In all fairness, Attorney Foreman did explain certain areas were open to the public and other areas which were not open, and the Council was to make the final decision. Months passed and the council failed to decide. Not only was Griffin told he could not come to the area designated to the public, but he could not attend public meetings either. Griffin was not the only one who had received a trespass notice. Apparently, a lady who had complained about her water bill was also given a Notice of Trespass.

But can the Town legally place such a notice against Griffin with the Hamilton County Sheriff's office? Was he really trespassing and if so, why wasn't Karin, his spouse, also trespassing since she was accompanying Griffin as his witness?

Griffin was in the area designated for the public to manage one's business affairs with the Town. That area is separate from the Town's offices and meeting rooms and members of the public are authorized to be there. Yet, Griffin only was considered a trespasser for being in an area of Town Hall which is designated as a public area. Had the Admin complied with GRIFFIN's initial request, there would not have been such a brouhaha in the first place.

Since the town never acknowledges receipt of emails or hard copy requests, one may not know if the clerk received them. They may be covered up in a pile somewhere for months and may not have been kept. So, I then went to town hall to get GRIFFIN's public records which he wanted. I stated the custodian could either acknowledge by replying with an email saying they were received by the custodian or give me notice on the hard copies saying they were received. The admin decided that each hard copy would be date-stamped, and a copy of each document given back to me. I heard Attorney Foreman say I did not need any acknowledgment or date stamp even though that is the law under 119.07.

The Town Manager then told the Front Desk Clerk that the clerk did not have to date- stamp each copy which the clerk did to appease me since I said it is under the Sunshine law that I receive acknowledgment. Further Foreman, who was on the line with the Town manager, asked the Town Manager if Griffin was in Town Hall and he was told by the Town Manager that Griffin was in the car. I was the only one in the public area. It is my belief that even though it was Griffin's right to be in the public area, at Attorney Foreman's behest, Griffin would have been arrested then or at our residence. Even the Hamilton County Sheriff's office understands the Trespass law, but they must appease their Municipal Government of the Town of White Springs. Thank you, Florida, for the "Home Rule."

2024 After Karin Left

On January 9th Griffin previously threatened suicide three times in two years to the VA and he did not get any help so he felt, he might as well do it. Griffin would always say that he intended to commit suicide, but that statement was to get attention. When Hamilton County Deputy arrived to do a welfare check on GRIFFIN, he was irate as usual with law enforcement's presence and did not want to cooperate. He also seemed to be delusional, stating there were more officers present than there were and had difficulty attempting placing phone calls. He eventually did infer that he had told the VA that he was contemplating suicide, and he lives at home alone. The officer did not observe any weapons, but GRIFFIN refused to talk to a counselor about his situation. EMS was called to transport him due to his immobility and he was transported to the Lake City VA,

Per the police' incident report, it was stated that "Griffin did intentionally run into Deputy Meeks and Herrera with his Scooter Chair and footage was taken."

Griffin's comment was that the deputies did not give him a reason that he could not go into the TV room or office. They held him hostage. He said he was denied the incident report stating he had bumped into two deputies. He said an assault by his wheelchair might be a violation of the Baker Act.

Deputy Fouraker was the reporting officer with Jason Herrera, Bradley Meeks, Jake Stephens and Larry Rodgers signing off on the report.

Prior to the report Griffin stated in a typewritten note, that he was assaulted twice in Gainesville; once on the second floor by staff and once by another patient on the Fifth Floor. He stated the staff, including the lead doctor denied any rights to speak to Griffin's attorney, at least four times.

Such Attorney contact was also denied on January 9, 2024, by the medical staff at the Lake City VA.

Griffin felt that when he was Baker Acted under the Ex Parte that it included a 72 hour hold but he was held in Gainesville for nine days with nothing sent to the judge and was not allowed to speak to an attorney. In his delusional mind, he said the baker act was because his wife says he not taking a daily shower is the reason to Baker Act him. The ex parte happened on October 30, 2023.

He then said on January 2nd, 2024, a clerk on the fourth floor at the Surgery Check-in desk in Lake City said, "*We'll get to you when we can*" despite the requirement the VA staff 'laid" on him for a noon appointment and that he should arrive 30 minutes before his appointment time". GRIFFIN arrived at 11:30 AM and was not seen by the doctor until 1:45 PM. The doctor and nurse told Griffin he should be thankful for the attention. The doctor told him, the procedure, removing his feeding tube, would take two minutes which he immediately agreed to. Griffin said the staff thinks he should be grateful for the waste of his time .... a two-hour wait for a two-minute procedure. He left the clinic without the removal of the feeding tube, I was told by Jim Smith that Griffin cut the tube off, himself.

> *Apparently when Griffin needed his bandage changed on his feeding tube, the staff at the ER said that a doctor's consult was required and that the doctor would see him in approximately one hour. Griffin left the ER without his bandages being changed.*

GRIFFIN stated "I have been told by two doctors at the VA that I will be in a wheelchair for the rest of my life due to the Assault that the Town Manager, at a public meeting, did to me, that the Sheriff will/would not investigate. The Sheriff says that he and he alone, will decide what violations of the law, he, the

Sheriff, will investigate. Legal case pending 2023-CA -102 in Hamilton County, Florida court. "

"After eight denials by the Sheriff's staff to produce the text that the Sheriff and the Deputies used to deny me the public Record giving me the right to an independent expert examination, provided by the court, and upon talking to the Clerk of the Court in Hamilton County, I got the Baker Act order" Griffin wrote.

> *Griffin contended he had not been given an ex parte order from any Judge or any Deputy for the incarceration at the Lake City VA. He truly felt he was Baker Acted without a reason. He said he was Baker Acted solely because he was filing a legal action against the sheriff, 2023-CA-102.*

Griffin comments on the order on petition for involuntary medical examination (Baker Act are highlighted below:)

<u>Mental Illness:</u> There is no reason to believe that the Respondent is mentally ill as defined by Chapter 394-455 (3).

Florida Statutes, FS394.455 (3) says as follows, 'Clinical record"

> *The Florida Statute cited by this judge has nothing to do with the requirements for a Baker Act. Respondent feels he was unjustly Baker-Acted by the judge's own statement. He wants the judge to resend the order issued by this court on 30th of October 2023 sought by Respondent's spouse who used the Baker-Act to get me out of the house.*

Refused Voluntary Examination.

> *Respondent did NOT refuse mental examination as known by Petitioner. He refused to go to a nursing home for confinement. A licensed facility is request-ed by*

Petitioner, a licensed facility for involuntary mental examination.

Inability to Make Self Determination:

The court CANNOT make a determination as to Respondent's ability to make a self-determination as to whether a mental examination was necessary only a licensed metical facility LICENSED BY THE STATE can make that determination according to the statute.

Patient Threat Of Substantial Harm

The Petitioner HAS NOT presented any threat of substantial harm to her filing with the court and Respondent totally disagrees with the courts finding and expects a hearing.

Griffin made his comments on the form as follows.

"This order presented on the number 5 item is well beyond the citing of the law and has not been cited by the court anywhere in its finding. The sheriff of HAMILTON COUNTY DID NOT baker-act to a state approved facility according to the facility that he had been taken to. All hospitals in the State of Florida are not approved, yet HCA Florida Lake City Hospital does not meet state standards for the nearest licensed facility as required by the judge's order. In fact, two hospitals are qualified for involuntary mental examination that are closer to Respondent's home of record.

Respondent prays that this honorable court resend the order of 30 October in case number 2023-12-MH. The recent mass shooting in Maine is all the proof this court needs to show that the damage done during extended mental health stay to the estate of the perpetrator of the illegal activities completely ruins the reputation of the *perpetrator; he was baker-acted for two weeks, and the press had a field day with his two weeks stay. "This court has set up the exact same falsehood for Respondent should Respondent ever be brought before the court of public opinion.*

Petitioner used this court's bogus order to prove that she may abandon Respondent without due process. Such is a violation of the US Constitution. Respondent believes, at a minimum, Item 2 following the court's order, and a judgment ordered and adjudged should have been held. It was not.

This court has cited no lawful reason why it had baker-acted me.

Joe Griffin, Respondent"

JOE TOOK OUT SEVERAL SUITS AFTER THE EX PARTE

Griffin felt he was above the law in that he felt his knowledge was superior to anyone else. He would not allow anyone to tell him he was wrong. Suing the Sheriff, the Judges and trying to say he had no due process for everything he has done is ridiculous. Yes, I did abandon him when the doctor advised that for my safety, I should leave and go elsewhere. I could take no more abuse, even if it was just verbal.

JUDGE Olin, Judicial qualifications committee, Docket No. 24-043

On January 25,2024, Grio n sent a letter to the Judicial quali..cation committee. His complaint stated: "Unless Judge Olin is in a conspiracy with the Town of White Springs, it's illegally Hired Out of the Sunshine attorney, or Respondents or some other party the only person I can fathom for her denial is my filing with your commission. She even placed the Town's name as a party to the legal action and they weren't even a party."

Also, in part he stated: She also dismissed my pro se suit against another party to case number 2023-CA-102 in Hamilton County without a single hearing or attempted hearing, she just did it. I am going to a civil rights attorney, and he wants any filings with your Commission and your letter of receipt to me. Please.

On March 26,2024 the Judicial Qualifications Commission advised Griffin that the investigative panel of the Commission had completed its review of his complaint and had determined that the concerns he had expressed are not allegations involving a breach of the Code of Judicial Conduct, warranting further action by the Commission but may be matters for review through the normal court process.

Joe Griffin V. Town of White Springs, Audre' Ruise and Vanessa George, Case No. 2023-96-CA

"This cause before the court upon the Defendants' Motion for Order to Show Cause to dismiss with prejudice and for sanctions file February 15, 2024. Upon consideration of the Motion, the record, and applicable law, this Court finds and concludes as follows:

*The Plaintiff has previously filed actions against these Defendants or their predecessors. In one such prior action, filed in this County (case number 2010-118-CA) the court , concerned with the number of previous lawsuits (18 of which are listed) **filed pro se by the Plaintiff, the voluminous filings by the Plaintiff contained within each, and the "redundant, ambiguous rambling, circuitous, unrecognizable, irrelevant and im-pertinent wording contained in most of the pleadings and motions filed in these cases ordered the Plaintiff*** *to show cause why he should not be prohibited from filing any future pro se lawsuits or Petitions in Hamilton County.*

*"**Order to Show Cause.**" This Order afforded the Plaintiff an opportunity to respond and be heard on the issues of concern raised by the Court. Rather than be heard, the Plaintiff stipulated to the entry of an Order "directing the Clerk of Court to not accept any future lawsuits, petitions, or pleadings in this court that are not filed by a member of the Florida Bar in good standing*

*"**Stipulation to Entry of Order prohibiting Pro Se Filings.**" As a result of this stipulation, the Court entered an Order prohibiting the Plaintiff from filing any future pro se actions or pleadings as a Plaintiff or Petitioner in Hamilton County. Order Prohibiting Future Pro Se filings. Such action is an inherent power of the courts to prevent the abuse of judicial process.*

The instant action was filed pro se by the Plaintiff against the same Defendants (or their predecessors) as each of the prior 19 actions (for which the Court raised serious concern and ultimately prohibited the Plaintiff from filing future pro se actions) it would not, however, matter if the action was filed against these Defendants or others. This plaintiff is barred from filing pro se as a Plaintiff or Petitioner in this County by an Order entered, in part, because of his own stipulation and which the Court had inherent authority to enter.

Although the Defendants have set a hearing on the Defendants' Motion to Dismiss, upon further consideration such a hearing would be a further waste of Court resources as it is not necessary to dispose of this matter, which has been conclusively resolved by the Court's Order prohibiting future pro se filings.

Therefore, it is ORDERED:

This case is dismissed

The hearing scheduled for March 21, 2024, is cancelled

The Plaintiff is reminded that he is prohibited from filing any pro se action in Hamilton County as a Plaintiff or Petitioner. He is further cautioned that any further such filings will result in sanctions.

The Clerk of the Court of Hamilton County, Florida, is directed to refuse to accept any future filings by the Plaintiff that are not signed by a member of the Florida Bar in good standing, in any cause of action for which he is the Plaintiff or Petitioner.

Signed: Melissa Gates Olin, Chief Circuit Judge

There were also pro se suits taken by Griffin against Attorney Joel Foreman, Town Attorney, Sheriff J. Harrell Reid and Deputies of the Sheriff's office, and others, including judges, all of which were dismissed prior or after his death/

BILLBOARDS CRITICIZING THE TOWN AND ONE JUDGE

While I was still in White Springs, GRIFFIN had asked his Power of Attorney (POA) and friend who he treated badly, Jim Smith to build sign billboards, like those at State Parks. Jim had one built in part and another in which only the posts were driven into the ground. Jim does great work, but I mentioned that as Griffin's POA he was to be responsible as a fiduciary, for Griffin's estate and that possibly the billboards being put up may not be a necessity. Jim agreed and let the sign billboards remain undone.

However, Griffin elected to have another carpenter build the billboards. It was his intent to advertise his disgust at the Town staff as well as certain judges. The information I am listing for you has been taken from the Lake City Reporter dated February 21, 2024.

The reporter Tony Britt showed photographs of the signage Joe Griffin put up while Griffin was sitting in front of the one sign which stated, **"White Spring's 3 Biggest Crooks,"** listing the names of Vanessa George, Anita Rivers and Audre'Ruise and photographs of each.

Then Griffin had Photographs of Judge Jamie Tyndal and Tisheena "Sheena" Rickerson on the second billboard. Under each photograph, respectively, **Griffin listed Tyndal as a bad guy and challenger Rickerson as a good guy.**

Griffin in his interview with the reporter stated, "I am very upset and disappointed in the political structure of White Springs and Hamilton County, so therefore I decided to redress my government for grievances, and you cannot get a fair trial on citizen grievances in Hamilton County."

Griffin also stated he did not consider either sign as slander or libel. He felt that his court cases which were filed, would show that the Town Staff of three were crooks and he mentioned the resolution he is seeking with the signs and judge's actions would be for officials to honor his requests. And of course, since he is a public records activist with tunnel vision, he **stated *he wished for the town to OBEY the public records laws*.**

As a result of the signs and publicity, a sign was posted on the door of Town Hall instructing visitors that the government office was closed for unspecified security reasons. Ruise when the staff reporter rang the doorbell at Town hall, said Town Officials were holding a safety / security meeting in the building regarding Griffin and his signs.

When I look back, I realize that I never wished to know how badly he treated others. I did not mean to place my head in the sand, but I had to survive. In fact, when I discussed my feelings of his vulgar writings, he seemed to calm down somewhat. But, in going back, I realize that Griffin told me one thing but did another. I stood by his side even though everything he told me was a lie. I was better at understanding the statutes and laws than he was. Although his ego would not allow him to admit it, I realized that is why he had me write his comments on the blog and in his letters. **He has gone too far in his negative treatment of officials and staff. There was nothing I could do, except allow the Universe to handle things as it would.**

In the meantime, I hired an attorney to assist me in dissolution proceedings:

I realized Griffin was going down hill, when he did not abide by any of the dissolution paperwork. Griffin did not hire an attorney or complete the paperwork. Instead, he sent the following letter to the Boudreau Law firm:

'Thursday January 18, 2024

Attorney Gayle Boubeau

Attorney Boudeau,

In case 2024-DR-10 in Hamilton County concerning Karin and Griffin Griffin and Karin's efforts to Dissolve the Marriage, I want you to know that I oppose this suit and seek marriage counseling instead. I have asked for Marriage Counseling from Karin on multiple occasions. She denied my request each and every time.

If Karin would just quit babbling all of the time we could make this marriage work. She made a promise to do that via a Notary statement. But she apparently would rather end the marriage than not babbling from her continued incessant babbling.

I made a promise to Karin when we took our vows. I intend to keep it at all costs. "Till Death do Us Part" and "In Sickness and in Health" mean something to me.

I am available for consultation with you or you and Karin about this matter at any time.

Joe Griffin Respondent"

For the higher education Griffin had, he neither had logic nor the ability to interpret what he read since his fall. It is said Narcissistic tendencies appear when a child is not receiving the love he or she anticipates. Griffin's sister mentioned that when their father was in the military, he told Griffin to take care of his mother and sister; that Griffin was the man of the house, and it was when Griffin changed. But I did not feel his change was to the detriment until his fall which caused him several mental injuries, in my opinion.

GRIFFIN'S DEATH

On March 15, 2024, Joe Griffin passed away and was found lifeless, slumped over on the floor, by his bed. His head was on an electric heater that had fallen over. Sheriff Deputy Fouracre who was also Jim Smith's nephew had found him and called Jim to the house. Jim then called me and Tamara, and I went to White Springs the following day to manage the funeral arrangements and stop the divorce proceedings for which I hired in Lake City.

Griffin died naturally from a cardiopulmonary arrest.

People asked me how I could have put up with the way in which Griffin treated me. The answer was somewhat simple. I apparently had a mechanism whereby I allowed his rants and comments to disappear from my mind. I IGNORED his criticisms of me because I knew who I was and was determined to live in my own world of sanity. I knew that I was correct, even though he said I was wrong. Just because I believed in working out a marriage did not mean that I would stay with such an abusive disgusting person which he turned out to be. I had my writings on the blog, my research, and art as well as duties I enjoyed such as outside work and creating things. Being on the computer probably saved my life and my mental state, If I had a bad state of mind, all I would have to do is dial the phone and speak to my daughter. She would have me laughing hysterically.

I now sometimes awaken expecting to hear him complain or call me names. Yet my anxieties were then mainly of a financial nature since he spent both his and my money for what he wanted. Once I was in my own apartment, everything seemed to be great. I was over the worst of it, and I was finally free. The assistance and kindness of a wonderful daughter was a blessing. Her consideration went far in my transition as did wonderful friends like Carin Copeland, Arlen Scott Gay. Farron Fylia, Jim and Teena Smith.

CHAPTER TEN – THE JLAC AND THE AUDITOR GENERAL

The Citizens complain to the Joint Legislative Audit Committee

Senator Cory Simon February 24, 2023, Letter to Chairs Pizzo and Caruso:

"I am requesting the Joint Legislative Auditing Committee to direct the Auditor General to perform an operational audit of the Town of White Springs (Town). Multiple constituents have contacted me about their concerns regarding the Town's operations. I understand that these concerns have been ongoing for at least the past couple of years.

Request for an Operational Audit of the Town of White Springs – March 9, 2023

"Senator Simon has requested the Committee to direct an operational audit of the Town of White Springs (Town) and requested that the scope of the audit, at a minimum, include the Town's controls and compliance with laws, rules, regulations, contracts, and other requirements in the areas of: 1 1 Letter from Senator Corey Simon to The Honorable Jason W.B. Pizzo, Alternating Chair, and The Honorable Michael A. Caruso, Alternating Chair, Joint Legislative Auditing Committee dated February 24, 2023 (on file with the Committee).

Background The Town of White Springs, Florida, was incorporated in 1885, and the incorporation was legalized in 1903 by the provisions of Chapter 5368 (No. 263), Laws of Florida. The Town is located in Hamilton County and has an estimated population of 766.

- The Town operates under a council-manager form of government and is governed by five elected Town Council members, each of whom are elected to four-year terms.
- All seats on the Town Council are at large seats, and the Town Council elects among itself a mayor and vice mayor.
- The Town Manager is appointed, by the Town Council and is responsible for the day-to-day management of the Town.
- The Town provides citizens with the following services: general government; public works; water, sewer, and solid waste disposal.
- and fire rescue and emergency medical service.
- Police service for the Town is provided by the Hamilton County Sheriff's Office.

Concerned residents of White Springs have contacted Committee staff, a number of times over the past few years regarding: 11 (1) lack of available current financial information, (2) requests for records from the Town yield insufficient or untimely information, and (3) conditions of the Town's water system and streets. Residents have also contacted Senator Simon's office regarding their concerns. In addition, at the Committee's meeting on February 16, 2023, a resident spoke to the Committee about the following concerns regarding the Town's operations:

- There is a **lack of available financial information**; there are no financial statements available at the monthly Town Council meetings.
- There has been <u>no real audit</u> of the Town since the fiscal year ended September 30, 2019, because the audit report issued for fiscal year ended September 30, 2020, had a disclaimer of opinion on the Town's financial statements.
- The current Town administration has said that, when they started, there were no financial records; however,

although the current Town Manager has been in place for almost two years, there has been no attempt to recreate the records forensically. Also, there was never a police report completed to document that Town records were missing.

- He is anxious because the **residents do not get any financial information from the Town; there is no financial accountability** to the State or the Town residents. In addition, the resident provided a copy of a letter from a member of the Town Council, which included the following concerns:

- Frustration with the lack of financial and operational transparency in the Town;

- Constituents' "repeated requests to the Town Administration for financial information with corroborating records, contracts, third party proposals, grant applications, third party professional reports, and governmental correspondence" over the last 24 months, that were made in the following ways: (1) "informal request at Town Council meetings;" (2) "via email;" and/or (3) "formal request Pursuant to State Statute 286.01114 (Florida Government in the Sunshine Law);"

- Denial of her requests for "access to information that would enable [her] to make more informed decisions" as a Town Council member. As an example, the letter stated: "Most recently, I have been asked to pass legislation to increase the [T]own millage rate, and increase water and sewer rates, without having sufficient justification for these adjust-ments. The justification I have been given is that 'the [T]own is broke.'"

- "The [T]own employs a Town Manager, [a] Town Clerk, and an administrative assistant. In addition, the Town has engaged an outside Bookkeeping firm to manage the finances on QuickBooks. This should be ample staffing for a [T]own of roughly eight hundred (800) citizens, to produce timely financial information to make available to the Town Council, outside Auditors, and Citizens."

- The Town is currently in arrears on financial reporting to the State and has forfeited sales tax revenue and municipal revenue sharing revenue for two years and is on the verge of a third year of forfeiture.

In summary, the audit scope based on the above-noted concerns appears to relate to the following areas: (1) financial reporting; (2) review of the Town's controls over purchasing and procurement processes and compliance with applicable laws and policies; (3) review of the Town's procedures for handling public records availability and access; (4) review of controls over water, sewer, and solid waste rates and testing as deemed appropriate; (5) evaluation of the financial condition and long-term sustainability

Prior Year Delinquent Financial Reports and Committee Action

The Town has not timely obtained annual financial audits of its accounts and records by an independent certified public accountant (CPA) and submitted such audit reports to the Auditor General's Office in accordance with Section 218.39(1), Florida Statutes. **The most recent financial audit report submitted to the Auditor General was for the 2019-20 fiscal year.** While this audit report was due by law no later than June 30, 2021, **the Town did not submit the audit report until July 26, 2022 (391 days late). Also, the Town submitted the financial audit report for the 2018-19 fiscal year (due by law no later than June 30, 2020) on October 6, 2021 (463 days later).** In addition, the Town has not timely submitted its Annual Financial Reports (AFR) to the Department of Financial Services (DFS) in accordance with Section 218.32(1), Florida Statutes. 16 **The Town submitted its AFR for the 2019-20 fiscal year (due by law no later than June 30, 2021) on August**

3, 2022 (399 days late) and its 2018-19 fiscal year (due by law no later than June 30, 2020) on November 15, 2021 (503 days late).

Due to the Town's failure to timely submit the above-noted AFRs and audit reports, in prior years the Committee approved to act against the Town if those financial reports were not submitted by dates certain. **As a result of this State action, the Town lost a total of $17,237.51 of Half-Cent Sales Tax monies and $13,154.52 of Municipal Revenue-Sharing monies that it would have otherwise received.**

In addition, Municipal Revenue-Sharing monies totaling $3,552.58 and $3,507.30 were withheld, but subsequently released to the Town in 2022 and 2021, respectively, after the delinquent FY 2019-20 and FY 2018-19 financial reports were submitted.

Financial Audit Report

The most recent financial audit report submitted to the Auditor General was for the 2019-20 fiscal year. However, although the Town had an audit performed for this fiscal year and submitted an audit report, **the CPA firm issued a disclaimer of opinion on the financial statements. The audit report states "Because of the matters described in the 'Basis for Disclaimer of Opinion' paragraph, however, we were not able to obtain sufficient appropriate audit evidence to provide a basis for an audit opinion.**

The Basis of Disclaimer of Opinion paragraph states: "Detailed property records have not been maintained and certain prior-year and current records and supporting data were not available for our audit. Therefore, we were not able to obtain sufficient appropriate audit evidence about the amounts at which capital assets and related accumulated depreciation are recorded in the accompanying Statement of Net Position at September 30, 2020, stated at $13,920,726 and $3,911,162 respectively, and the amount of depreciation expense for the year then ended stated at $385,637. We also could not verify the total of intergovernmental revenues stated at $745,291 on the accompanying Statement of Changes in net Position."

Audit Findings

The audit report included the current and prior year audit findings listed below and states that the auditors identified "certain deficiencies in internal control, described in the... schedule of findings as items that [they] consider to be significant deficiencies."

Current Year (for the fiscal year ended September 30, 2020)

- **Grant Revenue and Receivables**: "During the current year, [the auditors] found that the Town's financial records did not accurately reflect the grant revenue received and earned by the Town. This resulted in the Town not properly recording its grant revenue and related receivables earned in the financial statements. [The auditors] recommend that the Town establish subsidiary records to accurately reflect the grant activity during the year and that the financial records be regularly reconciled to these subsidiary records."

Documentation of Expenditures/Expenses:

- "From [the] audit test of disbursements, [the auditors] found disbursements that were inadequately documented as to retained invoices or other supporting documentation. [The auditors] recommend that the Town [retain] adequate supporting documentation...for all Town disbursements and that the documentation be filed in a manner that is easily retrievable."

Prior Year (for the year ended September 30, 2019

- **Available Cash:** "During the prior year, the prior auditor noted that the Town's operating cash accounts represented only two months of expenditures/expenses and had decreased approximately $100,000 during the year. During the current year the Town's operating cash continued to be inadequate to meet the Town's operating cash needs. [The auditors] again recommend that the Town take steps to increase its operating cash funds."

- **Town's Books:** "During the prior fiscal year, the prior auditor noted that the Town generally had inadequate financial records for the preparation of accurate financial statements. During the current year the Town retained an outside accountant to monitor and assist in the maintenance of accurate financial records."

- **Fixed Asset Listing and Depreciation Schedule:** "During the prior year, the prior auditor noted that the Town's fixed assets records were incomplete and inaccurate. [The prior auditor] recommended that the Town prepare and maintain a complete fixed asset listing including all relevant data of fixed assets. During the current year, [the auditors] found this finding to be unchanged and again recommend that the Town prepare and maintain proper fixed assets records."

- **Significant Budget Difference:** "During the prior year, the prior auditor noted that there were significant differences between the budgeted and actual amounts of expenditures in both the General and Enterprise funds. [The prior auditor] recommended that there be a more accurate preparation of the annual budget to better monitor the overall performance of the Town. During the current year, [the auditors] found this finding to be unchanged and again recommend that the Town more accurately prepare its annual budget."

- **Post-Employment Benefits other than Pension (OPEB):** "During the prior year, the prior auditor noted that the Town did not have an OPEB actuarial report prepared for the year. During the current year, [the auditors] found that under present circumstances, the Town was not required to have an OPEB actuarial report prepared."

In addition, the audit report included the following finding in the Management Letter, under the heading, Auditor General Compliance Matters: **"Deteriorating Financial Conditions –** From [the] audit procedures in the current year, **[the auditors] found the following conditions** which together comprise "deteriorating financial conditions" as defined by Chapter 10.550 Rules of the Auditor General:

Enterprise Fund:	9/30/2020
9/30/2019	
Net loss for the year ended	$(291,511)
$(153,343)	
Unrestric[t]ed cash reserve balance at year-end	
$(258,811)	$_____

To correct these deteriorating financial conditions, [the auditors] recommend that the Town implement strict measures during the subsequent budget cycles to assure that revenues are sufficient to fund expenditures and replenish needed fiscal reserves in the Enterprise Fund, as well as the General Fund.

Finances should be closely monitored during the current year to ensure that these objectives are met." The audit report did not include any written statements of explanation or rebuttal from the Town concerning the findings in the audit report, although required by Sections 10.557(3)(l) and 10.558(2), Rules of the Auditor General.

Excerpts of Financial Information Included in the Town's Audit Report:

- "99.5% of the Town's net position reflects its investment in capital assets (land, buildings, infrastructure, and equipment), less any related outstanding debt used to acquire those assets. The Town uses these capital assets to provide services to citizens; consequently, these assets are not available for future spending."
- "**Restricted assets** of $187,312 consist of earmarked funds as reserves for debt service and police training. The remaining balance of unrestricted net position $(142,188) may be used to meet the Town's ongoing obligations to citizens and creditors."
- For the **governmental activities**, **total revenues exceeded total expenditures** by $63,898, and ending net position as of September 30, 2020, was $3,735,062.29
- For the **business-type activities** (water, sewer, and solid waste operations), **total expenses exceeded total revenues** by $291,511, and ending net position as of September 30, 2020, was $5,327,678.

Other Considerations

The Auditor General, if directed by the Committee, will conduct an operational audit as defined in Section 11.45(1)(i), Florida Statutes, and take steps to avoid duplicating the work efforts of other audits being performed of the Town's operations, such as the annual financial audit. The primary focus of a financial audit is to examine the financial statements in order to provide reasonable assurance about whether they are fairly presented in all material respects. The focus of an operational audit is to evaluate management's performance in establishing and maintaining internal controls and administering assigned responsibilities in accordance with laws, rules, regulations, contracts, grant agreements, and other guidelines.

Also, in accordance with Section 11.45 (2)(j), Florida Statutes, the Auditor General will be required to conduct an 18-month follow-up audit to determine the Town's progress in addressing the findings and recommendations contained within the previous audit report.

The Auditor General has no enforcement authority. If fraud is suspected, the Auditor General may be required by professional standards to report it to those charged with the Town's governance and also to appropriate law enforcement authorities. Audit reports released by the Auditor General are routinely filed with law enforcement authorities.

Implementation of corrective action to address any audit findings is the responsibility of the Town's governing board and management, as well as the citizens living within the boundaries of the Town. Alternately, any audit findings that are not corrected after three successive audits are required to be reported to the Committee by the Auditor General, and a process is provided in Section 218.39(8), Florida Statutes, for the Committee's involvement.

First, the Town may be required to provide a written statement explaining why corrective action has not been taken and to provide details of any corrective action that is anticipated. If the statement is not determined to be sufficient, the Committee may request the Chair of the Town Council to appear before the Committee. Ultimately, if it is determined that there is no justifiable reason for not taking corrective action, the Committee may direct the Department of Revenue and the Department of Financial Services to withhold any funds not pledged for bond debt service satisfaction which are payable to the Town until the Town complies with the law

End of JLAC's request for an audit

I was pleased to find that prior to his death, Griffin had requested and received the Auditor General's findings and recommendations. This is something GRIFFIN had requested for years, and I am certain it brought him some satisfaction.

AUDITOR GENERAL'S FINDINGS AND RECOMMENDATIONS

Finding 1: Financial Condition

Deteriorating financial conditions negatively affect the ability of a local government to provide, on a continuing basis, services at the level and quality required for the health, safety, and welfare of its citizens. Auditor General rules require independent certified public accountants (CPA's) who perform a financial audit to assess the government's financial condition. The audit report management letter must include a statement that the CPA applied financial condition assessment procedures. If a deteriorating financial condition is noted, the CPA must disclose the government's financial condition is deteriorating and provide a description of the conditions causing the CPA to make that conclusion.

In the town's 2019-20 fiscal year audit management letter, the CPA showed a deteriorating financial condition because the Town's Enterprise Fund included a $291,511 operating loss (a $153,343 increase over the 2018-19 fiscal year loss) and a negative $258,811 unrestricted net position balance.

Although the management letter did not disclose a deteriorating financial condition in the General Fund, the 2019-20 fiscal year audited financial statement disclosed a deficit of revenues under expenditures of $195,588 and an unrestricted fund balance of $134,791.

In response to complete the Town's financial condition, Town personnel indicated that a water rate study performed recommended rate increases for water and sewer services over the next five years. In addition, the Town increased solid waste service rates to replenish depleted reserves in the Enterprise Fund. The Town has also generated new revenues through Internet cafes (Now shut down). Given the town's insufficient accounting records, various control deficiencies and instances of noncompliance disclosed in this report, there is an increased risk that the Town's financial condition may continue to deteriorate.

Finding 2: General Fund Unrestricted Fund Balance and Enterprise Fund Working Capital Requirements

To ensure that adequate funds are available to mitigate current and future risks, such as revenue shortfalls or unanticipated expenditures, it is **recommended the governments establish a formal policy in accordance with the Government Finance Officers Association (GFOA) best practices**. The policy should be set by the Town Council, articulating a framework process for how the government would increase or decrease the level of the unrestricted fund balance over a specific period, including how resources will be directed, to replenish the fund balance should the balance fall below the level prescribed. **The GFOA recommends, at a minimum, the government maintain an unrestricted fund balance in their general fund that is no less than 2 months of the regular general fund operating revenues or regular general fund operating expenditures.**

The Town personnel indicated that they were not aware that they needed these policies. The town had not adopted policies that address or provide an appropriate level of unrestricted fund balances to be maintained in the General Fund or an appropriate target amount of working capital to be maintained in the Enterprise Fund for the purpose of mitigating risks

Finding 3: Financial Audits

The Town should enhance efforts to comply with State Law and ensure that annual financial audit reports and annual financial reports (AFR) are timely completed and filed with the Auditor General and the Department of Financial Services (DFS) within 45 days of the completion of the audit report but no later than 9 months after the end of the fiscal year. The Town submitted its annual audit reports for 2018-19 and 2019-20, 463 and 391 days late respectively. According to the Florida Joint Legislative Auditing Committee records as of September 2023, the Florida Department of Revenue (DOR) and DFS had withheld from the Town half-cent sales tax revenues totaling $25,312 and municipal revenue sharing revenues totaling $23,935 for the untimely filed 2018-19, 2019-20 and 2020-21 fiscal year audit reports.

Timely audits are necessary to provide accountability and assurance to citizens and those charged with governance, help ensure that management and those charged with governance are promptly informed of financial concerns (e.g. deteriorating financial conditions), control deficiencies and financial-related noncompliance; and allow for timely review by appropriate Federal, State and county oversite agencies.

Finding 4: Financial Statement Preparation.

The Town should **contract for specified accounting services necessary to ensure that accounting records are properly prepared and maintained** and timely made available to the contracted CPA for financial statement preparation or alternatively, take appropriate actions to hire, train, develop and retain staff with the knowledge and capability to produce generally accepted accounting practices (GAAP) financial statements.

The Town personnel disclosed that, although the Town Charter states that the Town Clerk is responsible for accounting functions, the Town Personnel recognized that they did not have the knowledge and capability required to prepare GAAP financial statements for the 2020-21, 2021-22 and 2022-23 fiscal years. Although the town contracted with another accounting firm (J&S) to perform all accounting functions, twice per month, despite these efforts, the Town's accounting records included significant errors. Those errors contributed to the delays in submitting the financial audit reports and AFRs and demonstrate that the level of services provided for the accountant contract may not be sufficient for the performance of all the Town's accounting functions.

Finding 5: Accounting Records and Related Controls

The Town should establish and maintain a properly designated accounting system and related policies and procedures that requires and ensures the accurate and timely recording of all financial activity in the Town accounting records and the maintenance of appropriate supporting documentation. Records should be maintained in sufficient detail to support the amounts reported on the financial statement and to provide for periodic reconciliations of financial report amounts to the amounts recorded in the general ledger. There was an analysis of the Town's revenues recorded in the general ledger which showed **Significant understatements totaling $50,898 in ad valorem tax revenues during the 2019-20, 2000-21 and 2021-22 fiscal years.**

Certain tax revenues deposited in the Town's checking account were not recorded in the accounting records. Some deposits were entered into the accounting records twice, overstating ad valorem tax revenues recorded in the 2019-20 fiscal year by $10,291. This resulted in unreconciled differences between the Town's General Fund bank account and the General Fund cash balance in the accounting records. The Town's 2019-

20 fiscal year audit report also disclosed misstatements in "intergovernmental revenues."

The Town indicated procedures had not been established to require and ensure the accurate recording of financial activity or periodic reconciliations of financial reports to the corresponding general ledger and detailed subsidiary records. Town personnel believed that some differences could have resulted from year-end audit adjustments that the Town's contracted accountant had not posted.

Inadequate accounting records were noted by the CPA that audited the 2018-19 fiscal year financial statements. Although the Town contracted with an accountant in the 2019-20 fiscal year to maintain accurate records, the auditor noted significant deficiencies in the town's internal controls over financial reporting in that fiscal year. This included incomplete and inaccurate capital asset records, lack of subsidiary records to accurately reflect the town's grant activity during the fiscal year, and inadequate support for disbursements, resulting in a disclaimer of opinion in the auditor's report.

Without accurate and complete accounting records and reports, the Town cannot demonstrate proper accountability for activities or assure citizens and oversight agencies of the appropriate stewardship of Town Resources. In addition, the lack of accurate and complete accounting records may have contributed to deficiencies regarding financial condition monitoring, timely financial statement audits, financial statement preparation and the budgetary process, respectively. Timely and properly performed bank account reconciliations may have detected errors in the accounting records. The town's bank account reconciliation process was deficient.

Finding 6: Bank Reconciliations

The Town should establish appropriate policies and procedures to ensure that bank account reconciliations are properly and timely performed, reviewed, and approved. Such policies and procedures should require that reconciling items be documented and promptly and thoroughly investigated, explained, and resolved and any necessary adjustments to Town accounting records be timely made.

Bank account reconciliations verify that cash amounts included in the bank statement and the Town accounting records are accurate and complete and help provide for the timely detection of errors and fraud. Effective bank account reconciliation procedures require and ensure that:

- Employees performing, reviewing, and approving the reconciliation do not have cash handling and journal entry responsibilities.
- The identities of the employees who perform the reconciliation and the employees who review and approve the reconciliation are documented to properly affix responsibility for those functions.
- Reconciling items are documented and promptly and thoroughly investigated, explained and resolved.
- Reconciliations are timely completed and any related adjustments to Town accounting records are timely made.

As of March 31, 2023, the Town had six bank accounts, including the General Fund and the Enterprise Fund bank accounts, which accounted for most of the Town's financial activities. **As of that date, the balances in the six accounts totaled $1.7 million, including $1.2 million in the General Fund bank account, $72.959 in the Enterprise Fund bank account and $489,018 in the other accounts.**

As of May 2023, the General Fund bank account had not been reconciled since September 2021 and the Enterprise Fund bank account had not been reconciled since September 2020. Three of the other four bank accounts were last reconciled, in

August of 2020, October 2020, and February 2022 and the fourth bank account was opened in March 2023 and had not yet been reconciled.

The examination of the **General Fund bank account reconciliation for September 30, 2021**, disclosed numerous errors. For example:

- One check for $18,245 dated May 29, 2020, was voided and the Town subsequently issued a check for the same amount from the Enterprise Fund bank account. However, the Town did not record the check as voided in the accounting records. Consequently, expenditures were overstated, and cash was understated by that amount in the General Fund.

- One check for $5,000, dated March 16, 2021, listed as an outstanding **check, was posted twice** in the accounting records, overstating General Fund Expenditures and understating cash by $5,000.

- The reconciliation listed 89 items totaling $88,098 as deposits or credits in transit. Our scanning of these items identified six deposits in transit totaling $86,917 posted in the accounting records twice, resulting in uncorrected overstatements of the General Fund cash and revenues.

- Unrecorded deposits were not listed, as reconciling items on the bank reconciliation. According to previous bank statements, $50,773 in ad valorem tax collections were deposited, into the bank account, during the period October 2020 through September 2021, but had not been recorded in the accounting records as of June 2023, resulting in understatements of General Fund cash and revenues by the same amount.

The town personnel stated the contracted accountant is responsible for preparing bank account reconciliations. The

Town, however, lacks written policies and procedures for bank account reconciliations to be done, on a timely basis, and that someone other than the preparer performs a documented review of the reconciliation.

Finding 7: Budgetary Process

Pursuant to State Law "The Town must adopt a budget by ordinance or resolution each fiscal year and the total amount available from taxation and other sources, including balances brought forward from prior fiscal years, must equal the total appropriations for expenditures and reserves. The Town Council's adopted budget must regulate the Town's expenditures, and it is unlawful to expand or contract for expenditures in any fiscal year except pursuant to the adopted budget. The budget may be amended at any time during a fiscal year and within 60 days after the end of the fiscal year." Controls over budget preparation, recording, reporting, and monitoring should be improved.

Budget Preparation:

The 2021-22 and 2022-23 fiscal budgets were contrary to State law. Prior fiscal year-end balances were not included in the budget as available for appropriation. According to town personnel, the current administration's first budget cycle was the 2021-22 fiscal year and the **Town's financial audits for the 2018-19 and 2019-20 fiscal years had not been completed.** Consequently, the Town was unaware of what the fiscal year and balances were and **did not include any carryforward balances in the 2021-22 and 2022-23 fiscal year budgets.**

Fiscal year-end balances can be estimated and then later adjusted to actual amounts through the budget amendment process. Consideration of balances brought forward from prior fiscal years, provides for transparency of all available resources, increases the usefulness of the budget as a financial management tool, and enables the town to determine appropriate increases and decreases in revenues which may be needed to fund the Town's budget priorities.

The town personnel disclosed that neither the Town Charter nor ordinances defines the legal level of budgetary control. The Town Council-adopted resolutions for 2021-22 and 2022-23 fiscal year budgets did not specify the legal level of budgetary control; however, the adopted budget presented expenditures for each fund at the department level. Accordingly, it is not apparent how Town personnel and the town Council could readily determine whether resources were expended within budgeted amounts at the department level consistent with town Council intent. Although we inquired, **Town personnel did not explain why budget level of budgetary control had not been defined.**

Budget Resolutions:

To effectively manage expenditures, it is essential that adopted budgets be accurately input into the Town's accounting Records. The 2021-22 and the 2022-23 fiscal year budgeted expenditures had not been inputted into the Town's accounting records. The Town personnel did not explain why the approved budget amounts were not entered into the accounting records but responded that the amounts had been entered subsequent to our inquiry and were available to review. Without being properly recorded, there is an increased risk that actual expenditures will not be consistent with, or will exceed, approved budgeted expenditure amounts.

Budget Reporting and Monitoring:

According to GFOA. Recommendations, regular and frequent reporting is necessary to provide accountability, educate and inform stakeholders and improve confidence in the government. Communication and involvement are an essential component of every aspect of the budget process, and regular monitoring of budgetary performance provides an early warning of potential problems. And it gives decision makers time to consider actions that may be needed, if major deviations in budget-to-actual comparison results become evident. The Town Charter requires the Town Manager to keep the Town Council fully advised as to the financial condition and future needs of the Town by providing a financial and budget progress report at each regular monthly meeting and submit and make available to the public, a complete report on finances and administrative activities as of the end of the fiscal year.

Additionally, the Town Charter requires that the Town Manager quarterly review budget reports with department heads and advise or be advised, of any allotment which is in danger of being exceeded. If at any time during the fiscal year it appears that appropriate revenues will be insufficient, the Town Manager is to immediately report to the Town Council the estimated amount of the deficit and suggest remedial action to be taken.

The Town did not comply with the Town Charter budgetary reporting and monitoring requirements and GFOA recommendations:

- Town records did not evidence that the Town Manager prepared any of the required monthly financial and budget progress reports for presentation to the Town Council. The lack may have contributed to the town's deteriorating financial condition.
- Contrary to the Town Charter, **the Town records did not evidence quarterly budget meetings held with department heads** to ensure that budgeted amounts would not be exceeded. The Town Manager did not explain why the quarterly meetings were not held but indicated the Town would hold meetings going forward.
- **The Town did not amend the budget.** Our comparison of the Town-adopted 2021-22 fiscal year budgeted revenue and expenditure amounts to actual revenue and

expenditure amounts recorded in the **Town Accounting records disclosed significant differences as:**

- o Total budgeted revenues for the General Fund exceed actual revenues by $148,192 and total budgeted expenditures exceed actual expenditures by $175,867.
- o Total budgeted revenues for the Enterprise Fund exceeded actual revenues. by $119,537 and contrary to State law total actual expenses exceeded budgeted expenses by $408,029.

Town personnel did not explain why periodic budget amendments were not made to reflect actual revenues and expenditures that significantly differed from budgetary expenditures. Absent periodic budget-to-actual comparison reports, the Town Council and the public lack the information necessary to gain an appropriate understanding of the Town's financial status. Absent periodic budget amendments, the budget may not accurately reflect anticipated revenues and expenditures and there is an increased risk that the Town expenditures may exceed available resources, and that the Town will experience a deteriorating financial condition.

Recommendation: The Town should enhance controls over the budgetary process to ensure that:

- Balances are brought forward from prior years and included in the budget.
- The desired legal level of budgetary control is established for Town Budgets.
- Town Council-approved budgeted expenditures are properly recorded in Town accounting records.
- Actual expenditures are limited to budgeted amounts as required by State law.

- The Town Manager prepares and provides the Town Council with monthly financial reports reflecting budget-to-actual comparisons and meets quarterly with department heads as is required by the Town Charter.
- Budgets are periodically amended to reflect actual revenues and expenditures that significantly differ from budgeted amounts.

Finding 8: Utility Services Billing and Collection Practices

The Town provides water and sewer services to customers connected to the Town's water and sewer utility systems. Additionally, the Town contracted with a vendor to provide solid waste garbage services. The town Ordinance requires residents to connect to and use the Town's water and sewer systems and the Town's garbage collection services at fees established by the Town Council. **If any landowner within the Town limits refuses to connect to the sewer system after notification by the Town Clerk, the Town is authorized to make the connection at the owner's expense. However, the Town ordinance also allows owners of private sewage facilities to pay a monthly fee equal to the minimum usage fee rather than use the Town's sewer system.**

Although the town had no established written policies and procedures over the utility services billing and collection processes, **in practice, the Town requires customers to complete an application for utility services and pay the required deposit and any applicable fees. The Town personnel then enter the application information into the Town's utility billing system to establish a new customer account and enter the Town Council-approved billing rates.** Water and sewer rates are entered into the system on a per unit basis, and solid waste rates are dependent upon can or dumpster types. Town personnel read meters monthly and update the utility billing system for monthly consumption of water (in gallons), and the utility billing system calculates the monthly billings. The water and sewer charges billed include a monthly base charge plus actual usage charges based on meter readings, while garbage services are determined based on the contracted rate plus a markup.

As of December 2022, the town had 474 utility services customer accounts. Records were examined supporting utility billings totaling $2,406, before taxes, for thirty selected accounts, twenty-seven of which were active accounts, during the December 2022 billing period. The examination disclosed the following deficiencies which may have been caused, in part, by the lack of written policies and procedures.

- **Applications establishing services were not provided for twenty-five of the accounts, including twenty-two active accounts.** Town personnel indicated the twenty-five applications were related to accounts established prior to the current Town administration.

- While applications were provided for five active accounts, the information noted on the applications was not sufficient. During the audit period, and subsequently, the Town used two different application forms for utility services; one that detailed the services offered by the Town and required the applicant to select the services requested; and another that did not provide detail of the services offered nor require the customer to request specific services. The Town personnel could not provide an explanation.

The examination of the five provided applications found that:

- 2 applications were incomplete because, although required by the application, **the types of utility services requested were not specified.**

- 2 other applications did not require identification of the services requested.
- None of the five applications specified whether any additional fees were required or if sewer was available.

Absent properly designated applications for service that are accurately completed prior to entering the information into the Town's utility billing system. Town records did not establish a basis for a monthly utility charge to be assessed to the applicant.

- One account was **underbilled for sewer services** by approximately $60 per month due to the additional rate for water consumption over 1,000 gallons not being applied. **Town personnel indicated that the underbilling resulted from the account being incorrectly classified when established in 2019.** When errors made in setting up accounts in the utility billing system are not timely discovered, a continuous loss of revenue may occur.
- One account was not billed for water services for the month of December 2022. According to Town personnel, the customer requested services to be turned off for the month. In response to inquiries, Town personnel did not provide the legal authority for services to be suspended and reinstated upon a customer's request but indicated that it was customary practice in previous administrations. By allowing accounts to be suspended and reinstated upon request without apparent legal authority, the Town is foregoing revenue needed to cover costs of operating the water and sewer system.
- One account was not billed for sewer services, nor was it billed for the required minimum usage fee for nonparticipation. Town personnel indicated that, because they identified four other accounts not participating in the service and not being charged, the

required minimum fee, for consistency, they suspended the fee for the fifth account in March 2022. Town personnel lacked apparent legal authority to suspend billings of a required fee, and failure to assess the fee on the five accounts resulted in an additional loss of $1,039 in Town utility revenues.

- One account with no record of water consumption had not been billed for any service since November 2017. Town personnel indicated the account was closed; however, although there was a meter assigned to the property, Town personnel could not provide any evidence to support that the customer had been connected in the water and sewer system or that the customer had requested the account be closed.

- We expanded our procedures to scan billing system records for other accounts with no recorded water consumption and noted that in the month of December 3033, **the Town had 102 meters, approximately 30% of all meters assigned to addresses with no water consumption. Town personnel indicated that the accounts associated with the 102 meters were closed but did not provide records to evidence the closing of the accounts**. Absent, an investigation into meters assigned to properties without recorded water consumption, the Town has limited assurance that all property owners are connected to the Town's water and sewer systems (or, if just connected to the water system, paying the sewer minimum usage fee) as required by Town ordinances, that meters are operating correctly, and that the town is collecting all utility revenues to which it is entitled to cover the costs of operating the water and sewer systems.

- Although we did not note any instances of non-billing for garbage services, Town **personnel do not require property owners to sign up for garbage services, con-**

trary to **Town ordinances**. Rather the garbage contractor empties all garbage cans with the contractor's logo and places them out for pick-up within the Town and bills the Town based on a customary count periodically provided by Town personnel. However, **because the Town does not monthly update the count to reflect the number of garbage customers in the utility billing system, the Town may not be billing all customers served by the garbage contractor.** Consequently, there is an increased risk that garbage collection services are being provided to users who are not being billed by the Town., **Town personnel indicated they were not aware of the Town ordinance requirements.**

Recommendation: The Town should establish written procedures requiring **appropriately designed applications** to complete **prior to accounts being set up in the utility billing system**. In addition, the procedures should ensure that completed applications are maintained to support the fees charged for the services provided. **All properties required connection to the water and sewer systems are connected, accounts are properly set up in the utility billing system, all accounts are charged at least the minimum required fees and as required by Town Ordinances, and prompt investigations are conducted for meters with no recorded water consumption.** Also, Town personnel should **monthly reconcile the garbage contractor's invoices to active billing system account records to ensure that the Town is billing all customers receiving garbage services.**

Finding 9: Separation of Duties

Governmental organizations, to the extent possible with existing personnel, should separate duties so that no one employee has control over all phases of a transaction. Town personnel disclosed that duties were not always appropriately separated among employees. Specifically, the Utility Clerk, who is one of the town's four administrative employees, prepares and sends invoices for water, sewer and garbage services, collects cash and checks as payment, records payments to customer accounts in the utility billing system, prepares related bank deposits; and deposits the funds into the applicable bank account weekly. Although deposits are recorded in the accounting records by the contracted accountant because the Utility Clerk has control over the billing and collection process, she could divert collections for unauthorized purposes without timely detection.

No compensating controls are in place to mitigate the incompatible duties risk and Town personnel indicated that the **Town does not have funds to hire another employee to separate the incompatible duties.** Insofar as **the Town has four administrative employees, the Town could appropriately separate duties through realignment of position duties.**

Although the audit procedures did not disclose any significant errors or fraud, the inappropriate separation of duties, especially given lack of timely and complete bank reconciliations and lack of complete and accurate financial accounting records respectively, there is an increased risk that errors or fraud could occur and not be timely detected and resolved.

Recommendation: The Town should separate utility billing, collection and recordkeeping duties to the extent possible by realigning position duties among available administrative staff and the contracted accountant.

Finding 10: Procurement of Goods and Services

The Town is responsible for establishing controls that provide assurance that the process of acquiring goods and services is effectively and consistently administered. **A competitive procurement process provides a means for efficiently and equitably obtaining the best quality goods and** services at the lowest possible cost and reduces the appearance and opportunity for favoritism. In addition, the use of procurement documents, such as contracts or purchase orders, detail the goods or services being acquired, and evidence approval for the purchase.

Contractual arrangements for services should be evidenced by **written contracts** embodying all provisions and conditions of the procurement of such services. **Written contracts protect the interests, and identify the responsibilities, of both parties; define the services to be performed; and provide a basis for payment. Further, effective monitoring procedures are essential to ensuring that contractors comply with applicable contact terms and conditions and that the contractor's performance is acceptable and accomplishes objectives established in the contract.**

Town procedures require purchase orders be submitted to appropriate levels of authority for approval of purchases of goods and services. Approved purchase orders serve to document management's authorization to acquire goods and services, provide a basis for controlling the use of appropriated resources through encumbrances, document the specifications and prices of the goods and services ordered, and authorize vendors to provide goods and services.

Town procedures also specify that the Town Manager may approve purchases of $2,500 or less, but that competitive selection processes be used for purchases exceeding $2,500.

- Purchases of $2,501 to $4,999 must be approved by the Town Council and an unspecified number of telephone quotes should be obtained, when possible.
- Purchases of $5,000 to $24,999 require an unspecified number of written quotes or proposals and must be approved by the Town Council.

- Purchases of goods or services of $25,000 or more are to be made under a competitive sealed bit or Request for proposal (RFP) process, unless designated by the Town Council as a sole source, single-source, or emergency purchase.

During the period October 2021 through December 2022, **non-payroll Town expenditures totaled $1.3 million. 16 vendors were selected, each with payments greater than $2,500**, and examined Town records for payments totaling $94,888 of the $431.540 amount paid to the 16 vendors during that period. The Auditor General's examination disclosed that:

- Town records did not always evidence purchases of goods and services were made in accordance with Town competitive procurement procedures.

Specifically:

- Payments totaling $158,975 made to two vendors exceeded $25.000; however, Town personnel could not provide evidence that the goods and services were obtained pursuant to a competitive sealed bid or RFP process, or alternatively, that the purchases were exempted from competitive procurement.
- Payments totaling $74,145 for purchases of goods and services from 5 vendors, each exceeded $5,000 without evidence that written quotes or proposals were obtained.
- The Town could not provide evidence that telephone quotes were obtained for purchases of goods and services from two vendors with payments above $2,500 and below $4,999 and totaling $9,900.
- Contrary to good business practices and Town procedures, six of sixteen payments totaling $71,623 made to six vendors were not supported by a purchase order or contract. The absence of properly approved

purchase orders or contracts, increases the Town's risk of making purchases that are unauthorized, exceed budget authority, or inconsistent with the Town Council's intent. In addition, the lack of a written purchase order or contract clearly establishing the rights and responsibilities of both parties in advance of the provision of the goods and service may result in misunderstandings between the Town and its vendor.

- Contrary to good business practices, the invoiced amounts by six contract payments totaling $20,261 made to two vendors exceeded the contract prices by $1,802. In response, Town personnel could not explain why the amounts invoiced did not agree with contracted rates. Town procedures do not require Town personnel to verify the invoiced amounts agree with the contract rates, the terms and conditions and, absent of such verification, there is an increased risk that the Town may overpay for goods and services or that such goods and services may not comply with contract terms and conditions.

- Contrary to good business practices, invoices supporting three payments totaling $18,500 did not contain sufficient detail to verify services were provided in accordance with contract terms. The Town contracted with the Hamilton County Sheriff's Office (HCSO) to provide law enforcement services for $8,250 per month. The contract provided for at least one deputy to be on duty and within Town limits for at least 60 hours per week, especially during the hours of 6:00 PM through 2:00 AM, as allowed by call volume. Our review disclosed that the contract did not require and the HCSO invoices did not provide, detail of the deputy days and hours worked for the month, and the Town has not established alternate procedures for verifying that the HCSO had at least one deputy on duty for the hours required by the contract. When invoices lack sufficient detail of the services provided, there is an increased risk that the Town may overpay for such services or that the goods and services may not be received consistent with the Town Council's expectations and contract terms.

- Contrary to good business practices, **the Town did not have written procedures requiring documented receipt of goods and services** prior to payment. None of the records supporting the sixteen selected expenditures totaling $94,878 contained evidence, such as a signature and receipt date, indicating the goods or services were received by a Town employee having direct knowledge of the receipt of the goods and services. Absent evidence that goods and services were received, prior to payment, there is an increased risk that the Town will pay for unsubstantiated or improper expenditures.

Recommendation: Town personnel should follow established purchasing procedures and ensure that telephone quotes, written quotes, or sealed bids or proposals, are obtained as applicable. In addition, the Town should enhance the purchasing procedures to ensure that:

- Purchase orders, or contracts, are used, to document the approval of purchases and to clearly establish the rights and responsibilities of the Town and the Vendor.
- For expenditures pursuant to a contract, Invoices contain sufficient detail to demonstrate compliance with the contract terms and conditions and that Town personnel compare invoice amounts to contract rates and terms and conditions prior to payment.
- Evidence of receipt of goods or services be documented prior to payment.

Finding 11: Auditor Selection

Financial Audits performed by an independent CPA give assurance as to the reliability and completeness of Town financial statements; provide a means for evaluating the effectiveness of Town internal controls over financial reporting; and include a determination of the extent to which the Town complied with applicable laws, contracts, grant agreements, and Town ordinances, policies and procedures, non-compliance with which could have a direct and material effect on Town Financial Statement Amount. Consequently, **it is important for the Town to use an effective auditor selection process to obtain the services of a qualified auditor with the applicable skills and experience necessary to ensure adequate and appropriate audits**.

State law requires, prior to entering a contract for audit services, each municipality to establish an auditor selection committee, assign to the auditor selection committee responsibilities for evaluating and recommending an auditor, and use specified auditor selection procedures. Furthermore, every procurement is to be evidenced by a written contract embodying all provisions and conditions of the procurement of such services and include, at a minimum, a provision specifying the services to be provided and fees or other compensation for such services, a provision requiring that invoices for fees or other compensation be submitted in sufficient detail to demonstrate compliance with the terms of the contract, and a provision specifying the contract period, including renewals and conditions under which a contract may be terminated or renewed.

The selection of one CPA firm to perform the 2018-19 fiscal year audit and another CPA firm to perform the 2019-20 and the 2020-21 fiscal years audits indicated the CPA firms may not have been selected in accordance with State law.

- For the CPA firm selected to perform the 2018-19 fiscal year audit, Town Records, including the Town Council meeting minutes **did not evidence the advertisement of the RFP, how many and which firms responded** to the RFP, factors considered and **ranking of responding firms by the Auditor Selection Committee**, or **whether the Town ultimately contracted with the firm selected by the Auditor Selection Committee.** Additionally, although we requested, Town personnel did not provide the written contract for our review. Consequently, Town records do not demonstrate that the audit services, contract contained the required provisions and conditions required by State law. Town personnel indicated that the RFP occurred prior to the hiring of current staff, and the requested records may have existed at one time but could not be located.

- Because the Town Council was not satisfied with the CPA firm that performed the 2018=19 fiscal year audit, the Town Council selected another CPA firm to perform the 2019-20 and the 2020-21 fiscal year audits. However, contrary to State law, the Town did not establish an auditor selection committee and did not conduct an RFP based auditor selection process. According to town personnel, due to the urgency in getting the audits completed, the Town did not publicly advertise for audit services nor did the audit services contract provide for conditions under which the contract may be renewed.

Absent documentation evidencing that requests for audit services were publicly advertised, and responding audit firms were evaluated and ranked, based upon established factors, including, but not limited to, ability of personnel, experience, ability to furnished required services, and other factors as determined by an audit selection committee. Town records do not demonstrate that the audit services were procured pursuant to State law in a fair and equitable manner.

Recommendation: The Town should ensure and demonstrate that future auditor selections are performed in compliance with State law by establishing an auditor selection committee, publicly soliciting proposals, evaluating proposals based on establishing RFP criteria, and maintaining all documentation associated with the auditor selection. Additionally, the Town should ensure that audit services contracts include all required provisions, including a specified contract period and the conditions under which the contract may be terminated or renewed.

Finding 12: Personnel Policies and Procedures:

Effective personnel controls include the adoption of position descriptions that specify minimum education and experience requirements, verification of an applicant's employment, and maintenance of personnel files, which include personnel action forms or other appropriate documentation evidencing authorized personnel actions. Additionally, the adoption of a Town Council-approved classification and pay plan, including minimum and maximum salary ranges for each position, establishes authorized salary amount, by position, based on Town Council's intent.

The Town Charter requires the Town Council to establish personnel policies and procedures and requires the Town Manager to maintain a personnel manual. Accordingly, the Town established a *Personnel Policy and Procedures Manual* (Manual) that contains the Town's personnel and payroll policies and procedures. However, although the *Manual* contains several useful policies and procedures, our review of the *Manual* and Town payroll and personnel records identified enhancements that could be made. In addition, our procedures disclosed instances of noncompliance with *Manual* provisions.

Classification and Pay Plan:

The Manual provides that the pay of all employees be established by a classification and pay plan, which must include the minimum and maximum rates of pay for each position and which may be amended by the Town Council upon the Town Manager's recommendation. Contrary to the *Manual,* as of August 2023, the Town had not established a classification and pay plan. A classification and pay plan are essential to ensure that salaries are paid for employees in accordance with the Town Council's intent, and that all positions and rates of pay are authorized.

Position Descriptions:

Although not specifically required by Town policies or procedures, Town position descriptions that clearly established assigned duties and defined the minimum education and experience requirements were available for some established positions. However, we noted **Town Council-approved position descriptions had not been established for two active employees, and one position description did not align with actual employee duties.**

- Position descriptions were **not available for two positions (Utility Director and Road and Street Worker**). Instead, we were provided with a list of job duties performed by the employees in those positions. The documents provided **did not include minimum education, required skills or experience requirements for the positions and the actual position titles and classifications were not specified.**
- The Town Clerk position description required the Town Clerk to "maintain a regular record of all financial accounts of the Town and show, at all times, the financial condition of the Town. However, contrary to the position description, during the audit period

October 2021 through December 2022, the individual employed as "Town Clerk", did not maintain financial records and accounts of the Town. Instead, the Town contracted for accounting services and expended $42,622 for those services for the 2021-22 fiscal year.

Town personnel indicated that due to turnover in personnel, position descriptions had not been maintained or updated for these Town positions. Detailed position descriptions that specify maximum education, skills and experience requirements and actions to ensure that duties assigned to employees, correlate with the position descriptions established for their respective positions, help ensure that employees have the skills and education necessary to complete job duties required for their positions and that Town Council and management objectives will be met.

Verification of Employment History and Educational Requirements:

The Manual requires that **minimum education and experience requirements be established to qualify an applicant for appointment consideration**. However, neither the Manual nor other Town records include procedures for verifying and documenting applicants met their respective requirements before hire. **Only two of the nine employees' personnel files included evidence that minimum experience and education requirements were met. Absent verification of minimum experience and education requirements prior to hiring,** there is an increased risk that Town employees may lack the minimum qualifications or necessary knowledge and training to perform assigned job duties.

Personnel Action Forms:

Effective personnel administration necessitates the implementation of controls to document approval of all personnel appointments and personal actions through the use of personnel action forms (PAFs) or similar documentation. **Town policies and procedures do not specifically require PAFs, or similar documentation and we noted that Town records did not always contain documentation to evidence the approval of position appointments, salary changes, and other personnel actions.**

Documentation was not available to support the authorization of the current salary or position appointments for any of the seven employees in our payroll test. According to the Town Manager and Town Clerk, who were hired in November 2020 and January 2021, respectively, the Manual does not specifically require documentation for personnel actions and PAFs or similar documentation, have not been regularly used for personnel actions since their hire. Rather, Town personnel informed us that, in practice, the town Manager authorized the hiring of Town personnel, established pay rates, and otherized other personnel changes either verbally or through notes in the personnel files. Without properly approved PAFs or similar documentation. Town records do not demonstrate that appointments, salary changes and other personnel actions, were authorized by Town management, and the Town could encounter difficulty in resolving employment disputes should they arise.

Recommendation: To provide for efficient and effective personnel administration, the Town Council should:

- **Adopt a classification and pay plan** to establish minimum and maximum salary ranges for all authorized Town positions.
- Establish detailed position descriptions for all Town positions.
- Establish procedures to verify an applicant's educational and employment history prior to hire.

- Use PAFs or similar documentation to document authorization for all personnel actions.

In addition, the Town Manager should enhance the *Manual* accordingly.

The seven employees included the Town Clerk, Utilities Clerk, Bookkeeper, Utility Director, General Laborer, Street and Road Worker and Firefighter.

Finding 13: Time and Attendance Records for Salaried Employees:

Effective payroll controls include the required maintenance of a time record to provide the basis for issuing a payroll check by documenting hours worked and leave taken by each employee, whether salaried or hourly paid. Similarly, properly maintained leave records document sick, vacation, and administration leave earned and used, as appropriate. Then time records are not required and maintained, other documentation, such as employee-prepared activity reports detailing the employee's activities over a specified period, would provide some assurance that required services are being performed and would also aid in the evaluation of the employee's performance.

The Town Charter states that the Town Council, by majority vote of the total membership, shall adopt a Town Manager and enter into a mutually acceptable written agreement. The agreement may specify the terms, conditions, and benefits of the appointment.

The contract with the Town Manager dated November 2020 provided that the Town Manager shall devote such necessary time, attention, knowledge, and skills to faithfully perform her duties and responsibilities, and to exercise her powers under the agreement.

The Town Charter states that the duties and responsibilities of the Town Manager are to:

- Direct and supervise the administration of all departments, offices, and agencies of the Town.
- Prepare and submit the annual budget and capital program to the Town Council.
- Submit to the Town Council and make available to the public a complete report on the finances and administrative activities of the Town at the end of each fiscal year.
- Keep the Town council fully advised as to the financial condition and future needs of the Town by providing a financial and budget progress report at each regular Council meeting.

The Town Manager's employment agreement provided a fixed salary of $60,000 for the 2020-21 fiscal year and for the earning of leave benefits but did not establish a minimum number of work hours or specific job duties. As of September 2023, and since her hire in November 2020, the Town Manager did not maintain regular work hours at the Town and did not maintain a record of time worked or leave taken. Town personnel indicated that the employment agreement did not prescribe specific job duties and a minimum number of work hours, because, under the agreement, the Town Manager was required to fulfill all duties regardless of time worked.

However, based on the results of our audit, it is not evident that all Town Manager duties were being effectively completed in accordance with the Town Charter and employee agreement. For example, as of May 2023, and since her hire in November 2020, the Town Manager had not been providing monthly financial and budget reporting to the Town Council and Town citizens and had not ensured that Town activities were completely and accurately recorded in the Town records and reported or that Town bank accounts were timely reconciled to Town financial records.

We also noted that the Fire Chief was hired in June 2022, and six months later, In December 2022, the Town Council approved a contract establishing a fixed annual salary of $25,000. The Town Charter states that the Fire Chief shall ensure that the fire department is adequately equipped, provide inspections and training of personnel, ensure that an adequate number of fire hydrants are maintained in working order, provide emergency services, and ensure that all equipment is in working order. Our examination of payroll records and inquiry of Town personnel disclosed the employment contract dated December 2022 did not establish specific job duties or require a minimum number of work hours and the Fire Chief is not required to maintain time records or provide a monthly report detailing activities performed. Without established job duties and minimum work hours, records of time worked, or activity reports, Town records did not demonstrate the reasonableness of the Fire Chief's compensation based on the expected services or that the services performed met Town Council expectations.

The Town's Standard Operating Procedures require that hourly employees prepare time sheets to document time worked; however, no such requirement exists for salaried employees, such as the Town Manager and Fire Chief. Without documentation of salaried employee work efforts, such as established work hours and a requirement that employee time worked be documented, or activities performed be reported in detail, **Town records did not demonstrate the reasonableness of the Town Manager or Fire Chief's compensation based on expected services and there is an increased risk that employee services are not being provided consistent with established job responsibilities and Town Council expectations.**

Recommendation: The town Council should establish payroll documentation requirements for salaried positions that require documentation of work effort, such as detailed records of hours worked or activities performed and any leave taken, to ensure the basis for all compensation is documented and consistent with Town Council expectations. In addition, the Town Council should consider amending the Town Manager and Fire Chief employment agreements to include specific job duties and the minimum number of work hours required.

Finding 14: Sunshine Law – Public Record Requests:

Certain State laws require municipalities to provide transparency regarding their transactions and activities. These laws include the Public Records Act which requires the maintenance of public records and the Sunshine Law, which establishes requirements to provide public access to governmental proceedings and records upon request. State law also provides that the custodian of public records must acknowledge requests to inspect or copy records and respond to such requests in good faith in a timely manner. A person denied the right to inspect or copy public records under the Public Records Act may bring a civil action against the agency to enforce the terms of the law. Although the Florida Attorney General's *Government-in-the-Sunshine Manual 2022 Edition* (Sunshine Manual) does not provide any specific timeframes for responding to public records requests, it states that an unjustified delay in producing public records constitutes an unlawful refusal to provide access to public records. The *Sunshine Manual* further states that, where the delays are not justified "The Public Records Act holds officials accountable."

Our examination of Town records and discussions with town personnel disclosed that Town efforts to ensure compliance with the Sunshine Law and Public Records Act **could be improved. As of August 2023, the town did not have written policies and procedures to ensure that public records were promptly completed and documented, nor did the Town** maintain a record or log of public records requests received to monitor completion of all requests.

As of August 2023, the Town's Website included a **link to a form to make a public records request that would be emailed to the Town Clerk**. The Town Clerk, as the official Town records custodian, is responsible for responding to public record requests made through the Town's website or otherwise. Although the Town does not maintain a log of public records requests, the Town Clerk maintains physical file folders to document requests received.

To determine whether the town Clerk was promptly responding to public record requests, in May 2023, we requested public records requests received during the period January 2022 through April 2023. The Town **Clerk provided eighteen individual file folders that contained various records, including notes, and copies of emails and other correspondence, related to the eighteen public records requests received during that period.** Our review of each request and the related documentation included in the **eighteen file folders disclosed that Town records did not always demonstrate that the requested public records were promptly provided, as required by State law. Specifically:**

- The town could not document that an acknowledgment of the public records request was provided for sixteen of the eighteen public records requests.
- For five of the eighteen public records requests, received **during the period January 2022 through February 2023, Town records did not evidence that the requested records were provided**, and another two requests, received in August 2022 and March 2023, had only been partially completed as of May 2023.
- Records for eleven requests were provided to the requestor 43 days to 92 days later, an average of 53 days after the request.

The above-noted deficiencies may have been caused, in part, by the lack of written policies and procedures governing public records requests, including periodic monitoring to verify that requests are timely completed. **The failure of the Town to promptly respond to public records requests may subject the Town to penalties or litigation and limit the public's right to promptly access public records.**

Recommendations: The Town should establish written policies and procedures to ensure that public records requests are completed in compliance with the Sunshine Law and Public Records Act. Such policies and procedures should require logs be maintained to document each public records requests are completed in compliance with the Sunshine Law and Public Records Act. Such policies and procedures should require logs be maintained to document each public records request received, requests be promptly acknowledged, requested records be provided within an established time frame, and Town records evidence each request and that the requested records were provided.

Finding 15: Records Retention – Town Ordinances and Resolutions

Records of Town ordinances and resolutions are necessary to document the historical and ongoing managerial and administrative purposes; those activities, functions, programs, and events that are appropriate and allowable. Such records are necessary to provide current and future Town Councils with a basis to govern the Town properly and consistently, and the Town employees to properly administer Town business. Additionally, such records inform the Town's citizenry about the Town's governance decisions and provide a means to hold the Town Council and Town personnel accountable for their actions.

State law requires that upon the final passage by the governing body, every local government ordinance or resolution be recorded in a book kept for the purpose and be signed by the presiding officer and clerk of the governing body.

According to the State's records retention schedules, records documenting municipal ordinances and resolutions must be retained. permanently. Failure to maintain records in accordance with State law could result in Town officials being subject to the penalties specified in State law.

The Town Charter provides that the Clerk is to keep a record of all ordinances passed by the Town Council and is the custodian of all records, papers, and files of the Town. The Town Charter also requires a complete codification of ordinances to be prepared at least every 10 years. Further, the Town adopted a records retention policy as part of the Standard Operating Procedures, which states that ordinances shall be retained, codified, and made available for public review. However, the Town had not established written procedures regarding the retention of Town ordinances and resolutions.

As of June 2023, an index prepared during the 2018-19 fiscal year was the most recent record listing adopted Town ordinances and resolutions and, although we requested, Town personnel did not provide us a codification of ordinances. We were provided binders of ordinances and resolutions passed during the period November 2014 through May 2023 and, while subsequently reviewing other Town records, we located a codification of all Town-enacted ordinances that had been last updated in October 2013.

Town personnel cited turnover in personnel as the reason written procedures regarding retention of Town ordinances and resolutions had not been established and further indicated that existing Town personnel were not aware that the ordinances should be periodically codified. Absent an up-to-date and organized repository of Town ordinances and resolutions and periodic codifications of the ordinances, the Town cannot demonstrate compliance with the Town Charter and State law and may be subject Town officials to penalties. In addition, the lack of comprehensive records of Town ordinances and resolutions frustrated the public's access to information about local laws and Town Council actions.

Recommendation: The Town should maintain an up-to-date and organized repository of ordinances and resolutions, periodically codify the ordinances, and make available for public inspection comprehensive records of ordinances enacted and resolutions adopted by the town Council as required by State law and the Town Charter.

Finding 16: Anti-Fraud Policies and Procedures

Effective policies and procedures for communicating, investigating, and reporting known or suspected fraud are essential to aid in the mitigation, detection, and prevention of fraud. Such policies and procedures educate employees about proper conduct, create an environment that deters dishonesty, and establish controls that provide assurance of achieving management objectives and detecting dishonest acts. Specifically, anti-fraud policies and procedures identify actions constituting fraud, require individuals to report known or suspected fraud, provide guidance for incident reporting, establish responsibility and guidance for fraud investigation, and specify consequences for fraudulent behavior.

It allows individuals to anonymously report known or suspected fraud and provide an appropriate process for communicating known or suspected management fraud directly to those charged with governance or to an entity's legal counsel. Investigation procedures establish responsibility and the actions for investigating potential incidents of fraud, reporting evidence of such investigations and actions to the appropriate authorities, and protecting the reputation of persons suspected but determined not guilty of fraud.

As of June 2023, the Town had not established any anti-fraud policies or procedures due to personnel turnover. Absent such policies and procedures, there is an increased risk that potential acts of fraud may not be recognized, appropriately communicated, and investigated, and reported to the appropriate authorities for resolution.

Recommendation: The Town should develop and implement anti-fraud policies and procedures to aid in the mitigation, detection, and prevention of fraud.

OBJECTIVES, SCOPE AND METHODOLOGY

The Auditor General conducts operational audits of governmental entities to provide the Legislature, Florida's citizens, public, Town management, and other stakeholders unbiased, timely and relevant information to use in promoting government accountability and stewardship and improving government operations. Pursuant to Section 11.45(3)(a), Florida Statutes, the Legislative Audit Committee, at its March 13, 2023, meeting directed us to conduct this operational audit of the Town of White Springs.

Auditor General Disclaimer:

An audit by its nature does not include a review of all records and actions of management, staff and vendors and, as a consequence, cannot be relied upon to identify all instances of noncompliance, fraud, abuse or inefficiency.

Although Griffin and I made complaints to the state to no avail, finally complaints were posed by other citizens, including Arlen Scott Gay, AND A COUNCIL MEMBER, to the Joint Legislative Audit Committee. Other Senators were now in place at the JLAC since Senator Montford had resigned, so there was hope for White Springs. Neither Senator Montford, Democrat, and chair of the JLAC, nor Florida Representative Chuck Branford, Republican, would act on previous complaints regarding the Local Option Fuel Taxes. Had he still been alive, he would have been pleased that the multitude of complaints we made were all noted and more by the Auditor General's report.

www.ingramcontent.com/pod-product-compliance
Lightning Source LLC
Chambersburg PA
CBHW051131120626
46547CB00012B/755

* 9 7 8 1 9 6 6 5 6 5 3 3 8 *